THE Romantic TRADITION IN BRITISH POLITICAL THOUGHT

Jonathan Mendilow

BARNES & NOBLE BOOKS
Totowa, New Jersey

© 1986 Jonathan Mendilow
First published in the USA 1985 by
Barnes & Noble Books,
81 Adams Drive,
Totowa, New Jersey, 07512

Library of Congress Cataloging in Publication Data

Mendilow, Jonathan.
    The Romantic Tradition in British Political Thought.

    Bibliography: P.
    Includes index.
    T. Political Science—Great Britain—History.
I. Title.
JA84.G7M46   1985   320.5'094   85-22871
ISBN 0-389-20595-8

Printed and bound in Great Britain

ACKNOWLEDGEMENTS

This book would never have been completed without the encouragement, advice and help offered by my father. I also wish to thank Shlomo Avineri and Zfirah Porat who read parts of the manuscript and offered helpful suggestions for its improvement, and to Roslyn Langbart, Morissa Amitai and Sylvia Weinberg, the devoted team of typists who toiled to decipher my hieroglyphics and put me on my guard against slips in the notes.

A shortened version of part of Chapter 3 has appeared in *Libertarian Studies* (Winter 1982). The analysis of Marx and Carlyle in Chapter 4 relies heavily on my article 'Carlyle, Marx and the ILP: Alternative Roads to Socialism', published in *Polity* (Autumn 1984), while the study of *Sartor Resartus* and Carlyle's theory of revolution in the same chapter follows the lines of my article in HSLA (*Hebrew Studies in Literature and the Arts*) (XII (1984), pp. 26-45). I am grateful to the editors for permission to use this material.

CONTENTS

Acknowledgements

Introduction 1

1. The Political Message of Wordsworth's *Prelude* 16

2. Robert Southey and the Communal Values of Politics 47

3. The History Shelley Never Wrote 83

4. Thomas Carlyle's 'Marriage of Heaven and Hell' 112

5. Three Shades of Tory Radicalism 150

6. The Working Man as Hero: Hardie, Blatchford and the ILP 198

7. The Romantic Tradition in British Imperialist Ideology 235

Index 264

INTRODUCTION

When our first parents were driven out of the garden of Eden, Adam, wrote Dean Inge, turned to Eve and said: 'My dear, we live in an age of transition.' Ever since then transition has been a permanent feature of human life, and the clash of tradition and experiment the unending dialectic of society. However, the tempo of change is uneven. Shakespeare's dictum, 'time travels in divers paces with divers persons', is no less true of whole eras. There are periods when history seems to expand and creep at a schoolboy's pace. In others it seems as it were to contract, to collapse in on itself, till revolution, not only political, becomes the norm. It is especially at such times that thinking minds are stimulated to re-appraise the present in relation to past experience and future possibilities, and to re-examine the principles upon which personal and collective action should be based. Such periods are therefore conducive to the emergence of new trends in social and political thought.

A clear example is the era covered by the late-eighteenth and early-nineteenth centuries when many of the doctrines on which modern political thought rests battled for supremacy. As time progressed, people could not but become increasingly aware of the dislocation of established patterns of thought and behaviour under the pressure of those kaleidoscopic changes in all spheres of life which for convenience we lump together under the terms the Industrial Revolution and the French Revolution. The former was a protracted process the full significance of which could be appreciated only gradually. The feelings evoked by the latter were immediate and traumatic, for it could more easily be identified with a series of events restricted in time and place. The soul-searching it generated was not confined to statesmen like Burke, political agitators like Paine or philosophers like Godwin, all of whose major works were published within five years of the fall of the Bastille. For many decades thinking minds from all walks of life were obsessed with its effects, and the reverberations it set up constituted a powerful factor in shaping the response to the accelerating social transformation that marked the period after Waterloo. Thus Hazlitt could argue that the Lake school of poetry 'had its origins in the French Revolution, or rather in those sentiments ... which produced [it]'.[1] Years after the Napoleonic wars Shelley referred back to 1789 as the opening of a phase of civilisation when tyranny could no longer go unchallenged.[2] And still later Carlyle collated the two revolutions in one of the most famous descriptions of the temper of the time:

> ... there is a deep-lying struggle in the whole fabric of society, a boundless grinding of the New with the Old ... these two hostile influences, which always exist in human things, and on the constant intercommunion of which depends their health and safety, had lain in separate masses, accumulating through generations, and France was the scene of their fiercest explosion; but the final issue was not unfolded in that country; nay, it is not yet anywhere unfolded.[3]

The following study focuses on a configuration of social and political ideas stemming from the attempt by the leading Romantic writers (however the term is interpreted) to find solutions to the underlying problems presented by the French cataclysm and the emergence of a new industrial civilisation. It covers a period ranging from the end of the eighteenth century to the eve of the First World War. The discussion begins with the effect produced on the thought of the Romantic writers by the French Revolution and its aftermath, and the subsequent application of their conclusions to the conditions in the England of their time. It proceeds to consider their influence throughout the century on the development of the peculiarly British varieties of conservatism and socialism, and ends with their contribution, largely at second or third hand, to what virtually amounts to a philosophy of empire.

In no small measure, the impact of the French Revolution on the great romantics and on the generations that followed them can be explained less by the events themselves than by the principles underlying the grievances that sparked them. The overt cause of most earlier revolutions had been predominantly religious or dynastic. The Glorious Revolution heralded a new type of revolution by putting an end to royal rule by divine right in favour of parliamentary governance. The inversion of the metaphor of the hierarchy of power as rising from below instead of being imposed from above inevitably involved a re-evaluation of secular political philosophy as a guide to the exercise of authority. None of the preceding theorists of government and the conduct of rulers achieved the immediate influence of Locke's elimination of the supernatural from political theory. Despite the differences of their objectives, both American and French revolutionaries drew directly or indirectly on his writings in support of their demands, whether national, constitutional, economic or social. However, the impress of his ideas must be seen in the wider context of what may be called a shift in the mental sets that was progressively undermining the traditional view of the world.

The Elizabethan principle of order and degree, or 'Great Chain of Being' as Pope termed it, together with the doctrine of plenitude, incorporated a hierarchic value system as well as a structural scheme imposed by divine fiat upon the entire universe from the Godhead itself to inert matter. After the Copernican and Newtonian revolutions the fixed and finite world picture was gradually replaced by the conception of an infinite open universe in which everything was subject to impersonal scientific laws. A similar devalorisation was attributed to Descartes' dualism, attacked by opponents of Cartesianism as leading to pure materialism and even atheism. A further dimension of the same shift relates to the conceptions of space and time. The earlier tendency had been to view even temporal matters in terms of spatial qualities. The formal attributes of balance, symmetry and repose were applicable to verse, music or dance no less than to architecture, painting or landscape-gardening. Fixed prescriptive rules of composition, such as the dramatic unities, literary decorum, the steps of the minuet, neo-Palladian buildings or the geometrical patterns of the French garden, all carried similar implications. As the century progressed, the transition to new standards of apprehension and evaluation was marked by the consideration of even spatial forms in terms of temporal qualities. The freer rhythmic and thematic structures of poetry, the function of the discord in projecting attention forward to some anticipated resolution, the flowing movements of the waltz, the soaring spires and irregularities of the neo-Gothic architecture or Bridgeman's device of the sunken fence to obliterate the boundaries between the garden and outside landscape are only a few examples. Comparable developments were evident in the sciences, which were no longer devoted chiefly to mathematics, physics, classification, and the like. Henceforth increasing attention was paid to the life sciences and to such subjects as mythology and geology which indicated development, growth and change. Analagously, in the social and economic spheres new points of view and modes of behaviour came to the fore. The conception of the organic society where the estates were bound by mutual local interests, dependencies and responsibilities had already been weakened by the pursuit of policies of centralised state regulation and control over the economy in the interest of national power and aggrandisement. But around the mid-eighteenth century the French Physiocrats began to propagate the doctrine of 'natural' (*physis* in Greek) unrestricted economic activity, which came to be identified with the slogan '*laissez faire, laissez passer, le monde va de lui-même*'. While serving a death-blow to Mercantilism, it equally drove a nail into the coffin of organicism and local paternalism. Not long before the French Revolution and at the time that the Industrial Revolution was gathering force, Adam Smith, who had personally known many of the leading physiocrats, published his *Wealth of Nations* which was to have a profound influence on the theories that were to dominate social and economic thought and practice for nearly a hundred years.

By the end of the eighteenth century, such transformations formed as it were a highly saturated solution; the suspension of the beads of the American and French Revolutions provided the nuclei of large crystals containing all its qualities. England was plunged into protracted wars which were to a large degree wars of ideas and principles. They led to much inner questioning, to the analysis of conflicting motives and to a close consideration of the forces strengthening or weakening society, which increased in importance as the dangers to national existence grew. The sense of urgency did not cease, however, with the final defeat of the French, for the economic dislocations resulting from the cost of the war and the demobilisation of the army combined with a growing awareness of the extent of the effects produced by the spread of the manufacturing system.

The Lake poets and their school were by no means the first to recognise how far the pace of technological, industrial and commercial expansion was modifying the traditional way of life. In 1770 Goldsmith lamented the depopulation of rural England due to the increase in urban wealth through trade. Nearer the end of the century Blake fulminated against the 'dark satanic mills' and the vice created by poverty in the slums of London. Erasmus Darwin, on the other hand, prophesied at the time of the French

Revolution the invention of the steamship, steamcar, and 'flying chariots through the fields of air'.[4] But such fears and hopes were held only by percipient writers, and even they tended to focus on specific effects — chiefly economic and social. As the time span of change contracted, and the transformation in all spheres of life entered the general consciousness, critics came to view what a recent critic labelled 'the machinery question'[5] — an integrated complex of economic, social, political, philosophical, even religious, factors — as all reinforcing one another. The machine itself was euhemerised into an almost supernatural principle pervading spiritual and material domains of human activity alike, so that Carlyle could define his age as 'the age of machinery in every outward and inward sense of that word'.[6] The feeling was accentuated by the crises that plagued England during the first half of the nineteenth century. Periodic trade dislocations and unemployment leading to social misery and hunger, riots, disturbances and fears of revolution, the emergence of an urban working class and of a well-to-do middle class demanding a larger share in power, all these brought to the fore the differences between the values and forms of tradition and the directions of experiment.

Perhaps the best formulation of the resulting bifurcation of opinion would be in terms of two myths that were widely held to the very end of the century. The myth of the 'brave new world', to use the famous phrase of Miranda in *The Tempest*, expressed exhilaration and optimism, a vision of new horizons, and a belief in the infinite potentialities of the machine to bring wealth and happiness to all. There were, of course, temporary social displacements and difficulties, and something should be done to better the condition of the poor. But individual initiative, 'self help', thrift and all the virtues later associated with Victorianism through the good offices of Samuel Smiles would enable every honest man to rise in status and prosper. Thomas Tegg, for example, drew in his *A Present for an Apprentice* a nineteenth-century version of Hogarth's *Industrious and Idle 'Prentice* series, summed up in a 'moral and physical thermometer'. This ranges from commercial and domestic success linked to diligence and milk and water drinking, to suicide or the gallows linked to idleness and strong spirits.[7] The opportunities offered by the new age were, in short, available to all, and only frailty and self-indulgence stood in the way of Everyman becoming healthy, wealthy and wise. Indeed, the conception of both men and materials as resources to be exploited rationally for the benefit of mankind would lead in due course to the elimination of social injustices inherited from the dark ages that preceded industrialism, and to the opening of an era of social harmony. More still, expansion of overseas trade would disseminate the blessings to the whole world, ushering in a new phase of human development. The factory system would become 'the greater minister of civilisation to the terraqueous globe, enabling this country, as its heart, to diffuse along with its commerce the life blood of science to ... myriads of people still lying "in the region and shadow of death"'.[8]

The counter-myth of 'merrie England' sprang from the belief that the machine from being the servant of man was becoming his master, the Golem of the medieval Jewish folktale of a mechanical monster which destroyed its inventor, or the fiendish creation of Mary Shelley's *Frankenstein.* The natural attachment to traditional ways of life intensified into a yearning for the pre-industrial good old days when a community of values prevailed. These were diametrically opposed to the values that predominated as the machine tangled and tore the delicate web of social life till 'Oneness fled, and strife and schism triumphed in their stead'.[9] Reciprocal duties and mutual responsibilities, a communal economy and a social structure in which every member knew and respected the place of everyone else, were set against the atomism of individualisitic competition, the cash nexus and the mobility resulting from universal ambition to get on; the wholesome country life and vital contact with nature were the reverse of the artificialities of 'the great Wen', the city in which poverty bred vice and disease; the satisfaction and pride of the craftsman in his work were contrasted with the alienation of the factory hand, enslaved by the machine and turned into a robot-like extension of itself; and the spirituality of religious convictions was seen as replaced by the arid materialism that substituted Mammon for God.

However, the two myths by no means summed up the attitude of all Englishmen of the time. Many combined elements of both in varying proportions. In *Locksley Hall* (1837-8) Tennyson envisioned 'airy navies' transporting merchandise through the heavens, drawing the ends of the world together and heralding 'the Parliament of man, the Federation of the World'. Yet he acknowledged that the 'jingling of the guinea' was debasing the national spirit and that airships could become machines of war raining 'ghastly dew', to the destruction of mankind. Disraeli saw feudalism as 'the noblest, the grandest, the most magnificent and benevolent [system] that was ever conceived by sage or ever practised by patriot', but admitted that industry was 'the primary source of our wealth and greatness'.[10] Nor was this ambivalence restricted to the first half of the century. Towards the end of the second half, Morris dreamt of a return to the rural community with its social and personal values, but enjoying the benefits of modern technological invention, which, unseen and self-run, would perform the duller and more laborious functions of society. The Garden-City movement sought to create 'a new civilisation' in which 'the men and women of today [would] join hands with the men and women of yesterday, aye, and of the remote past'.[11] And the 'seismograph of the day', as a recent critic called the poet John Davidson, urged his generation to break out of the 'dark dungeon' of the present and 'Get out into the splendid Past/Or bid the splendid Future hail'.[12]

Neither those whose gaze was fixed on the distance horizons of the future nor those who looked back to a distant past, nor yet those who squinted in both directions, could ignore the immediate realities of the present. All had in common the need to find a way out of the shifting confusions of the contemporary situation towards a more coherent and stable future. The obvious sign of an age of transition, J.S. Mill wrote, is that 'the world of opinions is a mere chaos'. What with the division among the instructed, and the resulting loss of faith in them, 'the multitude are without a guide' and yearn for someone to provide them with spectacles through which to see more clearly the path to follow.[13] In the course of their interpretations of the 'signs of the times', the romantics therefore not only expressed their own apprehensions of the present and their visions of the future but were filling a general need. They were, of course, not the only ones. Moreover, they were not free from 'divisions'. Byron dismissed Keats in unprintable terms and damned the Lake poets for writing poems diluted, appropriately enough, 'with plenty of water'. Southey reviled Byron as leader of the 'Satanic school', and came to see Shelley as a pernicious immoralist. Carlyle had little use for either Coleridge or Wordsworth, while the latter regarded him as 'Power's blind Idolator'.[14] Examples could be multiplied to show that they contributed not a little to what Carlyle caustically called the 'fatidical fury spread[ing] wider and wider',[15] the plethora of opposing creeds, tenets and prophecies that were plaguing the country.

However, over and above their differences there was an overlapping area, a shared pattern of ideas acquired from one another, modified, developed and passed on from one generation to another, sufficient to justify the use of the loose term 'Romantics' to a distinct stream of nineteenth-century British political thought. As the century progressed, this romantic tradition came to influence important currents within both radicalism and conservatism, thus imparting to them something of a family resemblance.

Regarded in isolation, several of the components may be found in other schools of thought, notably German and French. What distinguished the great British romantics was the way they integrated the components into a complex structure which allowed them to bring the weight and meaning of the whole to bear on any particular, thereby creating 'a cosmos out of chaos', to use Carlyle's phrase about Tennyson. A brief outline might start with their epistemological position since it formed the prior assumption of their world-view. Half-way between idealism and materialism, it conceives human creativity not as restricted to mental activity but as equally manifest in the shaping of the world without. In Shelley's terminology, there is an 'unremitting interchange' between mind and matter;[16] mental activity forges its reality out of what is external to itself, each conditioning and being conditioned by the other as both cause and effect. Man and his environment, the romantics believed, are consequently the products of developmental processes of constant, mutual modification. Since society constitutes a part of man's environment, it too is subject to continual change.

These suppositions lie behind what could be called an axiological interpretation of society, the consideration of ethical, aesthetic, religious and other values as key factors in determining its nature. The romantics saw progress, material and social, as activated by universal and eternal truths implicit in such symbol structures as religions, myths or art. These are communicated by cultural agents — poet-prophets, 'Heroes', or representatives of established creeds — who give voice in particular time-bound terms to those objectives to which man should aspire as a dynamic being in an ever-changing world. They are translated into practical terms in the form of laws, institutions and customs which bind society together, prescribe the relationships among its members, and determine their use and their control of the 'universe of things'. However, the romantics did not regard evolution as continuous or steady; social and material changes affect the interpretation and execution of the values that motivate society by rendering the symbol structures that enshrine them obsolete, or by dulling response to them through habituation. Laws, institutions and other codes of action degenerate into empty rituals and periodically must be updated and reinvigorated. They therefore held society to be in a state of constant oscillation between two extreme conditions: that in which it is stimulated to advance by new symbol structures, and that in which it is kept static by habit and custom.

On such a foundation the great romantics developed a philosophy of history according to which society passes in its evolution through phases, each marked by the stages of birth, maturation, wearing-down and finally re-birth, but at a higher level. For them, periods of transition between death and re-birth constitute peripeties in the social drama. At such times the decline of symbol structures results in the loosening of the bonds that hold the people together, and shared values give way to the principle of 'everyone for himself'. This manifests itself in a growing gap between those who possess power and can exploit their fellow-beings and those who are reduced to mere instruments for satisfying the egotism of the strong. The exploiters seek to retain their power by clinging to outworn laws and institutions. The social order is frozen into a tyranny based on self-interest, and 'man's inhumanity to man' is justified by the claim that forms and codes are eternal. The victimised many resent the law and threaten to seek redress by a '*bellum servile*'. Society is thus torn between the twin dangers of despotism and anarchy. Such processes may come to a head in a fully-fledged social explosion of which the French Revolution provided a paradigm. But for all the sympathy for the suffering that sought release in violence, the romantics felt they could not ignore the dangers involved. Since the root causes of transitional crises are the breakdown of symbol systems, violence can at best play a part in sweeping away the debris of the past. In itself it can offer no positive substitute for the order it has demolished. On the other hand, it breeds general misery and indiscriminate destruction, and is liable to result in new forms of dictatorship.

The French Revolution was for the romantics a prophecy narrated as it were in the past tense. Society was again caught in a state of suspension in which traditional beliefs and codes of behaviour were no longer valid and the sense of communality had disintegrated. Their criticism of the capitalist system had many affinities with that of the early-nineteenth-century socialists. It also had important points of contact with the social idea implicit in the 'Gothic revival' or cult of medievalism. They repudiated political economy and utilitarianism as both responses to and stimuli of the predicament resulting from the loosening of shared values, the materialism and the withdrawal into what Adam Smith called 'self love'. Mammonism was taking roots as a new religion, and its rites involved the total abnegation of social duty and compassion. They could not but note the irreconcilable antagonism, the polarisation and the simplification of society into a class which possessed capital and the means of production and a class which owned nothing but its labour power. The few were growing richer, the many were being reduced into mere 'hands'.

However, the historical framework within which the romantics analysed their times led to the emergence of a recognisably distinct point of view. Notwithstanding their sensitivity to the seamy side of the Industrial Revolution, they interpreted social misery as the external manifestation of a weakening of the nation's moral fibre. Hence they did not allocate the blame to commercial and industrial expansion as such. Indeed, their epistemological doctrine made them alive to the potential good accruing from the realisation of man's inherent nature as a creator. They therefore tended to concentrate their attention on the upsetting of the natural balance between the material and the spiritual, and the remedy they sought lay in restoring to their rightful relationship man's inner and outer worlds. Ultimately, 'the mind of man' was 'the haunt and main region' of their political philosophy. More still, their understanding of historical patterns led them to see the new industrial order emerging from the pre-industrial one as itself constituting a transitional phase towards a future order which would incorporate and take further the best elements of those which preceded it. What hung in the balance was the means by which this change would be effected. If the classes continued to drift apart, and the workers became poorer, the workers would be provoked by despair to violence. Such a calamity could only be avoided by reform of the heart accompanied by judicious measures to eliminate injustice, revive community consciousness and reactivate society on a higher level. The great romantics all believed in the need for new spiritual guides to inspire and direct the people to subjugate their individual interests to the wider ones of the nation.

While they differed as to the nature, scope and modes of application of specific reforms, their contribution as a whole to English reformism, over and above the moral argument, was mainly the combination of two distinct approaches. One was the adoption of the principles of the manorial system to industrial conditions, ensuring the personal contact and reciprocal relations which make a community out of an aggregate of individuals. The other was the role of the state in initiating and controlling social change, justified by its being a supra-sectional entity standing for the entire nation, one which could express the elements that give the people and their culture an identity that could withstand vicissitude.

The writers chosen to illustrate this line of social and political thinking represent three generations, as defined by the period covering the composition of their major works: Wordsworth and Southey, Shelley and Keats, and lastly Carlyle. Wordsworth serves as a kind of paradigmatic figure. He was the only British romantic to have participated in person in the early stages of the French Revolution; indeed, had he not returned to England in time he might well have become a victim of the Terror. His greatest work, *The Prelude*, provides the earliest and fullest autobiographical account of the effects of this period on the development of his philosophy of life. Together with the semi-autobiographical books of *The Excursion*, it also offers the most detailed exposition of the psychological and axiological approaches to society which lay at the root of the theories of the other writers dealt with in this book. Southey was chosen because as a historian and a critic of current social and political events he built out of these approaches a detailed analysis of conditions in England which, in his *Quarterly Review* articles published during the Napoleonic wars, he developed into an overall philosophy of history. He also illustrates the way in which the initial romantic rebellious spirit could be harnessed to reinvigorate and reformulate conservatism. The seminal thought of Coleridge permeates the discussion of both these figures. If he has not been selected for fuller treatment it is because so many of his opinions overlap those of his two friends. Moreover, his main addition to the ideas he held in common with them was in the area of metaphysical and theological speculation, which lie beyond the scope of this study. With certain exceptions, especially in *The Friend* and the *Lay Sermons*, he was less involved with the pragmatic issues of the day. Some of his theories, such as that of the organic society, largely a distillation of German and

French writings, were undoubtedly influential, and have been touched on in relation to their counterparts in the theories of the other romantics. On the whole, however, his mark on practising politicians as well as on the political ideas of the following generations of British romantics was less than Southey's.

Shelley has been taken as the chief representative of the second generation because in poetry, prose and at first in action, he devoted so much of his brief life to the issues of the day and to the development of a philosophy which would explain their direction. His early death prevented the realisation of his plan to write a full history of the growth of human civilisation, but enough remains to show how he intended to develop further the moral premises in the doctrines of his predecessors, concentrating on the role of ethical and aesthetic values in the evolution of social systems. He also illustrates how romantic thought could reinvigorate and reformulate radicalism. Keats was added because his most important longer work dealt with the theory of the succession of culture cycles to explain in a way reminiscent of Shelley's doctrines the application of the principles underlying the classical theomachy to contemporary life. Byron, on the other hand, has been omitted in spite of his being more directly involved in the revolutionary movements of Italy and Greece, and the excitement he aroused among the reading and writing public at home and on the continent. The reason for omitting Byron is that the sensationalism of his life and death which set up such shock-waves was caused by his actions and personality rather than by his theories. Goethe said of him that for all his greatness when he thought he was a child. This explains why his impact on social and political thought was brief and limited, whereas Shelley's writings increased in influence, from Benjamin Disraeli and the Chartists of the mid-century to the socialists at the end of the century.

Of the third generation only one writer is dealt with, Carlyle. His works, especially those written during the 1830s and 1840s, brought into sharper focus both the conservative and radical elements that sometimes lived in strange symbiosis in the doctrines of the earlier romantics. He also introduced into his philosophy of history a theory of revolution, of the nature of leadership, and of man as *Homo Faber*, all present in embryo in the teachings of Wordsworth, Southey and Shelley. Tennyson has regretfully been passed over. Although in youth he contributed in some degree to the revolutionary movement in Spain, his political opinions did not differ significantly from those of his friend Carlyle, and his lifelong work on the rise and fall of the Christian culture, *The Idylls of the King*, recalls, although far more fully and pessimistically, the *Hyperion* of Keats. Moreover, his political impact was negligible compared with that of his friend Carlyle, the great populariser of the romantic tradition in the Victorian age. As Frederic Harrison wrote, 'Carlyle had so much to do with the birth of the new movements in religion, in socialism, in art, in history, in criticism and even poetry' that few escaped his influence 'even where they have greatly improved on the strong impulse which he first imparted'.[17] Among those who fell under Carlyle's sway, at least at some period or other of their lives, were men of the calibre of Dickens and Gissing, Tyndall and Huxley, Mazzini and Mill, a veritable *embarras de richesse*. It is impossible therefore to appreciate the spread of the romantic tradition and its place in British political thought without following the scope and significance of Carlyle's doctrines.

The later chapters of the book are devoted to the analysis of the way in which the essential traits of the tradition were transmitted chiefly through Carlyle to his disciples, and by them to theirs. Chapter 5 sketches the views of three avowed conservatives who expressed different shades of what came to be known as Tory radicalism or Tory democracy. Disraeli, the leading figure of nineteenth-century conservatism, illustrates the general line of the thesis, appropriating in his early writings elements of both Shelley's and Southey's philosophies and later, under the influence of Carlyle, fusing them into the doctrine of the Young England movement. Kingsley, rather than Maurice, was taken to represent Christian Socialism, firstly because he regarded himself as a direct follower of Carlyle who personally helped him in his career and, secondly, because he in turn influenced the socialists of the late century. Further, more than his fellow Christian socialists, he extended his religious and social views to form an entire philosophy of history. Finally, the choice of Ruskin was inevitable. With Froude he was one of the closest friends of Carlyle, and probably the most influential of all his disciples. What he developed was the aesthetic, anti-industrial streak in the romantic tradition, which extended its impact to embrace another stream of thought well represented by such figures as Morris and Blatchford. He also took further the conception of the state as the supra-sectional initiator and administrator of reform, investing it with almost totalitarian powers. This may explain in part why he, although a declared Tory, had such a profound effect on late-nineteenth-century socialists.

Chapter 6 focuses on the romantic element in the ideologies propounded by Keir Hardie, Bruce Glasier, his successor as leader of the Independent Labour Party and editor of its weekly paper, and Ramsay MacDonald, who was to become the first Labour Prime Minister. Even if the latter was exaggerating when he claimed that British socialists were 'overwhelmingly standing by the attitude taken by the ILP' and that its rivals were 'grotesquely' overrated,[18] it remains true that it was by far the most popular socialist grouping within the Labour movement. Blatchford has been included in this chapter for purposes of comparison. Himself a founder of the ILP, he became the leader of the Clarionites, and his writings, in particular *Merrie England*, were the most widely read of all socialist literature of the time. Although he was a bitter enemy of Hardie, their common indebtedness to Carlyle, Ruskin and Kingsley explains the fundamental similarity of their views.

The last chapter, on the British idea of empire, serves in effect as a summary of many of the leading elements of the romantic tradition. It shows how the epistemological and axiological pillars on which it was based constituted the cornerstones of an ideology of empire which sought to restore a lost unity by fusing the vision of a return to the pre-industrial patterns of society with that of a progress towards an industrial utopia. The chapter opens with an analysis of the imperialist doctrines of some of the romantics themselves: Wordsworth, Southey and Carlyle. It proceeds to discuss similar traits in the thought of three thinkers of the period preceding the First World War. Kipling was an obvious choice because of the enormous popularity of his fiction and verse; Milner was an important colonial administrator whose opinions were reinforced by practical experience; Kidd was the most widely read of those who based their doctrines on empire on evidence adduced from the social sciences. Kidd also exemplifies the disillusionment that overtook so many with the realisation that with the Great War an era had passed, and the dream of reconciling 'merrie England' with a 'brave new world' was no longer possible. Since then the empire has vanished, and the patterns of domestic and public life have changed beyond recognition. The romantic tradition made a valuable contribution to British political thought during the nineteenth century. How far its influence in our day is still potent is greatly in doubt, but perhaps, as Tennyson wrote,

> The old order changeth, yielding place to new,
> and God fulfils himself in many ways,
> Lest one good custom should corrupt the world.

Notes

1. W. Hazlitt, *The Complete Works of William Hazlitt*, P.P. Howe (ed.) (London: Dent, 1930-4), vol. V, p. 161.
2. P.B. Shelley, *Shelley's Prose, or the Trumpet of a Prophecy*, D.L. Clark (ed.) (Albuquerque: University of New Mexico Press, 1954), p. 236.
3. T. Carlyle, *The Works of Thomas Carlyle in Thirty Volumes*, H.D. Traill (ed.) (London: Chapman and Hall, 1907), vol. XXVII, p. 82.
4. E. Darwin, *The Botanic Garden, a Poem in two parts* (London: J. Johnson, 4th edn, 1799), vol. I, ll. 289-96.
5. M. Berg, *The Machinery Question and the Making of Political Economy 1815-1848* (Cambridge, London and New York: Cambridge University Press, 1980).
6. Carlyle, *Works*, vol. XXVII, p. 59.
7. T. Tegg, *A Present for an Apprentice* (London: William Tegg, 1838), frontispiece.
8. A. Ure, *The Philosophy of Manufacturers, or, an Exposition of the Scientific, Moral and Commercial Economy of the Factory System of Great Britain* (London: Charles Knight, 2nd edn, 1835), pp. 18-19.
9. J. Manners, *England's Trust* (London: J.G.F. and J. Riverson, 1841), p. 5.
10. T.E. Kebble, *Selected Speeches of the Earl of Beaconsfield* (London: John Murray, revised edn, 1928), vol. I, p. 163.
11. E. Howard, 'Preface' in G.M. Harris, *The Garden City Movement* (London: Garden City Press, 1906), pp. 14-15. See also E. Howard, *Garden Cities of To-morrow* (London: Faber and Faber, n.d.), p. 131.
12. J.B. Townsend, *John Davidson, Poet of Armaggedon* (New Haven, Conn: Yale University Press, 1961), p. viii; J. Davidson, *St. George's Day* (New York: John Lane, 1895), p. 8.
13. J.S. Mill, *Mill's Essays on Literature and Society*, J.B. Schneewing (ed.) (New York and London: Collier-Macmillan, 1965), pp. 36, 47.
14. W. Wordsworth, *Sonnet: In Allusion to various recent histories and Notices of the French Revolution.*
15. Carlyle, *Works*, vol. XXVI, p. 58.
16. P.B. Shelley, *Mont Blanc*.
17. F. Harrison, *The Choice of Books and other Literary Pieces* (London: Macmillan, 1887), p. 192.
18. In a letter to Algie M. Simon, April 16th, 1915, Algie M. Simon Papers, *State Historical Society of Wisconsin.*

1 THE POLITICAL MESSAGE OF WORDSWORTH'S *PRELUDE*

I

Writers of biographies and autobiographies, whether historical or fictional, are confronted with a major problem: at what point should they begin their narrative? The birth of the protagonist seems an obvious choice. But to the analysis of his early conditioning and environment there should be added his inherited characteristics, and to deal fairly with these the author is led further and further back in time. Sterne, in his pseudo-autobiography, *Tristram Shandy*, chose to start not with his birth but with the moment of his conception, and this drew him into such a wild goose chase that he himself barely enters the story at all. In the recent debates on abortion, medical, religious and legal authorities have been at variance on this same issue of when a person begins. However, both conception and birth do constitute physiological events that offer a beginning of sorts.

The same cannot be postulated of ideas. In taking some prominent figures of what is commonly called the school of British romanticism as fathers of a specific kind of political theory in nineteenth-century England, we are really starting *in medias res*. The only justification for any claim of paternity is that they were the most distinguished propagators of a distinctive social and political brand of thought. If William Blake is excluded on the grounds that he was barely known till long after his death, the oldest and perhaps most influential is Wordsworth, although where he begins and Coleridge ends or vice versa is a question as difficult as that of origins. *The Prelude*, the work which most clearly illustrates Wordsworth's philosophy, and to which he devoted so much of his life, was not published till 1850. Nevertheless, the ideas developed there can be traced back half a century to the *Lyrical Ballads*, the Preface of which (1800) has been termed 'the manifesto of English romanticism'. They also appear in *The Excursion* (1814) and permeate most of his shorter poems. In focusing on *The Prelude*, therefore, we come to grips with the most extended and explicit exposition of his views. The intention of this chapter is to show that at the heart of this work lies a social and political doctrine that challenged the various contemporary schools of political thought and was designed to serve as an answer to the underlying problems posed by the French and Industrial Revolutions.

That Wordsworth was deeply interested in social and political matters is well known. He went so far as to state that he had given 'twelve hours of thought to the conditions and prospects of society for one to poetry'.[1] However, the critics interested in his political views concern themselves for the most part with the early radicalism of the 'Letter to the Bishop of Llandaff', the later nationalism of 'The Convention of Cintra', and the increasing conservatism that followed his acceptance of a government sinecure (1813). *The Prelude* has been valued as a biographical record containing an aesthetic philosophy and a doctrine of Nature. Wordsworth's experiences in revolutionary France are usually drawn upon to confirm or explain ideas he came to accept, but not as the expression of an original political theory which is a major strand in the whole poem. Lindenberger has summed up the common attitude in his pronouncement that notwithstanding all the space the poet devoted to the revolution and its aftermath, 'the *Prelude* has as little real concern with politics as perhaps any longer work in our literature'.[2] Such a comment is the more surprising since it stands in contradiction to Wordsworth's general holistic philosophy, to his belief that his own experiences blended to form the unity of his personality and to his avowed doctrine of the integration of man, nature and society.

A possible reason for the common failure to appreciate the full significance of the social and political message of *The Prelude* is that it is presented not in discursive prose but in blank verse, often of great poetic intensity. However, one of its cardinal points was precisely that the emotional medium of verse was best fitted to 'systematically lay down rules for the actions of men'. In an unfinished essay on 'moral habits' written shortly before starting on the epic, Wordsworth categorised Godwin, Paley 'and the whole tribe of authors of that class' as impotent. The rationalising faculty, he maintained, is secondary to the deepest levels of our feelings, and when abstracted from the matrix of the instincts and emotions produces a series of sterile propositions which fail to deliver their message and 'presenting no image to the mind can convey no feeling which has any connection with the supposed archetype or fountain of the proposition existing in human life'.

Denying therefore both the methodology of these authors and the claims deriving from it, he planned to provide a substitute in the form of a 'system of moral philosophy written with sufficient power to melt into our affections, to incorporate itself into the blood and vital juices of our minds' and thereby actively to influence daily behaviour.[3] In effect, he was taking sides in the 'old quarrel between philosophy and poetry' referred to in *The Republic*, by which the exclusion of poets from the ideal city was justified. Speaking as a philosopher, Socrates warned that 'poetry mustn't be taken seriously as a serious thing laying hold of truth', and that if the muse is allowed to influence politics, 'pleasure and pain will jointly be kings in our city instead of law and that argument which in each instance is best in the opinion of the community'.[4] Wordsworth in the Preface to the 1800 edition of the *Lyrical Ballads* enlisted the authority of Aristotle's view that poetry is the 'most philosophic of all writings' since 'its object is truth, not individual and local, but general, and operative'.[5] He even went further to argue that creative imagination is the primary quality of the human mind, that poetry is this quality in its highest form, and hence that it is the poet's vision that pierces beyond the contingential and accidental to hold up to the rulers the true principles that should govern social behaviour.

Another explanation of the neglect of political theory in *The Prelude* may be the autobiographical nature of the poem. As the title supplied by Wordsworth's widow indicates, and as the Prospectus to the 1814 edition of *The Excursion* (written in 1800) confirms, the author in the course of composition accepted Coleridge's suggestion that the story of his life should serve as an introduction to a longer work, a 'philosophical poem on Man, Nature, and Society' to be called 'The Recluse', of which only the opening book was in fact written. What might be called Wordsworth's justificatory *curriculum vitae* was published posthumously with the sub-title 'growth of a poet's mind, an autobiographical poem'. However, as has just been noted, for Wordsworth a poet is an exemplary representative of human nature who in no way differs 'in kind from other men, but only in degree', and who stands for humanity at large.[6] The hero of the work is therefore not only Wordsworth but in a sense all of mankind. He conforms to the definition offered by Coleridge (to whom the poem was addressed) of the symbol as having value for itself as a concrete particular, but also serving as a translucent medium for a universal principle. The truth of the biographical detail is consequently of secondary importance. As Wordsworth himself admitted:

> I cannot say what portion is in truth
> The naked recollection of that time
> And what may rather have been call'd to life
> By after-meditation[7]

There is a circular argument involved in the very selection of the incidents narrated. The work opens with a preamble dealing with Wordsworth's feelings on leaving Bristol in 1795, although mostly written several years later, describing the author's hesitations as to whether he was capable of a great work and as to the subject he should choose. Were these doubts, he asked, the extinction of all the advantages and promise of his early years? The final books show that the answer to the question was in the asking of it, for his life itself pointed to and illustrated the thesis he had sought. It also indicated the source of his poetic powers and his qualifications to 'teach [and] inspire'.[8] This new awareness was fully formed not earlier than 1799, when he conceived the idea of writing the poem. His subsequent selection, refractions, emphases and revisions for nearly half a century were therefore already conditioned by a prior theory which he nevertheless represented as the outcome of the matter treated. The result is that the philosophy and its exemplification through the autobiographical medium are so involved in each other that each is fully comprehensible only in terms of the other.

Finally, it could be argued that the minor importance attached by critics to the political ideas is due to the fact that the thesis of Wordsworth's life-work, as proclaimed in the prospectus of that other fragment of 'The Recluse', *The Excursion*, suggests that his themes were psychological, aesthetic, philosophic and religious. What is insufficiently noted is that these themes were so closely interwoven with his social and political theories that they constitute a single unitary conception of human nature and behaviour. What he called his 'high argument' may be summed up in three propositions. First, that contrary to the contemporary idealist school,

> ... the individual Mind
> (And the progressive powers perhaps no less

Of the whole species) to the external world
Is fitted.

Second, that contrary to contemporary mechanistic materialism, 'the external World is fitted to the Mind'. Third, that just as God is the Creator of the Universe, so man, blending the powers of his mind with the forces of nature, is the creator of his own universe: the two forces 'with blended might' accomplish 'creation (by no lower name/Can it be called)'. However, the three propositions are followed by what amounts to a fourth: that any discussion of them must shed light on 'the tribes/And fellowships of men'. The application of this connection was particularly important at a time when society was in turmoil and its structures in danger of collapse, since only through it could solutions be offered. Indeed, what triggered his interpretation of his life in terms of the propositions were his personal experiences, both in France and in England, of societies torn by 'madding passions mutually inflamed'[9] and his pondering on the causes, the course and the ultimate meaning of such upheavals. The examination of the political ideas in *The Prelude* must therefore start with a consideration of the situations which played such a large part in their formation.

II

Reduced to the barest essentials, the description of Wordsworth's experiences in France and the eddies they set up in his mind fall into three phases which form a distinct progression in his emotional and intellectual development and in his appreciation of his relation to society. The first covers his meetings with the revolutionaries and monarchists as an uninvolved spectator. The second shows how he took sides as a partisan in the struggle. In the third, after an interim period of total disillusion and despair, he found his true role as a poet-prophet-philosopher entrusted with the mission to bring home to his compatriots the way to the good society which he himself had so painfully learned. Concurrently, his understanding of the principles operating behind social realities unfolded from unreflecting reactions conditioned by his early environment during the first phase, through his concentration on socio-political factors such as leadership during the second, to the understanding of society as inseparable from nature and the mind of man in the third.

The first phase dates from 1790, when Wordsworth and a fellow-student set out on a walking tour on the continent. Europe at that time rejoiced,

> France standing on the top of golden hours,
> And human nature seeming born again.[10]

On their way they were befriended by a group of revolutionary delegates returning from commemorating the first anniversary of the fall of the Bastille. Infected by the general euphoria the two young foreigners joined in their revelry, but later, proceeding alone, they were shocked at the sight of the ransacking of the ancient convent of Chartreuse by revolutionary troops. Nature itself, Wordsworth wrote, recoiled from the sacrilege, and his early upbringing in the Lake District, among people rooted in faith and tradition, led him to reject the iconoclastic ideal of breaking with the past in the name of liberty.

The same causes determined his rejection of the monarchist cause. During his second stay in France (1791-2) he struck up a friendship with a band of royalist officers of the Blois garrison who tried to win him over to the side of the *ancien régime*. His instinctive sympathy lay, however, with the common man, and he was repelled by the 'pomp of orders and degree'.[11] In Cumberland, he wrote, he had never come into personal contact with anyone who was granted special privileges through claims of wealth and blood. Nor as a student in Cambridge, so he claimed, did he ever meet with 'attention and respect' granted other than on the basis of intellectual achievement. His childhood and youth thus enabled him to seize upon two cardinal elements at issue between the warring camps — on the one hand, the traditional gulf between the common people and the members of the *ancien régime*, the perpetuation of which was fought for by the monarchists; on the other, the wrenching of a nation from its past and tradition by the revolutionaries. However, judging events in terms of his native environment, he was oblivious to the nature and magnitude of the clash he was witnessing and to the universal principles at stake. Faced by 'conflicting passions' and unable to identify with either, he felt himself an outsider for whom 'all things were .../Loose and disjointed, and the affections left/Without a vital interest.[12]

The second phase began with his friendship with Beaupuy, the only officer of the garrison to espouse the revolutionary cause.

Between the two there was an immediate affinity, the young commoner put off by the doctrinaire extremism of both monarchists and republicans, and the older revolutionary-aristocrat balancing with wide toleration both 'custom and habit, novelty and change'.[13] Their 'heart bracing colloquies' on the ends of government and the lessons of the past enabled Wordsworth better to apprehend the weaknesses he had sensed in the arguments of both sides. He became aware that they resembled each other in denying the principles of unity and continuity, the one with the present, the other with the past. The dogmas of the revolutionaries had therefore to be mitigated by a deeper knowledge of history, while the vices of the old order could be eradicated by the social idealism of the revolutionaries. The seemingly contradictory sentiments which had both attracted and estranged him now complemented each other to form a united conception of social change.

The effects of these lengthy discussions gave greater depth to his perception of the significance of ordinary experiences. A decade or so later, when he was writing *The Prelude*, a particular event remained especially fresh in his memory. During one of his walks with Beaupuy on the banks of the Loire, they chanced upon a 'hunger bitten girl' leading a cow tied to her arm while knitting in a heartless mood. This obviously was not the poet's first encounter with poverty. One may compare his reactions with those evoked at the sight of 'The Cumberland Beggar' during a walk in his childhood. Like the girl in France, this meeting too was 'observed, and with great benefit to my own heart'. But the beggar, although 'helpless in appearance', was grasped as a symbol of the warmth of an organic community which gave him alms as of unquestioned natural right. The girl, by contrast, appeared as a symbol of victimisation and social injustice. 'T'is against *that*/that we are fighting',[14] Beaupuy exclaimed; and the political abstractions took on for Wordsworth flesh and blood. It now came upon him that the revolution was not directed merely at local reform but was a battle for 'better days/For all mankind', so that poverty 'would in a little time/Be found no more'.[15]

In this confident mood he left for Paris, passing the square where the September massacres had taken place a few weeks earlier. The events were not unknown to him, but he had regarded them as regrettable consequences of revolutionary fanaticism which 'were past,/Earth free from them for ever'.[16] Now, however, his presence at the very place of carnage so worked upon his mind that he could see and touch the lifeless corpses strewn on the ground, and in a trance he heard a voice crying to the whole city 'Sleep no more'.[17] As with the ransacking at Chartreuse and the sight of the half-starved girl, the place triggered something akin to what he called 'spots of time', moments of illumination when we see 'into the heart of things'. He now realised that his earlier confidence was misplaced. The extremes of reaction and of revolution had equally to be resisted, and he could no longer stand outside the struggle. Since 'the destiny of Man still/Hung upon single persons',[18] he became convinced that only a strong moral leader could keep the people under control and clear 'a passage for just government'.[19] Such a leader, if he is not to degenerate into a tyrant, must be a man of 'self-restraint', aware of the 'solid birthright'[20] of the people and anxious to put an end to their suffering, yet conversant with the 'example given/By ancient law-givers'.[21] The only party that held such principles and had such leaders were the Girondins, and so Wordsworth decided to join them.

However, in December 1792 he had to return home,[22] and before he could go back, England, to his horror, declared war on France. From afar he watched the fate of a country controlled not by the ideal leader he dreamed of, but by tyrants drawing from

> ... a terrific reservoir of guilt
> And ignorance filled up from age to age,
> That could no longer hold its loathsome charge,
> But burst and spread in deluge through the Land.[23]

Nevertheless he continued to believe that if only France could overcome the crisis a new society could still emerge that would serve as a model for all nations. His identification with the enemy was the stronger because he saw at home the very vices of oppression and injustice that had brought about the revolution in France. The shepherds of the English nation 'Thirsted to make the guardian Crook of Law/A tool of murder'[24] and

> ... leagu'd
> Their strength perfidiously, to undermine
> Justice, and make an end to Liberty.[25]

The death of Robespierre seemed to vindicate his confidence. The Terror had put a stop to the resurrection of hope following the winter of the *ancien régime*; but now the fall of the Jacobins presaged 'blossoms of a second spring'. Although the new authorities took as yet little positive action, he believed that the 'Great, universal, irresistible' tide of revolution would soon sweep all before it.[26]

Events, however, proved his faith misplaced. The French, intoxicated by power, took advantage of their military strength to conquer and dominate Holland, Spain, Italy and Germany. 'Oppressors in their turn' they

> ... changed a war of self defence
> For one of conquest, losing sight of all
> Which they had struggled for.[27]

Despite the extent of his disappointment, Wordsworth refused to forgo his ideals. Rather, he embarked on a study of political philosophy in order to provide a rational basis for his 'passionate intuition'.[28] But the conflicting views he encountered in the books, far from inspiring him with renewed confidence, discouraged him yet further. Trying out the approach of the theoreticians and examining every social value as an abstraction in the light of pure logic, he found that one could prove or disprove anything by rational manipulation. Each thinker formulated his system in the light of his own prejudices and ambitions, thus rationalising the immediate and accidental instead of exploring the permanent and essential. In practice, this also meant that it was vain to hope for a leader who would be 'Sage, Patriot, Lover, Hero'.[29] Like the philosophers, even the best men of power, for all their talk of abstract reason and absolute systems of government, 'were not free from taint/Of something false and weak'.[30] 'Sick, wearied out with contrarieties' he 'yielded up moral questions in despair', and forswearing the world like a monk sought consolation in the natural scenes that had delighted him in youth, and in poetry which deals with 'purer creatures' and dreams of perfection.[31]

This escape from the world of politics led paradoxically to the third phase, in which Wordsworth began to see his vocation as the propounder of the true values of social and political life. Learning to understand the principles animating the 'Soul of Nature',[32] and under the healing influence of his sister and of Coleridge, he found that the same principles have analogues in the operation of the human mind, the external world as apprehended through our senses and the relations binding man to man. He used the term 'right reason', probably taken from Price, to stand for the leap of the creative imagination to the intuition of truth, as distinct from the 'false reasonings' of logical dissection.[33] It taught him that there are permanent forces shining through the transitory sensible phenomena. The 'feeling intellect' intuits the Power of Nature and reveals to

... the mind intoxicate[d]
with present objects, and the busy dance
of things that pass away a temperate show
of things that endure[34]

Similarly, in society there are two co-existing 'kindred' dimensions — that of 'vicissitude' and that of 'permanence'. Such knowledge, he asserted, is the source of distinction between the moral and the immoral, and the sense of 'true proportion'. It is, therefore, the key to right social behaviour.[35]

This conception was in effect a realisation of the full significance of the voices Wordsworth heard in the Chartreuse and the Square of the Carrousel episodes. It also provides a clue to the reasons for the failures of the French. Revolutionaries and monarchists alike relied on 'abstract principles, drawn out of the laboratory of unfeeling philosphists'.[36] Manipulating logic to legitimise their predilections and prejudices they brought divisiveness to extremes, thus breaching the continuum of social existence. By contrast, the 'power/That is the visible quality and shape/And image of right reason'[37] teaches that the transient is rooted in the enduring and change in tradition, just as 'the spiritual world' holds 'fit converse' with 'sensible impressions', and as higher minds can relate to the 'generations of mankind/Spread over time, past, present, and to come'.[38]

The pattern of Wordsworth's development, it has been held, follows that of Dante's *Divina Commedia*: the Purgatory of his youth, the Hell of his early maturity, and the final achievement of Paradise. Such a progress was not uncommon in English literature, and Milton, Bunyan and Blake may serve as representative examples. Coleridge, in his *Table Talk*, commented to the same effect on the plan of 'The Recluse' as falling into the stages of 'man in contact with external nature, the present state of degeneracy and vice' and finally 'the whole state of man and society being subject to, and illustrative of, a redemptive process in operation'.[39] Some critics have suggested that after Wordsworth's sojourn in hell and passage through the city of destruction he attained the paradise of seclusion, far removed from the evils of politics. Closer examination reveals, on the contrary, that his recovery from despair came with the discovery of the true springs of social action leading to a new political philosophy. This, unlike earlier theories, did not take as its starting point the view that the distinguishing characteristic of man lies in his reason. Rather, what marks him off is the way he relates through the two-way creative activity between him and eternal objects or Nature, to the Power imminent in, yet transcending, the phenomenal world. Society, Wordsworth held, is one aspect of this mediated relationship which reflects at the same time as it influences man's interaction with Nature.

III

To follow Wordsworth's theory of man's interaction with Nature and its social and political implications, one must mention, if only in briefest outline, two of the main influences on his thought that have already received extensive attention. The first is the empirical tradition of the Lockean school. Perhaps the clearest example of the early impact of sensationalism upon him comes in a fragment from a notebook (1789-90), in which the senses are described as powers that

> ... colour, model, and combine
> The things perceived with such an absolute
> Essential energy that we may say
> That those most godlike faculties of ours
> At one and the same moment are the mind
> And the mind's minister.

Whatever the degree of his familiarity with Locke's writings, one may note that in 1787 he used his metaphor of the mind as a *tabula rasa*, a 'mental tablet' upon which 'Life ... throws Each Beauty' known to art and nature.[40]

More apparent, however, is the effect of Hartley's *Observations on Man* which, although Wordsworth had probably read it already as a student,[41] assumed greater importance through Coleridge's enthusiasm during the early days of their friendship. One example of the impression left on Wordsworth by his version of what Locke termed 'the association of ideas' may be seen in the description of the poet in the Preface to the *Lyrical Ballads* (1800) as one who 'by obeying blindly and mechanically the impulses' of his 'habits of mind' is bound to 'describe objects and utter sentiments' which will strengthen and purify the understanding and affections of the reader. Although Wordsworth came to reject important constituents of this psychology, he never relinquished it *in toto*. Admittedly, in the 'Immortality' Ode he seemed to deny the basic premise of the mind at birth as a blank page, but the doctrine of prenatal qualities does not recur elsewhere. Some two months after composing the poem on the rainbow, which prefaced the Ode, and which includes the famous line 'the Child is father of the Man', he again emphasised the principle of early conditioning in the statement that the 'practice and exercise of [our] senses' in childhood are 'the fathers of [our] passions'.[42] The theme is woven into the texture of the entire *Prelude*, most markedly in the passages dealing with his childhood. Thus he described with an interesting double sense of the word 'composed', how as a babe in arms the River Derwent which flowed by his house 'made ceaseless music [which] compos'd my thoughts'.[43] And, as has been seen, the composition of his mind under the impress of his childhood environment determined his initial reactions to both revolutionaries and monarchists in France.

Yet Wordsworth's early works, even before he met Coleridge, already show evidence of a coexisting mystical and idealistic streak in his thought. For example, in April-May 1794, when correcting 'An Evening Walk' first published in the previous year, he wrote that a heart that vibrates in harmony with

> ... all forms that Life can take
> ... sees not any line where being ends;
> Sees sense, through Nature's rudest forms betrayed
> while a secret power those forms endears
> Their social accents never vainly hears.

This again was presumably strengthened by his discussions with Coleridge, who was undergoing a shift towards idealism before the birth of his two sons, Hartley and Berkeley. The change in

Coleridge's thought can be clearly detected in 'The Destiny of Nations' (1796) where Joan of Arc is

> Urged by the indwelling angel-guide, that oft
> With dim inexplicable sympathies
> Disquieting the heart, shapes out Man's course.

By December of the same year he asserted roundly: 'I am [not] a Materialist; but ... a Berkleian'.[44] Reference to the discussions of the two poets on these matters is provided by Coleridge's letter to Thomas Poole, dated 16th March, 1801.[45] More telling is a remarkable passage in *The Prelude* in which Wordsworth sums up the idealist element in his philosophy, attributing it to his discussions with Coleridge at the time of his recovery from his breakdown. To him he owed the belief in 'the life/Of all things and the mighty unity/In all which we behold, and feel, and are',[46] so that

> The rapture of the Hallelujah sent
> From all that breathes and is, was chasten'd, stemm'd
> And balanced by a Reason which indeed
> Is reason; duty and pathetic truth;
> And God and Man divided, as they ought,
> Between them the great system of the world
> Where Man is sphered, and which God animates.[47]

These ideas were already present in the *Lyrical Ballads*. In 'Lines written in Early Spring', for examle, he wrote of the 'thousand blended notes' that link in harmony everything that exists in the active universe, and pondered on the part played by man in the fulfilment of 'Nature's holy plan' sent from heaven; and in 'Expostulation and Reply' he suggested in nascent form the passage in *The Prelude* narrating his recovery upon realising the forces behind Nature which are revealed to the intuition (or as he called them in 1798, the 'Powers/which of themselves our mind impress').

What is less commonly appreciated is that throughout the *Lyrical Ballads*, written on the reawakening of the true poet in him as described in *The Prelude*, there runs a central theme presenting an intermediate position between materialism and idealism, drawing on both yet critical of each as excluding the other. This was to form the core of all his later major works, and contains in germ the social and political theory which was to be elaborated later. As we have seen, it was expressed in the two propositions concerning the 'Kindred mutations' of the mind and nature, and the third proposition defining creation as the result of their interfusion. In the Preface to the *Lyrical Ballads* (1800) the argument was phrased thus: 'man and the objects that surround him [are] acting and reacting upon each other ... man and nature [are] essentially adapted to each other'. Coleridge took a similar stand by criticising both idealism and materialism as being 'grounded in the impossibility of intermutual action between things altogether heterogeneous'.[48]

Both Wordsworth and Coleridge found it impossible to apprehend sensuous reality merely through observation and to determine that it is as it is known to us. The mind itself is not 'nothing, a mean pensioner/On outward forms',[49] wrote Wordsworth, while Coleridge attacked Newton because for him the mind 'is always passive — a lazy looker-on an external world'.[50] Both agreed that the mind, on the contrary, is active, shaping and giving meaning to what is outside us according to our needs and disposition. Whereas Locke and Hartley held that it has no control over the sense impressions entering consciousness, Wordsworth endowed it with the power of sifting from the welter of sense data what shall enter the consciousness. Further, whereas 'the doctrine of mechanism', as Hartley called his theory, saw the relations of the mind to external objects as morally neutral, Wordsworth held that the mind informs the sense data it selects with meaning and organises them into value structures. In brief, each of us sees the world through a private grid, what Wordsworth called in the Preface to the *Lyrical Ballads* (1800) the 'Structure of [the] mind', which determines the scope and nature of our perceptions. As formulated later in *The Prelude*:

> Though reared upon the base of outward things
> Structures like these the excited spirit mainly
> Builds for itself.[51]

Thus Michael in the *Lyrical Ballads* could hear and fill with meaning 'the subterraneous music' of every gust of wind which city dwellers are incapable of noting. Further, Wordsworth argued in *The Prelude*, our knowledge of what is outside us is the knowledge of ourselves, but we see ourselves too through the structures of our own minds. Like the written paper pinned on the chest of the blind

London beggar outlining the story of his life, our worlds are selective interpretations of a reality which we can only see 'through a glass darkly': 'The label seems of the utmost we can know/Both of ourselves and of the universe'.[52] Recurring to his French experiences, one can see how he detected and interpreted both the good and the bad in the revolutionary and monarchist camps according to his personal refractive vision. He remained, however, an onlooker rather than a participator, for his attitude was already determined by his past. The meeting with the girl and the heifer, on the other hand, acquired special significance owing to his awareness of the modifications in his 'grid' following on his discussions with Beaupuy.

However, it is equally impossible to take the human mind as a point of departure and to assume part self-awareness independent of social and physical environments. Michael's range of perceptions and the significances he attached to them were a function of his upbringing and needs as a mountain shepherd; and Wordsworth himself attributed his perception of the two points of view in France and his reactions to them to the values which were the product of the conditions of his life in the Lake District and Cambridge. The constructs of our minds, in other words, are not *ex nihilo* creations but are built up out of our conditioning and circumstances. It is therefore only in the abstract that we can differentiate between subjective mind and objective nature. In 'Tintern Abbey' all the 'Mighty world/Of eye and ear' is described as what we 'half create/And what perceive'. In *The Prelude* perception is defined as a two-way process of cause and effect in which man is both active and passive, creator and created,

> A balance, an ennobling interchange
> Of action from within and from without.
> The excellence, pure spirit, and best power
> Both of the objects seen, and eye that sees.[53]

So far the theory appears to be purely psychological. But since Wordsworth held that reality has both its spiritual and its material facets, he concluded that human creativity is not confined to mental activity but manifests itself equally in our shaping of the world outside us, and that the two spheres are interinvolved. Man 'on earth/... daily spreads abroad/His being'[54] not only abstractly but also sensuously, that is, concretely. In 'Lines to My Sister' the poet promises to 'frame the measure of our souls' in accord with the 'power that rolls/About, below, above'; and in the 'Lines written in Early Spring', as already mentioned, he laments that man, instead of carrying out 'Nature's holy plan', has in his social relations distorted it. A similar idea recurs in *The Prelude*, where man is described as 'an agent of the one Mind/[that] create[s]'.[55] Yet a later example of the give-and-take between man and nature comes in *The Excursion*, where the Wanderer, who represents Wordsworth's philsosophy, discusses the industrial revolution. His character and intellect were formed by 'the solid frame of earth/ And ocean's liquid mass', the mountains and streams among which he lived. But he could also exult in man's 'intellectual mastery exercised/O'er the blind elements' that imparted 'almost a soul to brute matter', the results of which in turn conditioned and shaped the mind of man for better or for worse.[56]

Again we have the cross-fertilisation of materialism and idealism. The former was essentially spatial in character, reflecting the exact sciences of the seventeenth and eighteenth centuries. It lacked therefore the evolutionary outlook of the new biological sciences. Idealism, by contrast, gave full credence to the conception of constant human activity and development. Activity, however, was restricted to that of the mind. As Marx was to argue in his criticism of Feuerbach, of the French and English schools of materialism, and of Hegel's idealism, 'in contradiction to materialism, the *active* side was set forth abstractly by idealism — which, of course, does not know real sensuous activity as such. Feuerbach wants sensuous objects ... but he does not conceive human activity itself as *objective* activity'.[57] Marx too, therefore, nearly half a century later, synthesised the conception of reality as mental activity, 'the enstrangement of self consciousness', with the conception of the mind as a passive perceiver, to arrive at something akin to Wordsworth's doctrine. However, Wordsworth's belief in a 'Supreme Existence' led him to regard man the creator as analogous to God the Creator. Thus he could write of himself:

> ... Of genius, power,
> Creation and divinity itself
> I have been speaking, for my theme has been
> What pass'd within me.[58]

More centrally, although Wordsworth referred among others to the economic aspects of life, he stopped short of extending his doctrine to include an economic interpretation of history. Marx and Wordsworth were at one, however, in identifying society not as a quantitative aggregate of individuals but as a qualitative evolving whole, and in regarding the network of relations within it as an essential expression of the man-nature symbiosis. Whatever is to be read into the phrase 'social accent' in the passage quoted earlier from 'An Evening Walk', this association of man and nature with society was one of the earliest, and certainly the most persistent, aspects of Wordsworth's world view. Memory, of course, tends to shape the things recalled according to the dispositions of the rememberer at the time of recall. Nevertheless, it is noteworthy that he described himself in 'Michael' as one who from boyhood was led by the 'power of Nature' to 'think on man ... and human life'.

The connection may be viewed from two vantage-points. The first relates to group identity in the ontological sense. Common environment has a similar conditioning effect on people subjected to it. Consequently, the 'perennial forms' of Nature[59] are conducive to the creation of a permanent bent that links individuals and generations through common attitudes and values. In earlier times the social unity was territorially restricted. With greater mobility and developed communications the units combined to form a single greater though looser unity, which is the nation. This became the common denominator for all the groups, each retaining many of its local biases. Describing the matter in detail Wordsworth wrote in June 1802:

> ... tracts of country ... will make themselves felt powerfully in forming the characters of the people, so as to produce a uniformity of national character ... It was so formally, no doubt, in the Highlands of Scotland; but we cannot perhaps observe it in our own island at the present day, because, even in the most sequestered places, by manufactures, traffic, religion, law, interchange of inhabitants, etc., distinctions are done away which would otherwise have been strong and obvious. This complex state of society does not, however, prevent the characters of individuals from frequently receiving a strong bias, not merely from the impressions of general nature, but also from local objects and images.[60]

The other vantage-point relates to societies as historically developing entities, whose changes mark 'what man has made of man'. Since man is not only conditioned by his environment but also modifies it, man is not only moulded by society but also moulds it. Such a subject-object 'interfusion', to use one of Wordsworth's many 'inter-' words, means that the man-nature-society relationship has a historical dimension. 'The Child is father of the Man' applies no less to nature and society, in the sense that they are subject to both continuity and development. Each is the product of their past interrelations just as their continued interchange produces their shape to come.

The concommitant conception of the individual as inseparable from his social context, and of society as the evolving totality of all its components, bears a close resemblance to the theories of Burke. This probably explains the early eulogy of Burke's genius and wisdom in an unused passage of the 1805-6 version of *The Prelude*. Wordsworth may have also been affected by the organic theory of society as 'the totality of human affairs, their union into a living whole'[61] propounded by the German romantics and disseminated in England by Coleridge. There were important differences, however, which can best be grasped by comparing the principle of dynamism on which all their social theories hung. Burke and the Germans anchored it in the permanence of the nation, or even humanity at large. This allowed them to generalise about large-scale historical trends, impossible when the unit is the individual. Wordsworth, on the other hand, took the individual as his starting point in the manner of the contract theories held by the eighteenth- and early-nineteenth-century radicals. However, his epistemology enabled him to see the individual as a developmental being in creative relationship with his environment:

> The mind of Man is fram'd even like the breath
> And harmony of music. There is a dark
> Invisible workmanship that reconciles
> Discordant elements, and makes them move
> In one society.[62]

It was this conception which lay at the root of his theory of social growth. An early example is 'Lines Left upon a Seat in a Yew-Tree' which was begun in 1787 but not finished till 1797. The poem presents the negative side of the doctrine. It treats of a man who secluded himself in a desolate stretch of country, 'far from all human dwelling'. He had opted out of society and removed himself from those for whom 'the world, and human life, appeared a scene of kindred loveliness'. He did nothing to improve the 'barren rocks with fern and heath,/And juniper and thistle sprinkled o'er', tracing in them 'an emblem of his own unfruitful life'. All he did was to train the 'barren boughs' of a single Yew-tree, traditionally planted in graveyards and associated with death, to shade a seat — 'his only monument'.

The poem illustrates another central belief which derives from Wordsworth's epistemology. Divisiveness is a contravention of the universal unity, a negation of the life principle. It breeds sterility and what Coleridge called 'dejection'.[63] Conversely, to act and feel in harmony with the 'one Life' is to be fulfilled, to experience 'joy' and be alive to 'the glory' (also in the sense of halo) that emanates from all things. This is the theme of Wordsworth's major ode, 'Intimations of Immortality'. The first four stanzas were written in 1802, lamenting his loss of total identification with nature, so that 'the things which I have seen I now can see no more'. The 'visionary gleam' of childhood has fled and 'there hath *past* away a glory from the earth'. Two years later the Ode was completed in a spirit of optimism. The poet found compensation in the awareness of the seamlessness of life, for in a world that is a whole, each starting-point can provide an avenue to every other. Whereas his sensitivity to people came in youth through his sensitivity to nature, now, in maturity, he found that his lost sensitivity to nature can be regained through sensitivity to society. Similarly, his involvement in the material aspects of society gained depth from the 'obstinate questionings' in youth 'of sense and outward things'. The 'years that bring the philosophic mind' thus brought home to him the truth that the past must never be severed from the future, that love of man, nature and society lead to one another, and that every part contains the whole.

What emerges is a positive social outlook, the negative side of which Wordsworth had already felt intuitively when he rejected the points of view of the monarchists and of the revolutionaries in France. Under the influence of Beaupuy, and later in England, he tried but failed to develop a conception of the good society. Disillusioned by events and the conflicting theories of the philosophers he became convinced that no such thing was possible. However, during the period of his escape to nature he found what he had been looking for: a theory based on his own experience. In France he could not confront with equanimity the divisiveness that separated the classes, the refusal of the monarchists to accept progress and their insensitivity to the sufferings of the poor, and the rootlessness of the revolutionaries shown by their insensitivity to the past. Now he arrived at a view of the good society, one in constant growth yet resting on tradition, where men are in accord with the world in which they live, and are united by a community of values and concern for one another's needs. One of the summaries of such a view comes as the conclusion of Book VII of the 1850 version of *The Prelude*,[64] which formulates more clearly the parallel passage in the 1805-6 version. It is here presented as far as possible in his own words. 'Among all regions', he wrote, 'the powers and aspects' of 'the forms perennial' of Nature 'shape for Mankind, by principles as fixed', similar 'virtues'. Likewise, 'the changeful language of Nature' stimulates the mind and produces behind 'multitudinous' activities 'order and relation', so that even 'self-destroying, transitory things' are brought into 'ennobling Harmony'.[65] The identifying characteristic of the good society then is the equipoise among four cardinal elements: the enduring features of Nature, the fundamental character of the social group, the transitory aspects of the phenomenal world and the dynamics of social development. The interaction of any one with each of the other issues in a synchronised gradual change which partakes of the self-fulfilment of the Divine Power. This sensitive balance is sustained by 'love', the product of which is 'joy'. It is the sense that all that exists constitutes a totality, it is the group feeling of individuals conditioned by similar environments, inheriting a similar culture, and heirs to the same tradition as links in a historical chain. In the words of *The Prelude*, love is the power that links 'transitory qualities' to 'permanent relations'. It feeds the 'creative sensibility', leading to

> ... the great social principle of life
> Coercing all things into sympathy.

IV

The principles that Wordsworth enunciated as essential to the good society provide further evidence for his argument, elaborated in his description of his psychological crisis of 1794, against political philosophy as a guide to social and political life. The search for abstract and absolute systems of government, he claimed, is the error of those who fail to understand the dynamics of the man-nature-society relationship, and who consequently cannot distinguish between 'what would last/And what would disappear'. Such men

> ... thrust themselves upon this *passive* world
> As Rulers of the world ...
> Even when the public welfare is their aim, [their policies are]
> Plans without thought, or bottom'd on false thought
> And false philosophy.

Institutions, constitutions, laws and all other codes are changing means to foster the unimpeded creativity of the mind of man in its interfusion with all that is outside it in a changing world. They must therefore be subject to constant reinterpretation and modification. This aspect of the balance between the absolute Law of the Universe and the relative laws of government provides a clue to the puzzling dream of the Arab on the dromedary bearing the stone and the shell.[66] The stone was 'Euclid's elements', described in Book VI (lines 134-5) as an image of 'the one/Surpassing Life ... out of space and time', and more clearly in the 1850 version as 'a type, for finite natures, of the one/Supreme Existence', or the 'permanent and universal sway' of 'Nature's laws'.[67] The shell held to the ear, expressed in 'an unknown Tongue' the voice of 'a God, yea many Gods/[with] Voices more than all the winds', the 'blast of harmony' interpreted by different societies and different times.

The failure of the philosophers to hear the varied music of the shell, moreover, may be costly. As the gap between changing reality and political arrangements widens there develop

> ... [social] differences, the outward marks by which
> Society has parted man from man
> Neglectful of the Universal heart.[68]

The gap is reflected in the break up of society. The powerful, wishing to hold on to their interests and privileges, oppose change. Those who feel discriminated against wish to wipe the slate clean and start afresh. Their iconoclasm reinforces in turn the fear of change, and a vicious circle of revolution and reaction sets in. Such extremism resulted from the rigidity of the *ancien régime*, and the 'rulers of the [English] state' who turned the shepherd's crook into 'a tool of murder' were risking a similar fate.[69] Wordsworth's opposition to the liberal doctrines of those he called 'the modern statists' rested ultimately on the same principle. They too denied the divine element in man which is the basis of society by reducing his glorious potential to self-centred material interests, 'animal wants and necessities', thereby negating the spirit of social 'love' and promoting the division of society into antagonistic camps.[70]

The alternative was closely connected with the revolution Wordsworth effected in English literature, as expressed more discursively in his critical essays and resulting from the same psychological crisis out of which his political philosophy emerged. The usual conception and practice had been of poetry as exclusive, written by and for the educated classes in a special diction and dealing with restricted themes. In contrast, Wordsworth proclaimed that true poetry is not an escape into private satisfactions, nor a mere imitation of an imitation of ultimate reality as Plato had maintained in *The Republic* (Book 10), but the expression of deep involvement in the central issues of society. It is inclusive, ranging the entire gamut of humanity throughout its history — from the scholars familiar with the great authors and works of all time to the 'low and wren-like warblings, made/For cottagers and spinners at the wheel', from the tunes for the little ones to those for 'old Men who have surviv'd their joy', and from the compositions of known figures to the 'nameless' singers of the folk.[71] The poet, therefore, is 'a man speaking to men' in terms that all can understand, of matters that touch the interests of all. He can detect under life's everyday appearances the eternal laws governing man's relation to external objects and to other men and, by exalting 'the enduring and the transient both',[72] so guide the people that 'the acts of daily life'[73] are brought into 'communion with the invisible world'.[74] Poetry binds society together as one of the Powers

> ... only less,
> For what we may become, and what we need,
> Than Nature's self, which is the breath of God;[75]

and poets are 'even as Prophets, each with each/Connected in a mighty scheme of truth'[76] which they must transmit to society so that 'justice may be done'.[77] In brief, poetry in the universal sense should replace social and political philosophy as a signpost pointing the way to the good society, and the poet should replace the philosopher as the guide of the politician.

Implied is a conception of the true poet and the good statesman as working to the same ends, although from different directions. Both are the guardians of the good society, the one by cultivating 'creative sensibility', the other by directing it into practical channels. The parallel is pointed up by the similarity of Wordsworth's criticism of the function of poetry to his criticism of the function of the ruler. This already appears in a passage inserted into 'The Ruined Cottage' (1798) and later incorporated into *The Excursion* (Book I, lines 365-81), where he contrasted the Wanderer who 'could *afford* to suffer/With those whom he saw suffer' and hence was rich 'in the wisdom of our daily life', with the 'unthinking masters of the earth/As makes the nations groan'. The wise and good governor, he wrote in 'I Grieved for Bonaparté', must not stand apart on an eminence but must involve himself in daily affairs, keeping his fingers on the pulse of the nation and being attentive to 'the talk/Man holds with week-day man in the hourly walk/Of the mind's business'. His ultimate duty is to morality, to 'the universal heart' and 'men as they are men within themselves'. Hence also the attack in *The Prelude* on the warped judgement of those who 'blazen with the pompous names/Of power and action', or as he put it in the 1850 version, 'the Historians .../... [who] blazen power and energy detached/From moral purpose'.[78] Indeed Wordsworth, who explicitly identified himself with the Wanderer, saw himself as combining 'some of the faculties which belong to the statesman with [the kindred faculties] which belong to the poet'.[79]

The common mission of the poet and the statesman may now be defined more clearly as maintaining the delicate balance of the four elements which regulate man's behaviour as an individual and as a social being. As emissaries of the Supreme Power they complement each other in waging constant war against all that brings man to 'substitute a universe of death ... in place of that which is divine and true'.[80] The forces of evil, operating against Love by inducing withdrawal into the self and by deadening the sensibilities, lie in wait from earliest childhood. Growing up itself, Wordsworth wrote in the 'Immortality' Ode, involves 'endless imitation', till 'the vision splendid' dulled by habit fades, and 'shades of the prison-house begin to close' upon the boy. Familiarity blinds us to the true nature of the world; 'the tendency ... of habit [is] to enslave the mind', and 'custom lies upon [us] with a weight/Heavy as frost, and deep almost as life'. In social terms, rigid laws, customs and conventions do not bind society together but harden the heart and inhibit vital contact between man and his fellow-beings. We are

> ... follow'd, watch'd and noos'd
> Each in his several melancholy walk
> String'd like a poor man's Heifer at its feed
> Led through the lanes in forlorn servitude;
> Or rather like a stalled ox shut out
> From touch of growing grass.[81]

Unconcern for others and rampant egotism, as we have seen, divide society into the exploiters and the exploited. Where 'oppression worse than death/Salutes the Being at his birth'[82] and 'labour in excess and poverty/From day to day pre-occupy the ground/Of the affections'[83] man is alienated from his world, for human energies are reduced to mere animal existence and 'there, indeed/Love cannot be'.[84] Furthermore, commonly allied with poverty is lack of education which develops sensitivity and imagination, links the knowledge of all times with the present and provides a sense of belonging to a group bound by common traditions and values. When 'grace/Of culture hath been utterly unknown',[85] therefore, man, oppressed 'by the laws of vulgar sense',[86] can only maintain material contact with nature and other people. However, it is not only the poor who lead unnatural lives. No less isolated are 'the wealthy Few, who see/By artificial lights'.[87] *The Excursion* treats of the 'wealthy, the luxurious, by the stress/Of business roused, or pleasure' hurrying in their chariots or on horseback, oblivious to the beauty of the countryside, whereas he who goes on foot can savour at leisure all that he beholds, his 'spirit braced', his thoughts 'pleasant' and 'pure'.[88] Worse still, even the education of the rich is soured by sycophantic authors who, creating a false culture built on social division, 'debase/The many for the pleasure of those Few'.[89]

Typically, Wordsworth saw each of these aspects of 'the Universe of death' as leading to a loss of contact with nature, just as insensitivity to the external world leads to the withdrawal into the self:

> ... why is it/that we feel

So little for each other, but for this,
That we with nature have no sympathy.[90]

We have seen how the transient aspects of nature and of society are as essential as their enduring aspects, and that the proper equipoise of the four must be preserved. Thus the effective exploitation and control of the riches and the forces of nature by 'earth's thoughtful lord'[91] is a necessary condition of civilisation, while the modification of social forms is a necessary condition of group-life. Similarly, the conditioning of men by the enduring aspects of nature is as important as their conditioning by social continuity and tradition. Upsetting of the balance, as through the denial of change by the French monarchists, or the over-acceleration of change, as by the French revolutionaries, was the main menace to contemporary society. In fact, each of these brings about the other. Equally dangerous were the loss of contact with nature in the industrial centres and the over-exploitation of nature by the expansion of mines and industry, and again each was both cause and effect of the other.

The node of all four evils was the City, which assumed for Wordsworth a symbolic, even mythological, quality. The negative aspect of modern progress, 'the darker side of this great change',[92] was the concentration of commerce and industry in huge urban metropolises, whose inhabitants were wrenched away from natural objects, had lost their social ties and were driven to 'all the strife of singularity'. The city had become the Vanity Fair of *The Pilgrim's Progress* or the Inferno of Dante, a 'monstrous ant-hill on the plain/Of a too busy world', where Love cannot thrive, the 'human heart is sick', and 'the whole creative powers of man asleep'.[93] The political consequences were frightening. Organised society was endangered by 'Mobs, riots, ... anarchy and din/Barbarian and infernal', where the sole link was mass excitement 'when half the City shall break out/Full of one passion vengeance, rage, or fear'.[94] In summary of the discussion above of Wordsworth's world-view as formulated in The Recluse, it was noted that he stressed the importance of appreciating the connection of man, nature and society as the more fateful when social bonds were threatened, when one could 'hear Humanity in fields and groves/ Pipe solitary anguish' and 'the fierce confederate storm/Of sorrow, barricaded evermore/Within the walls of cities'.

This suggestion of a solution to the deepening crisis became the central theme of a group of sonnets written in 1802-3, and later incorporated in the collection entitled *Poems Dedicated to National Independence and Liberty*. In these England was depicted as at the crossroads. On the one hand, 'the good old cause/Is gone'. The people have lost their 'inward happiness', and moral integrity has degenerated so that 'the wealthiest man among us is the best'. On the other hand, poets and moralists like Sidney, Shakespeare, Milton and Marvell had earned for British freedom the 'world's praise, from dark antiquity'. Although fallen on evil days, the country could still remain a 'Bulwark for the cause of men', especially at a time when the French, who never had the guidance of 'such souls as we had then', were intent on putting out 'the only light/Of liberty that yet remains on earth'. The need to reform and purify was therefore not for the sake of England alone, but for all mankind whose 'best hopes rest all with Thee'. Wordsworth's belief ten years earlier that if only France could overcome its trespasses she could still be a light to the world was thus transposed. This time it was France that was 'far more abject', while England, if only another great poet were to rise, could still lead the nations to the 'faith and morals' that it had once enjoyed. 'Milton', he wrote, 'thou shouldst be living at this hour/England hath need of thee'.[95]

The significance of the conclusion that Wordsworth arrived at in the final passages of *The Prelude* now becomes clearer. His analysis of his experiences and his development had shown him that he had gained the 'powers' and the 'knowledge' that would make him 'capable/Of building up a work that should endure',[96] defined in the Prospectus to 'The Recluse' as 'a philosophical poem containing views of Man, Nature, and Society'. Perhaps on Wordsworth had fallen the mantle of the prophet-poet.

The Prospectus and the bulk of Book I of 'The Recluse' were written in 1800. Some months later he sent a copy of the *Lyrical Ballads* which, as has been suggested, already contained the basis of his thesis, to Charles James Fox as heir of the 'good old cause' and of the parliamentarian sympathies of Milton and Marvell. The accompanying letter expressed the affinity that every 'true poet living in England' must feel for a statesman such as him because of his 'sensibility of heart' and concern not merely with 'men in bodies and classes' but with individuals. Such a leader, Wordsworth believed, would appreciate the portrait of the common man and his lot depicted in the volumes, and act against the social alienation and loss of domestic affection resulting from the over-rapid extension of industry and commerce, the expropriation of the small holdings of the peasant-farmers, and the hard-hearted complacency of industrialists and 'the present Rulers of this country'.[97]

The direct plea of the poet to the politician proved unavailing. However, Wordsworth's life-task cannot be said to have failed. His interpretation of the nature and function of the poet as the supreme example of the creative principle in all men, falling in with similar trends in German philosophy, had a tremendous influence on following generations of writers. It gives point, for example, to the final sentence of Shelley's 'Defence of Poetry', 'Poets are the unacknowledged legislators of the universe', often misunderstood because poetry is being used in the universal sense. At two removes, it illuminates Disraeli's quotation of Shelley's sentence even before the essay was published. It may too have prepared the ground for Carlyle's assertion, following Fichte, that the men of letters are a 'perpetual priesthood', and his extension of the idea in the development of his theory of the Hero. Fundamentally, Carlyle wrote, 'Prophet and Poet well understood ... [are] the same; in this most important respect especially, that they have penetrated both of them into the sacred mystery of the universe'.[98] It is unnecessary to look for further examples. What is indisputable is that Wordsworth was one of the greatest figures, if not the greatest, of the English romantic movement, the political importance of which cannot be overestimated. Far from being an escapist movement, it had a major impact on the development of the peculiar British varieties of both socialism and conservatism. Although not directly, and in ways he could not have foreseen, Wordsworth was himself proof of his thesis of the creative artist as guide of the people.

Notes

1. Cited in F.M. Todd, *Politics and the Poet* (London: Methuen & Co., 1957), p. 11.
2. E.g. L.F. Chard, *Dissenting Republican* (The Hague: Mouton, 1972); H. Lindenberger, *On Wordsworth's Prelude* (Princeton University Press, 1966), p. 262.
3. G. Little, 'An Incomplete Wordsworth Essay upon Moral Habits', *Review of English Literature*, II (January 1961), p. 12.
4. *The Republic of Plato*, trans. A. Bloom (London and New York: Basic Books, 1968), pp. 290-1.

5. Ibid.
6. W. Wordsworth, Preface to *Lyrical Ballads*, 2nd edn (1800).
7. W. Wordsworth, *The Prelude*, 1805 version, Bk III, ll. 645-8.
8. Ibid., Bk XXI, ll. 645-8.
9. W. Wordsworth, 'The Recluse', Pt I, Bk I, ll. 63-80. Cf. the contention in the Preface to the *Lyrical Ballads* (1800) that one cannot discuss fully the 'theory upon which the poems [are] written ... without retracing the revolutions, not of literature alone, but likewise of society itself'.
10. *The Prelude*, 1805 version, Bk VI, ll. 352-4.
11. Ibid., Bk IX, ll. 211-12.
12. Ibid. ll. 105-7.
13. Ibid., l. 331.
14. *The Poetical Works of William Wordsworth*, E. de Selincourt and H. Darbishire (eds.) (Oxford: Clarendon, 2nd ed, 1949), vol. IV, p. 445.
15. *The Prelude*, 1805 version, Bk IX, ll. 531-2, 521-2.
16. Ibid., Bk X, ll, 34-5.
17. Ibid. l. 77.
18. Ibid., ll. 138-9.
19. Ibid., l. 154.
20. Ibid., l. 187.
21. Ibid., ll. 188-9.
22. In following Wordsworth's own account, I pass over the personal reasons related to Annette Vallon for his coming to England and his intention to return to France.
23. *The Prelude*, 1805 version, Bk X, ll. 437-40.
24. Ibid., Bk XI, ll. 646-8.
25. Ibid., Bk X, ll. 655-7.
26. *The Prelude*, 1850 version, Bk VII, l. 6; 1805 version, Bk X, l. 586.
27. *The Prelude*, 1805 version, Bk X, ll. 792-5.
28. Ibid, l. 588.
29. Ibid., Bk XI, l. 64.
30. Ibid. ll. 65-6.
31. Ibid., ll. 69, 76. Cf. his attack on the 'Moralist' in 'A Poet's Epitaph' as:

One to whose smooth-rubbed soul can cling
No form, nor feeling, great or small;
A reasoning, self-sufficing thing
An intellectual All-in-all

32. The term calls to mind Shaftesbury, but might be more clearly understood when compared with Deism, by which Shaftesbury himself was also influenced. Like the Deists, Wordsworth maintained that one can infer the existence of a divine power from nature without appealing to supernatural revelation or Biblical authority. However, the Deists saw the objects of the finite world as illustrations of laws established by God in the primal act of creation and left thereafter to operate on their own. Wordsworth, on the other hand, conceived the world in terms of an unceasing process of becoming, and the supreme Power as imminent in, although not limited to, natural phenomena themselves.
33. R. Price, *A Review of the Principal Questions in Morals*, D. Raphael (ed.) (Oxford University Press, 1948). Coleridge made a similar distinction, using the terminology 'reason' and 'understanding', translated from the Kantian *Verstand* and *Vernunft*; *The Prelude*, 1805 version, Bk XII, l. 26.
34. Ibid., ll. 33-6.
35. Ibid., l. 42, ll. 63-5.

36. W. Wordsworth, 'The Convention of Cintra', *Political Tracts of Wordsworth, Coleridge and Shelley*, ed. R.J. White (Cambridge University Press, 1953), p. 130.
37. *The Prelude*, 1805 version, Bk XII, ll. 24-6.
38. *The Prelude*, 1850 version, Bk XIV, ll. 106-10.
39. S.T. Coleridge, *Table Talk*, T. Ashe (ed.) (London: Bell, 1884), p. 171.
40. *Works*, vol. V, Appendix B, p. 340; 'The Value of Esthwaite'.
41. See B.R. Schneider, *Wordsworth's Cambridge Education* (Cambridge University Press, 1957), p. 109.
42. *The Early Letters of William and Dorothy Wordsworth*, (1767-1805), E. de Selincourt (ed.) (Oxford University Press, 1935), p. 293.
43. *The Prelude*, 1805 version, Bk I, ll. 279-81. Cf. the verses on the same river written in 1798 in the Alfoxden note-book:

... I hear thy voice
Beloved Derwent, that peculiar voice
Heard in the stillness of the air,
Half-heard and half-created

Works, vol. V, Appendix B, p. 340.
44. *Collected Letters of Samuel Taylor Coleridge*, Earl L. Griggs (ed.) (Oxford: Clarendon Press, 1956-9), vol. 1, p. 534.
45. Ibid., p. 707.
46. *The Prelude*, 1805 version, Bk XIII, ll. 253-5.
47. Ibid., ll. 262-8.
48. S.T. Coleridge, *The Philosophical Lectures*, K. Coburn (ed.) (London: Routledge and Kegan Paul, 1950), p. 60. See also p. 116: 'There are ... essentially but three kinds of philosophies and more are not possible: the one ... give[s] the whole to the subject and make[s] the object a mere result involved in it; [the other] ... give[s] the whole to the object and make[s] the subject ... the mere result of that; and lastly [there are] those who, in very different ways, have attempted to reconcile the two opposites and bring them into one'.
49. *The Prelude*, 1805 version, Bk VI, ll. 666-8.
50. *Collected Letters of Samuel Taylor Coleridge*, vol. II, p. 709.
51. *The Prelude*, 1805 version, Bk VII, ll. 650-2. A clear contrast between private versions of the universe comes in 'Peter Bell', ll. 298-350:

A primrose by a river's brim
A yellow Primrose was to him
And it was nothing more,

While the concluding lines of the 'Immortality Ode' are

To me the meanest flower that blooms can give
Thoughts that do often lie too deep for tears.

52. *The Prelude*, 1850 version, Bk VII, ll. 645-6.
53. *The Prelude*, 1805 version, Bk XII, ll. 376-9.
54. Ibid., Bk IV, ll. 158-61.
55. Ibid., Bk II, ll. 272-3.
56. *The Excursion*, Bk I, ll. 201-2; Bk VII, ll. 203-16.
57. F. Engels, *Collected Works* (New York International Publishers, 1975), vol. V, p. 3.
58. *The Prelude*, 1805 version Bk III, ll. 171-4. Furthermore, he was less

impressed by the heaven and hell created by man's inadequate imagination of the Powers than by the nature of the creating imagination itself. See the Prospect to

The Excursion:

> Jehovah — with his thunder, and the choir
> Of shouting Angels, and the empyreal thrones —
> I pass them unalarmed. Not chaos, not
> The darkest pit of lowest Erebus ...
> Can breed such fear and awe
> As fall upon us often when we look
> Into our Minds, into the Mind of Man.
>
> Such outrage done to nature as compels
> The indignant power to justify herself;

59. *The Prelude*, 1805 version, Bk VII, ll. 725-6.
60. *The Early Letters of William and Dorothy Wordsworth*, pp. 293-4.
61. H.S. Reiss (ed.), *The Political Thought of the German Romantics 1793-1815* (New York: Macmillan, 1955), p. 157. One must remember that Edmund Burke's *Reflections on the French Revolution* appeared in German translation at about the time Wordsworth and Coleridge were in Germany.
62. *The Prelude*, 1805 version, Bk I, ll. 351-5.
63. The different versions of Coleridge's 'Ode to Dejection' and its relation to Wordsworth's 'Intimations Of Immortality' have been fully discussed by numerous critics and need not be elaborated here.
64. *The Prelude*, 1850 version, Bk VII, ll. 745-70.
65. *The Prelude*, 1805 version, Bk II, ll. 310, 12, 79, 408-9.
66. Ibid., Bk V, ll. 70-140.
67. Ibid., Bk VI, ll. 134-5; 1850 version, Bk VI, ll. 133-4, 131, 124.
68. *The Prelude*, 1805 version, Bk XII, ll. 217-19.
69. Ibid., Bk XI, ll. 646-8.
70. Ibid. Bk XIII, l. 94.
71. Ibid. Bk V, ll. 208-26.
72. Ibid., Bk XIII, l. 97.
73. Preface to the *Lyrical Ballads* (1800).
74. Ibid., Bk XIII, l. 105.
75. Ibid., Bk V, ll. 220-2.
76. Ibid., Bk XII, ll. 301-2.
77. Ibid., l. 236.
78. Ibid., Bk XII, ll. 48-9; 1850 version, Bk XII, ll. 42-5.
79. Cited in A. de Vere, *Essays Chiefly on Poetry* (London: Longmans, 1887), vol. II, p. 281.
80. *The Prelude*, 1805 version, Bk XIII, ll. 141-3.
81. Ibid., Bk V, ll. 238-43.
82. Ibid., Bk XII, ll. 194-5.
83. Ibid., ll. 197-9.
84. Ibid., ll. 200-1.
85. Ibid., ll. 195-6.
86. Ibid. Bk XIII, l. 140.
87. Ibid., Bk XII, ll. 209-10.
88. *The Excursion*, Bk II, ll. 97-110.
89. *The Prelude*, 1805 version, Bk XII, ll. 209-10.
90. *Works*, vol. V, Appendix B, p. 340.
91. *The Excursion*, Bk VIII, l. 164.

92. Ibid., ll. 151-2. See the description of the city as nature's revenge on man's breach of the universal bond:

Yea, to avenge her violated rights,
For England's bane. (Ibid. ll. 153-6)

93. *The Prelude*, 1805 version, Bk V, l. 573; Bk XII, l. 202; Bk VII, l. 554; 1850 version, Bk VII, ll. 149-50.
94. *The Prelude*, 1805 version, Bk VII, ll. 675, 659-60, 645-6.
95. W. Wordsworth, *Poems Dedicated to National Independence and Liberty*, Nos XII, XVII, XV, XVIII, XXI, XVI, XIV.
96. *The Prelude*, 1805 version, Bk XII, ll. 277-8.
97. *The Early Letters of William and Dorothy Wordsworth*, pp. 259-62.
98. T. Carlyle, *The Works of Thomas Carlyle in Thirty Volumes*, H.D. Traill (ed.) (London: Chapman and Hall, 1907), vol. XXVI, p. 58; vol. XX, p. 102.

2 ROBERT SOUTHEY AND THE COMMUNAL VALUES OF POLITICS

I

'I wish you would buy the *Lyrical Ballads*', wrote Robert Southey to his life-long friend Grosvenor Charles Bedford on 22nd March, 1806; 'you will see in the Preface and Postscript my critical creed.'[1] Far from being a sudden illumination, this identification with Wordsworth's revolutionary doctrines which, as we have seen, cannot be dissociated from his political views, implies a confirmation of opinions Southey had held years earlier and was to retain throughout his life. By 1798, the very year in which the first edition of the *Ballads* appeared, and two years before the Preface was published, he had already modified his *Joan of Arc* to introduce ideas of social and political import directly comparable to Wordsworth's 'creed'. In fact, they were present in the germ even in the first edition of the poem, drafted some five years earlier and constantly revised before being published in 1796. At the time Southey had only briefly met Wordsworth, who disapproved of his poem, a compliment returned by Southey in an unfavourable review of the first edition of the *Lyrical Ballads*. Any speculation on possible influences of one on the other is, however, immaterial. Our concern is with Southey's special contribution to the formation of a political approach which was to be held with variations by all three 'Lake poets' and was to leave a considerable mark on later theorists.

A common pattern in the development of Wordsworth, Coleridge and Southey is easily discernible. Like the two other poets whose lives became so intimately intertwined with his, Southey's whole outlook was powerfully affected by the French Revolution. 'Few persons but those who had lived in it', he wrote in middle-age, 'can conceive or comprehend what ... a visionary world seemed to open upon those who were just entering it ... Old things seemed passing away, and nothing was dreamt of it but the regeneration of the human race.'[2] The fervour with which he embraced radical doctrines led him to join with Coleridge in the scheme of a pantisocracy, as it had led Wordsworth to take up the

Girondin cause. In 1809 he could still be outraged by Coleridge's attack on Jacobinism, a general term that in England included all those of whatever faction who supported revolution: '... if he was not a Jacobin ... I wonder who the Devil was. I am sure I was, am still, and ever more shall be'.[3] Adopting an attitude to the war with France identical with that of Wordsworth, he half wished that England might be defeated, for the French stood for 'the cause of Liberty', and England for reaction.[4]

And yet, again like Wordsworth, there was a moderating tone in his early radicalism, in favour of conserving much of the past and against mob extremism, just as his later conservatism was accompanied by a radical social reformism and opposition to reactionary extremes. In May 1793 he saw an affinity between his views and those of Bedford, who blended 'Aristocratic principles' with 'Democratic motives': 'I am far more proud of this similarity than if system or enthusiasm taught us both to bellow God save the King, whilst Priestley's house was on fire or to yell out *Ça ira* whilst poor Louis was on the scaffold.'[5] Southey's revulsion against Napoleon came sometime after that of Wordsworth or Coleridge, but he too came for a time to 'yield up moral questions in despair'. As he wrote to Coleridge in 1799: '... at present I have the true cynic growl, softening down into Stoical not Epicurean apathy. All the nations are so detestably governed that I see no preference except it be in the amount of taxes.'[6] With the collapse of the peace of Amiens in 1803 he took sides once more, but this time clearly justifying the British. Just as he had approved of the opposition of Fox to the war in 1793, so now he approved of Granville's suspicions of peace with Napoleon.[7] He, like Coleridge and Wordsworth, had come round to see England as the bulwark of the world against the tyranny of a military dictator. Wordsworth discussed with him his proposed work on the Convention of Cintra, and he himself joined the *Quarterly Review* 'with the view of counteracting these base politicks, which would make us betray Spain and Portugal, and lay us at the feet of Bonaparte'.[8] Thereafter, his political outlook became increasingly conservative till he, Wordsworth and Coleridge were branded by many of the younger generation of romantics as turncoats, 'lost leaders', to quote the title of Browning's Sonnets on Wordsworth.

Nevertheless, for all the similarities, there was a fundamental difference in the attitudes of the three to social and political issues. In *The Prelude* Wordsworth described the 'different roads'[9] by which he and Coleridge had 'gain'd/The self-same bourne'[10] as explaining their different approaches to the same problems. Brought up in the isolated wilds of the mountainous Lake District, Wordsworth had experienced daily the 'Presence of Nature, in the sky/And on the earth ... visions of the hills/And souls of lonely places'.[11] Through them, he claimed, he had learned the 'great social principle' which was to dominate his major works. He was therefore 'less aptly skill'd' in abstraction and philosophical argument. For him, as later for Keats, 'axioms in philosophy are not axioms until they are proved upon our pulses'.[12] Trying to explain to himself the effects of nature upon his early childhood and the mystical experiences of his 'spots of time', he arrived at a psychology based on the 'interfusion' of the self and the outer world. Coleridge, on the other hand, grew up in the great city. Although surrounded by multitudes he sought 'the truth in solitude', developing his metaphysics by extensive intellectual study and deep introspection. His theories remained on a high level of abstraction, reinforced, as he stated in the 'Dejection' Ode, by circumstances that compelled him 'by abstruse research to steal/ From my own nature all the natural man'. Such differences lay behind the fructifying influence each had on the other and their successful collaboration. A well-known example is the division of work in the *Lyrical Ballads*, as described in the *Biographia Literaria* (Chapter XIV). Coleridge was to transfer 'a human interest and semblance of truth' to 'persons and characters supernatural, or at least romantic'. Wordworth was 'to give the charm of novelty to things of everyday' and, by arousing the mind from the 'lethargy of custom', to 'excite a feeling analogous to the supernatural'. Similar differences of approach mark their common doctrine of man as creating and created by his world of external objects. Notwithstanding his discussions on practical politics, especially in the *Friend*, Coleridge was always tempted to consider the metaphysical and theological foundations of the universe and the implications of the philosophical assumptions underlying human behaviour. Wordsworth's interest in natural environment as conditioning the mind from birth led him, by contrast, to a theory of the way everyday man actually behaves in relation to other men.

Southey, less introspective than either Coleridge or Wordsworth, concentrated his attention not so much on individual psychology or metaphysical speculation as on actual events and processes, their origins, course and results, more suited to his interest in the past, historical researches and poetry on mythological themes. Such an approach probably owed much to his experiences as a rebellious idealist tamed by material circumstances. The eldest son of an unsuccessful Bristol shopkeeper, he was brought up in Bath by a fashionable snobbish aunt, wholly indifferent to the nature and needs of a sensitive child. His resentment against authority came to a head at Westminster School from which he was expelled for publishing a savage attack on the flogging practices of the teachers, ministers of the Church of England whom he described as following the idolatrous 'abominations of the children of Moab'. Sent thereafter to Oxford by his uncle, he underwent a prolonged crisis as to his future, caused by his refusal to take orders and the consequent necessity of fending for himself. Financial problems were to plague him for many years, aggravated by his taking on himself responsibility for numerous dependants in addition to his own family. Of necessity he acquired a streak of careful prudence and grasp of practical detail that contributed more to his life as a private person and literary hack than to his qualities as a poet. The implicit assumption underlying his social and political thought was not dissimilar to that of Wordsworth and Coleridge, namely, that what we think and how we act are each the cause and effect of the other, and that both are conditioned by and affect the external world. However, he was mainly interested in examining the current situation in England from the perspective of long-term trends in social and political developments and in deducing remedies for abuses that had grown up under the pressures of industrialism and the wars with France. This was to lead him not only to formulate specific policy proposals, but to develop a fully-fledged theory of history which complemented the general principles of the political philosophy common to the Lake School.

The analysis in this chapter will centre chiefly on this theory of history as the most provocative, original, yet neglected aspect of his writings. Already discernible in his early works, it can be deduced most clearly from the *Quarterly Review* articles, from his 'Life of the French Revolutionaries' and 'Inquiry into the Poor Laws' of 1812 to 'The Poor' and 'Parliamentary Reform' of 1816. It was summed in 1817 in the 'Letter to William Smith, M.P.' and in the *Colloquies*, begun in the same year. In all these he offered a restatement of contemporary conservative thought which, though owing much to Burke (whom he had been rebuked for abusing in an essay while at school[13]), diverged from his philosophy on several main issues. First, their conceptions of history were very different. Burke saw history as the record of the slow building-up of habits, opinions and sentiments common to a society, which constitute a broadly consistent national character. His concern was therefore more with the products of historical evolution than with the analysis of actual processes that lead to them. Southey, witnessing the collapse of established traditions and the dramatic changes in the patterns of living, focused on the processes giving rise to social and political transitions in history with a view to identifying repetitive rhythms in order to predict the direction of change in his own day. He saw history as marked by alternating periods of slow and rapid economic development which determine changes in the structure of society. Such structures condition moral and social attitudes, and these in turn affect social, economic and political developments. Another divergence from Burke lay in Southey's conception of the relationship between the individual and society. Like Wordsworth and Coleridge he accepted Burke's view of society as based on a bond linking its members in a community of values and interests. However, for Burke the bond was a given, an essential ingredient of human nature, while Southey saw it as subject to the vagaries of socio-economic conditions. Rapid economic development, however beneficial it may be, weakens the sense of communality and disrupts the social order, threatening society with disintegration. A third difference was over the relationship between state and society. Like Burke, Southey held political authority to be a trust on behalf of the nation. The former, however, maintained that 'a wise Prince ... will act upon the circumstances of his states as he finds them'[14] and preserve the established character of society as revealed in its institutions, modes of life and values. Southey saw these as varying configurations, and argued that especially in periods of rapid socio-economic change government should intervene to mould general opinion so as to serve the interest of the nation as a supra-temporal entity. Finally, again like Wordsworth and Coleridge, Southey believed that this demanded the abandoning of the ideal of a balanced constitution and limited government in favour of strong initiating leadership.

It was perhaps as a consequence of his more concrete cast of mind and the publication of his ideas in the *Quarterly Review*, the leading Tory journal, that Southey was able to influence the Tory circles with his variety of conservative radicalism more directly than the other two poets were able to do. Lord Ashley, for example, wrote to him on the threshold of his political career: 'I have derived the greatest benefit from the study of your works, and I think that the world also is largely indebted to your genius and industry!'[15] Similarly, George Smythe, Disraeli's associate and one of the founders of the Young England group, asserted that Southey was the 'real founder of the movement', and that his writings were the main source of its inspiration.[16] But Southey's impact was far from being restricted to what Randolph Churchill called 'Tory Democracy'. As will be shown in the following chapters, Shelley, although disagreeing violently with Southey, nevertheless propounded a theory of history which resembled Southey's in many respects, and Carlyle avidly followed Southey's writings and was deeply influenced by them. Southey, in sum, although much neglected as a political thinker, was an important link in the development of the political philosophy of the leading romantics, as well as having a formative influence on the modification of British conservatism to suit the new industrial society that emerged during the nineteenth century.

II

Southey's theory of history as elaborated in the *Quarterly Review* articles and later writings was, as has been mentioned, not a sudden deviation from ideas held during his early radical period, but rather the fruition of these ideas. Of special interest is his first major work, and the first of its kind for many years, *Joan of Arc*, a political epic which he planned as 'my legacy to this country' that may 'preserve my memory in it'.[17]

The narrative, though set in France of the early fifteenth century, carried a clear message to the England of the writer's time. The presentation of the English as waging an unrighteous war against the French obviously reflected the war that had broken out between the two countries in 1793. But the work was also of more general import, pointing to the moral crises which generate bloody upheavals, and prescribing a non-violent cure of the evils that by implication were now also racking England.

Southey's moral and political thesis appears early in the epic, in the form of a debate between the Maid and the Arch-Priest on the nature and function of religion, which fifteen years after the first draft he still held to be among the best things he had ever produced.[18] A superficial reading might easily gloss over the clear implications of the claims and counterclaims, especially if one bears in mind the observation of Southey in a letter to Bedford a few days before he actually began to write. He had just come across a passage in Rousseau which expressed 'some of my religious opinions better than I could do it myself'. The lines he quoted describe the ecstasy that must strike the one who contemplates the works of God in nature, and refer to the Bishop who said of the old country woman's simple exclamation 'O!' that it was a truer prayer than any he could devise.[19] Joan herself exemplifies Rousseau's 'compagnards et surtout solitaires'. Southey insisted that her greatness was due to 'the working of her own mind' and not to supernatural powers which would 'destroy the obscurity of her character, and sink her to the mere heroine of a Fairy Tale'.[20] In her rebuttal of the charge of heresy she insists that she is a simple country girl, different from others in degree but not in kind, and only in her sensitivity to nature which made her conscious of 'the God within me'.[21] Nevertheless, the essence of her argument is far more subtle, resting on an epistemological approach which closely resembles that of Wordsworth and Coleridge. The phenomenal world is a material expression of the divine power, 'th' eternal energy which pervade[s]/The boundless range of nature'. However, we can only perceive God and his manifestations in terms of our limitations. The primary source of our knowledge of His world is our sense impressions. But what we see is equally the creation of our own minds, the result of an active collaboration that exists between the one who sees and the thing seen. The objects of sense pass through the grid of our minds which is formed by our conditioning by the environment of our early days, our experiences and the patterns of thought and values impressed upon us by current codes and beliefs. Thus religion is a major influence in producing our conceptions of the world we live in. To Joan, brought up as a shepherdess in the solitudes of the 'mountain valleys', all nature's voice proclaimed 'the all-good Parent'. Nature was the expression of the spirit of universal Love which embraces all that exists, from the sun which 'pour[s] life and radiance' to 'the lowliest flower in the field'. To the priest, who lived his life under 'the high arched roof', restricted by 'the bonds ... which confine the path/Of orthodox belief', God is 'a God of Terrors' and 'nature can teach to sin' only.[22]

The debate is not merely one of principle but has a direct bearing on human action. If our behaviour is conditioned by our perceptions of the external world, so the external world is affected in turn by our behaviour. Joan's 'love for whate'er was beautiful and good' induces her away from herself to concern for others, from seeking the wounded lamb 'to bind his wounds, and bathe them with [her] tears' to liberating the people and the nation as a whole. The Arch-Priest, on the other hand, concerned with original sin, guilt and penance, withdraws from a world of evil and limits himself to 'teach remorse' and warn against 'the penal fires of purgatory'.[23] The social implications are clear. Southey, as Shelley was to put it later, considered love to be 'the going out of our own nature and an identification of ourselves with the beautiful which exists in thought, action, or person, not our own'. It is the operative force that makes society cohere in a community of values, joint action and consideration for one another. In its absence we have the elevation of the self over the common interest which is the antithesis of social feeling. Joan, in effect, accuses the Church of producing a system of thought and action which is subversive of social good.

Her words, however, are not aimed at denying any social role to the Church. Although her 'feeling of religion' was gained directly through the works of God and not through the medium of the 'forms of devotion' and 'the ordinances of the holy Church', few are they who can communicate so directly with the divine energy, and who 'from aught evil and deform'd ... shrink/Even as with instinct'. The truths must therefore be communicated through religious symbolism to ordinary men at two removes. Thus the music of the mass should have the same function as the bird's song, which to him who hears it aright is a prayer of thanksgiving to God.[24] But with time religion became overlaid by elaborate forms and rituals. With constant repetition the spiritual essence ebbed away, till only the outer husk of faith remained. The symbols became self-generating entities which had lost the living contact with the work of God and isolated man from it. The music of the high mass no longer related to the song of the bird, 'The chanted mass,/The silver altar and religious robe,/The mystic wafer and the hallowed cup,/God's priest-created' became the essentials of religion, and the edifice of the church came to reflect merely the skill of the architect. A growing body of theological metaphysics based on hair-splitting arguments separated the priest from the congregation as well as from the everyday world which it sought to control through terror and penance. To Joan, the ecclesiastic argument that 'Nature can teach to sin,/But 'tis the Priest alone can teach remorse' is 'blasphemy against the Holy one'.[25]

In the second edition of *Joan of Arc*, a significant contrast is added. Joan recalls the small derelict chapel of a nearby hamlet sacked by the uncaring soldiery. The distant sound of its bells had once awakened in her a sense of comfort and holiness as she tended her sheep. Among its ruins one night she had a vision — or was it a dream? — of St Agnes who drew her attention to the simple altar and cross, now overgrown with moss and weeds. Later, whenever she passed the threshold of a great house of worship she felt 'a cold damp chill', till she fled to make 'the lonely grove' her 'temple'.[26]

Criticism of the degeneration of true religion is not restricted, however, to the practices of the Church but is extended to its social effects. A parallel is drawn between the abrogation of its duty of unifying the people in spiritual love and the neglect by the rulers of their temporal responsibilities. The 'court vermin' wrested 'to their own ends the Statutes of the land/Or safely [broke] them',[27] and rampant selfishness bred poverty and misery 'as shall one day with damning eloquence,/Against the mighty plead'.[28] A vicious circle was set up. As the attitude of the exploiters affected the material conditions of the people, so the material conditions of the exploited affected their attitudes. Those who were brought up in an environment of squalor and deprivation were condemned to vice. 'I agree with Godwin', Southey wrote in December 1793, 'that society makes the crime and then punishes it.' In the same letter he extended the specific historical framework of his diatribes to an observation on his own day. The 'artificial distinctions' of contemporary society resulting from the injustices of government have bred poverty, 'the nurse of vice', and turned the world into 'a world of woe'.[29] The inevitable consequence of such deterioration is the loss of common purpose and social cohesion which issue in lawlessness and internal strife. These in turn invite outside intervention and foreign invasion, as happened in France of the early-fifteenth century. In a section of the poem excluded from the second edition and published separately under the title 'The Vision of the Maid', Henry V confesses he was tempted by the weakness of France and, beholding it 'by faction tempest torn', thought it would fall an easy prey.[30] As one who had heard the voice of God directly without the intervention of the Church, Joan of Arc sets out therefore to reform the country both spiritually and socially, and thereby to lead it as its military saviour and rid it of foreign domination. Just before embarking on the actual writing of the poem, Southey wrote that his plan was to show how she rescued the French from a combination of related evils: 'Ambition, Hatred, Envy, Slaughter, Injustice and the English'.[31] The coronation of Charles VII in the great Cathedral of Rheims and her final address to him express her knitting together again the Church and the people, the ruler and the ruled, religion and authority. The poem ends with the words: 'Thus the Maid/Redeemed her country. Ever may the All-just/Give to the arms of freedom such success.'[32]

The role of Joan as reformer raised, however, the contentious issue of how reform should be achieved. This question was taken up in her confrontation with Richmond and in the speech to the King in the coronation scene ending the poem. Southey's wrestling with it points to a feature of what Wordsworth called the 'structures of his own mind'[33] which explains much of his later theory of history. As more than one of their biographers have pointed out, both poets hid beneath their reserved and self-controlled exterior unusually passionate spirits tending even to extremes. Part of this control lay in their being aware of other pulls within themselves, and even of opposite bands in the spectra of their own views, no less than of the antagonistic views of others. The outcome was often ambiguity or an attempt to 'reconcile/Discordant elements' and 'make them cling together/In one society'.[34] This clearly applies to the early radicalism of the two friends. During the *Joan of Arc* period Southey was under the powerful influence of Godwin, though already in the first years of the nineteenth century he came, like Wordsworth and Coleridge, to recant his admiration. In 1794 he wrote to Bedford that if he wished to see 'the philosophical principles which form the basis of my character ably elucidated read Godwin'.[35] This is evident in the emphasis laid on the ethical foundation of politics and on social reform in *Joan of Arc,* as against the concentration on political reform in Tom Paine, the Society for Constitutional Information and even the plebeian London Corresponding Society. It is also noticeable in Southey's consideration of how reform should be put into practice. Whereas radicals like Paine and the members of the London Corresponding Society appealed directly to the masses, incurring thereby the charge of revolutionary incitement, Godwin preached long-term evolutionary change through educational means which would bring about a change of social consciousness. Joan too saw her mission as awakening the social consciousness and conscience of France. Nevertheless, there were significant differences in the conceptions expressed through Joan's lips and those of the philosophical anarchist Godwin. One involved the central role of religion as the channel through which social compassion and brotherhood is transmitted. In 1803 Southey wrote of his former guide: 'I abominate the cursed mingle-mangle of metaphysics and concubinism and atheism with which he polluted it.'[36] Equally important was the difference in Godwin and Southey's attitudes towards Law. For Godwin, the greatest danger to society lay in the tendency of institutions to render absolute the codes and structures of belief and behaviour, thereby countering the natural tendency of the human mind to develop freely and sowing the seeds of ills which are liable to end in violence and revolution. Southey, on the other hand, maintained that it was not the unchanging nature of the 'Statutes of the land' that was responsible for social evil but their evasion or distortion at the hands of the powerful for their selfish ends. Implicitly, the Law should apply equally to all and thus serve as a brake on egotistic exploitation. He used the term 'tyranny' to indicate authority which abuses its trust and is arbitrarily employed for the personal gain of the strong. For him, therefore, tyranny did not relate to the extent of political authority, but to the ends to which it was put. It was presumably such an approach that led him to extol even the freethinker Paine as a 'tireless Priest of Liberty! Unbought teacher of the poor!', and to proclaim 'the truth and Divinity' of his doctrines.[37] Society could not afford merely to wait for the slow Godwinian processes but also must be reformed by determined political action. Politics, moreover, had itself to be reformed and institutions brought into line with the growing needs of society. When writing *Joan of Arc* Southey, then, wished to work through both education and politics in order to revolutionise the moral and social basis of society, yet without revolution, and to reform the political structures of authority, yet without contravening Law.

The difficulty of advocating all these admirable ends at one and the same time is reflected in the depiction of Richmond who, in defence of the common people, destroyed the 'guilty ones above the law'. Although his purposes were those of Joan herself, she nevertheless expressed her strong disapproval of his violence. His justification was that the first duty of the shepherd is to slay the wolf that attacks the defenceless flock. To shed the blood of the 'Wolves of State' was therefore no crime. Further, he had no alternative since the 'Court Parasites' had the ear of the King and were immune to legal prosecution. Joan rebutted his argument by pointing to a two-way pattern of cause and effect between tyranny and social injustice on the one hand, and general lawlessness on the other. The issue turns on the old problem of ends and means. Southey never abandoned his firm belief that the vices of despots and exploiters generate deprivation and resentment in their victims, leading to crime, the rejection of authority, and finally anarchy and revolution. But, in a variation of Plato's paradox of freedom, once law collapses all restraints are removed and nothing can prevent the powerful from becoming exploiters and despots. This is the vicious circle that Joan implied in her answer to Richmond: his unlawful actions, although directed against the enemies of the people, taught by example that right and wrong were confounded. Men learn 'to execute what deeds of blood/ Their will or passion sentence', and power thus becomes the sole arbiter.[38] The same line of thought underlies the Maid's warning at the ceremony of the coronation at Rheims. It is the duty of a King to preserve social justice and prevent those who wield power from manipulating the law for their own private interests. A society whose ruler betrays this trust is open to tyranny and exploitation by the strong and rich, and to poverty and suffering for the poor and weak.[39]

But if the way of a Richmond will not purge society of its ills, Southey's sole solution is a Joan of Arc, a charismatic person whose sincerity and burning faith are great enough to ignite the nation to follow her vision of selflessness and social love. The weakness of such a solution is revealed in Southey's bringing in a *deus ex machina* as proof of the 'miraculous power' of 'the mission'd Maid' to convince the doubtful: the recognition of the Dauphin, or the blue flame that starts out of the tomb, and the sound of the clash of arms within.[40] He chose to end the epic on a note of Joan's triumph. Had he continued her story, he would have had to confess that her subsequent failure to lead a unified nation in the spirit of love and her burning as a witch could hardly provide the model for the creation of the good society.

The need for supernatural intervention to gain credence for Joan, especially in view of Southey's rejection of the voices and visions as an explanation of her power, and her reduction thereby to the status of a heroine of a fairy tale, points to a doubt in his own mind as to the satisfactory nature of his alternative to violent change. This cannot be divorced from the unusual ambivalence he showed in his estimations of many of the leading events and leaders in France. Already in 1792 he noted the cause and effect pattern of tyranny and anarchy that had set in since the execution of Louis XVI. 'The [French] people have changed tyrants',[41] he wrote, and the 'mobocracy' would inevitably end in 'blind submission to [a] military despot'.[42] Just before he began the first draft of his political epic he prayed for the downfall of Marat, Robespierre and the other leaders of the revolution. Yet he added 'vive la République', following this with 'my Joan is a great democrat or rather will be'.[43] In *The Fall of Robespierre*, written in collaboration with Coleridge, he contributed the final lines in the words of Barrere on the way violence breeds violence. The speech lists the tyrants who had successively met their fate on the very scaffold where Louis had been executed, and describes Robespierre as the last and worst of them all. With his death France would be free of 'matchless villainy' and would 'blast/The despot's pride, and liberate the World'.[44] But Southey had another comment on Robespierre's death: 'this great man' had been sacrificed by 'fools and cowards ... a man so situated must not be judged by common laws, Robespierre was the benefactor of mankind and ... we should lament his death as the greatest misfortune Europe could have sustained'.[45] Such ambiguity was to play a crucial role in the development of Southey's brand of conservatism. He came to distinguish between radicals and revolutionaries. Already in the 'Hymn to the Penates' (1796) he called on the 'crusaders for mankind' to return to their household gods and avoid being involved in the 'spaniel race/That licks the hand that beats them, or tears all/Alike in frenzy'. It should be noted that the crusaders were English volunteers in the cause of liberty, while the 'spaniel race' were the French. After the collapse of the Treaty of Amiens the national element took precedence. A clear example is the 'Poem Written Immediately after Reading the Speech of Robert Emmet on his Trial and Conviction for High Treason' (1803). The English radicals were still 'idealists', but he warned them against subversive activities, the triumph of which would allow 'the ruffian slaves' of Napoleon to impose their dictatorship on Europe.

Another expression of the hesitations and doubts in *Joan of Arc* as to the means of reforming society related to the nature of society as reformed. During the period Southey was dealing with *Joan of Arc* he held the perfect society to be one where there obtained complete political, social and economic egalitarianism. This led him to embrace enthusiastically the pantisocratic scheme of a communist settlement on the banks of the Susquehanna river as that system which could alone prevent future convulsions such as the French Revolution. Long after the plan had been abandoned he still maintained the principles on which it was based. As late as 1808 he recapitulated them, although this time emphasising their Christian rather than their Godwinian sources. The words of Jesus, he wrote, were meant to lead to 'nothing short of a total revolution', and the establishment of a new order 'in which no man is to exercise authority over another' and all would share the benefits of common labour.[46] Any other system 'tends to counteract the morals of Christianity ... its main institutions are thus at war with the revealed will of [the] Maker'.[47]

But could a scheme feasible perhaps in a new society restricted to a few individuals such as the Pantisocracy be broached for a large established society as in England? In *Wat Tyler* (1794) Southey expressed the same naive hopes as in *Joan of Arc*: 'The electric truth shall run from man to man,/And the blood-cemented pyramid of greatness/Shall fall before the flash.'[48] Facts of history, however, raised serious doubts. In *The Fall of Robespierre* the argument of the French dictator and his followers was that only by ruthless means could a new ideal society be erected on the ruins of the old.[49] Some years later Southey raised the issue again with regard to Baboeuf. At the height of the blood-bath 'the system of total equalisation would have been wise ... and incited insurrection all over Europe', but he delayed too long, and the cause was lost.[50] In the final analysis, then, Southey was caught on the horns of a dilemma: without violence the ideal society could not be established, yet violence cannot lead to the ideal society but breeds tyranny.

The way out was to strike a balance between impractical ideals and realisable goals. In *Joan of Arc* the chapel was at one remove from the universal energy expressed directly in nature, but it was closer to God than the great house of prayer. Similarly, the society of preceding ages was closer to the ideal than the one of Joan's time. Since the ideal society could not be reached, one could at least revive the earlier principles that lie at the foundation of a good society: obedience to law, responsible authority, reciprocal privileges and duties, selfless acceptance of one's position and the organic coherence of the people in social 'Love'. The pseudo-writer in *Letters from England* (1806) was to sum up the desirable order as an 'equipoise' analogous to the celestial hierarchy of imperceptible gradations.[51] In the same spirit, Joan, the 'delegate of Heaven' entrusted with crowning the 'Representative of Heaven', sought to expound to Charles the duties of the good king. The positive injunctions are few. He should see himself as 'Chief servant of the people', protector of the lowly, provider of the poor and father to the orphan, evoking in return the gratitude, love and loyalty of the people.[52] Significantly, the bulk of the speech deals with what he should avoid doing. He must not yield to the lust for power by wars of conquest which result in mass slaughter of his subjects. He must not yield to the lust for wealth, leaving the people in misery and poverty. He must not be complacent, concerned with his own greatness instead of with the lot of his people. He must be directly involved with their problems and not allow the court flatterers to intervene between him and them. The list of admonitions rises to its climax in the final lines of the poem, the warning against tyranny which breeds revolution to which attention has already been drawn. Although the Maid's words refer only to the King, the principles apply equally to the lower ranks of authority. The positive aspects of her advice are illustrated, for example, through the vignette of the ideal form of the lord-retainer relationship pictured earlier in the poem. The 'well-beloved' English servant who had dwelt in his lord's castle, treated as one of the family, goes to war 'following the lord he loved', and is slain defending his master.[53] A similar description occurs in the fragment *Robin Hood* (1805), where the retainer's duty to his 'earthly liege-lord', the 'just, the bountiful, the good' and 'blessed', is compared with that which all men must discharge to God.[54]

Such views led Southey to idealise the old ways of pre-industrial England and to contrast them with the poverty and social alienation that marked the new age of the machine with the 'infernal noises ... infernal fires ... [and] infernal occupations' of its industrial cities which 'the devil has certainly fixed upon ... for his own nursery-garden and hot house'.[55] 'The Retrospect' (1794) laments the reduction of the old manorial hall, where the 'jovial Squire/Once called his tenants around the crackling fire', to a school over which the master 'in petty empire ... held despotic rule'. Conversely, 'The Old Mansion-House' (1798) offers a vision of a future incorporating the best of the past. The outer appearance of the ancient manor house is being totally modernised, but the new squire promises the grieving old tenant that within, the spirit of the past, based on mutual trust and co-operation, would again prevail.

One may at this point recapitulate in brief some of the socio-political positions common to the Wordsworth of *The Prelude* and the early Southey. A few of these Southey did not take further: the conception of nature as the material manifestation of the Divine Power; the moral sensibility produced by those in constant and direct contact with natural phenomena; and the moments of transport, or 'spots of time', which the Maid experienced in her visions. Other positions he developed and modified in his later writings, especially the *Quarterly Review* articles of the second decade of the nineteenth century. What he retained was the epistemological approach which saw Man as both created and creator of his world; the moral view of the inter-activity of the Divine Power and Man which determines social activity; the belief that the relationships of the inter-involved physical and spiritual worlds are in constant change, although beneath the transient manifestations of each there exist principles that are permanent; the recognition that automatic responses, habit and routine make for the freezing of codes and conventions from which tyranny is born; the doctrine of the vicious circle in which tyranny breeds revolutionary anarchy from which another tyranny emerges; and the assertion that contemporary society had reached a critical turning-point where tyranny evoked, or threatened to evoke, anarchy and revolution. One major point of difference was the significance of the place of worship and the symbols of religion as the mediating power between the moral and the social worlds and as serving to bring society together. These, together with further elements, most notable of which was the economic dimension, were to provide the foundations upon which Southey was to build his philosophy of history.

III

While one cannot assign dates to the changes in Southey's ideas, they were clearly in evidence in 1810, a year which he saw as fraught with danger. At home, the controversy over the replacement of George III hinged on the likelihood of a switch from a Tory to a Whig government, which the Regent was reputed to support. In the light of the traditional Whig questioning of the wisdom of British policy towards France this might well have spelled a relaxation of the war effort, which Southey regarded as a coming to terms with foreign tyranny. 'The affair of the Regency could never have been more unhappily timed ... God preserve us from the peace-mongers', he wrote to Bedford a little later; and at about the same time he commended Charles Pasley's belligerent call for the intensification of the war as 'the most important political work that has ever appeared'.[56] Meanwhile, the French blockade and the failure to open up markets in South America gave rise to an economic slump resulting in considerable social restiveness. 1810 was also the year when Southey undertook to contribute to the *Edinburgh Annual Register*. As he wrote: 'now that it becomes my business to be better informed, I have spared no pains to become so'.[57] His researches prompted him to shift the emphasis in his tyranny-lawlessness equation, from the danger of social injustice and despotism to the danger of a collapse of authority. Three issues henceforth assumed central importance for him: the functions of Government in periods of national danger, its relations with the Opposition, and the role played by industry.

Fear of internal disorder and of the rise to power of a Whig government induced him to denounce the Opposition as 'a regular party organised against the government of the country, and consequently in semi-alliance with the enemy'.[58] His justification of the war policy led him also to deny that the blockade had weakened the national economy. This involved a reassessment of his attitude to the manufacturing system which was to colour his entire outlook. He no longer found fault with it as such; on the contrary 'it [is] industry acting on sufficient capital which constitutes the strength of a nation'.[59] He still stressed the paradox that characterised the new order: in proportion as the country grew wealthier and more powerful, the majority of its people grew poorer and weaker, mere 'two legged beasts of labour.[60] However, he began to recognise that industry contained within itself the remedies for the ills it had produced. Machinery rendered idle large numbers of workers, but the manufacture of more and better machinery was already beginning to increase employment and raise the standards of living. What was required was time and wise leadership to allow the beneficial process to unfold itself. But meanwhile popular discontent was growing, and with it the threat to order and all hope of progress. The Opposition, then, was not only playing into the hands of the enemy without, but by undermining government was reinforcing the enemy within.

Moreover, governmental power, Southey insisted, should be strengthened on moral no less than on pragmatic grounds. Social discontent was a symptom of an injustice that must be eradicated. The fulfilment of the responsibilities of government for the wellbeing of the people demanded therefore that it intervene in the economic and social spheres to restore the spiritual and material health of the nation. The argument brought into sharper focus two conceptions of social misery and of the state, which were already latent in Joan of Arc's final address to the King. Poverty and unemployment are not to be regarded as private misfortunes or individual bad luck, nor the products of ignorance and idleness. Rather, they are collective ills generated by the malfunctioning of the socio-economic system, the stability of which they threaten if allowed to continue unchecked. It is worth mentioning that there are critics who attribute the emergence of such a view to the end of the nineteenth century. But even if one points to earlier versions, such as may be found in Oastler's weekly *Fleet Papers*, Chadwick's *Sanitary Report* or J.S. Mill's *Political Economy*, one must still remember that Southey had already advanced this thesis during the Napoleonic wars; it came to form an important element in the theories of writers like Shelley, and like Carlyle who influenced Oastler, helped edit the Chadwick report and of whom Mill was 'during a long period one of his most fervent admirers'.[61] In the *Annual Register* for 1809 the point was buttressed by the reminder that it was the rejection of remedial action by the *ancien régime* that had brought about the revolution in France. In the *Colloquies* the view is given trenchant form. Montesinos states that the lesson to be learnt from the dangers besetting society is that social evils should not be conceived as pertaining merely to individuals but are 'collectively created' and should be collectively rectified. To this Sir Thomas More replies: '... enforce upon your contemporaries that truth which is as important in politics as in ethics, and you will not have lived in vain'.[62] This approach is directly connected with a conception of the State as a supra-individual entity transcending particular time-bound manifestations of society and charged with initiating and implementing changes that would realise the collective goals of the nation. It contains also a nascent theory of revolution in line with Joan's final warning — revolution arises when three conditions are prevalent: social injustice, a widespread demand for redress and a persistent refusal by government to provide it. In a letter to his brother dated January 1811, Southey wrote that when revolution threatens, 'there is no way but the recourse of the traveller in the savannahs of America — when the grass is on fire behind him to set fire to it before. Kindle the combustible materials yourself and direct them to your own purpose, or you will be cornered by them.'[63]

The reforms he proposed at the time are further indications of his thinking. His interest in social reform was far from new. In 1798 he had proclaimed the need for convalescent homes and welfare advice bureaux for the poor, and a general reconsideration of the provisions of the poor law. In the *Annual Report* for 1809 he listed further areas calling for state action, such as the criminal code. His correspondence shows he was also mulling over the redivision of landed property and 'a proper scheme of income taxation'.[64] However, the main thrust of his argument was a development of the thesis advanced in *Joan of Arc*. There he had asserted that the functions of the purified Church and the good King must supplement each other in ensuring the moral and spiritual welfare of the population, which were the primary concern of the Church, and the consequent social reciprocity and national unity, which were the primary concern of the King. Now he regarded both domains as the responsibility of the state, acting through the church and the administrative bodies of the country. Universal education would allow all members of society to better their condition. Religious instruction would cement society by inculcating common values and mediating between the classes. Therefore he pleaded, as Coleridge recently had (*Friend*, essay 8), for a 'national school system conducted upon the principles of national religion'.[65] The concept is akin to that of Burke's identification of Church and State, but Southey's view of the national church as a constitutional organ for the attainment of state goals gives it a further dimension. This explains the ecumenical suggestion, in the above quoted letter to his brother, for 'an Eclectic Church, combining all that is good in each, yet so philosophically framed that as the world grew wiser it would be adapted for a Catholic, i.e. — a universal faith'. The idea was first expressed in 1793, just before he embarked on *Joan of Arc*, when he wrote that if he were a legislator he would have established a 'national creed', acceptable to all believers in 'The One Eternal Universal God'. This indeed was another expression of the desire for unity and fear of divisiveness which marked the poem and his entire outlook. It also lies behind his mixed reaction to the Evangelical sects. He admired their work on behalf of the poor, but deplored their 'bigotry' which 'is nourished at the expense of national spirit'. However, there was perhaps a lack of urgency in his admission that he could have drawn up the scheme for an Eclectic Church but for 'the multiplicity of my employments, or the interest which I take in them, and the importance that I have ... attached to them'.[66]

Prime Minister Percival's assassination in May 1812 marked the beginning of the final phase in Southey's political thought. Coming on top of the Luddite activites, he was now convinced that 'nothing but the army preserves us: it is the single plank between us and the Red Sea of English Jacquerie, — a *Bellum Servile*'. His first reaction was that the balanced constitution must be replaced by a 'dictator who is to save the commonwealth'; the Prime Minister should be given unquestioned authority to implement the necessary policies.[67] This is actually no more than a forceful expression of the doctrine of the social equipoise and the role of the state in safeguarding it. Previously he had argued that in England it was the vice of unregulated wealth and power that bred the vice of lawlessness, whereas in France it was the anarchy of the masses that led to Napoleonic tyranny. Now that the country was on the verge of following the French model the need was for an authority strong enough both to stamp out revolt and to impose the reforms necessary to prevent social injustice, thereby restoring the national balance.

First, the malady had to be diagnosed and its causes investigated. The procedure was outlined several weeks after the assassination, in the *Quarterly Review* article 'Lives of the French Revolutionaries'. Again he insisted that suitable reforms 'by a strong government and an able minister' could have averted revolution in France. The final paragraph promised at some future time to prescribe remedies to counteract the spread of the French infection in England. Meanwhile Southey presented his conclusions and the premises on which they were based. Human history records a general direction towards 'amelioration', that is, the realisation of those potentials which it is our mission on earth to fulfil. However, human development advances not in a straight line but in zig-zags of alternating progressions and regressions. In the long run, 'amelioration' can be measured only as the sum of positive and negative developments taken as a whole. The rate of change varies considerably. It may be slow and incremental, or rapid and qualitative. Short-term evil consequences are most likely to arise in the latter case. For example, 'it was expedient for the welfare of mankind' that the Roman Empire should be subverted, though few living at the time would have agreed; and the same applied to the French Revolution and its effects. However, social misery at such times is not inevitable. By the study of history we may deduce the laws governing the development of societies and promote the good in change while acting to reduce the evil. In short, Southey was proposing the use of history as an instrument of social investigation, whose aim is not only to forecast possible directions of future development, but to help steer society in the most desirable direction. He was, in effect, heralding what Karl Popper has designated as 'Historicism'.[68] As the century progressed and the sense of drastic change became more general, earlier social models were felt to have lost their validity and such an approach became widespread. Thus, by the 1830s Carlyle could point to a prevailing tendency to guess at the future by appealing to history as 'Philosophy teaching by Experience'.[69]

Southey's new concern with historical processes is reflected in the 'Inquiry into the Poor Laws' of December 1812, where his theory took the form he was to maintain henceforth. In a letter written some months later he explained his reasons for publishing the article in the anonymity of the *Quarterly Review*. He could have published it in his own name, he stated, but this was the best channel for drawing attention to a 'most momentous topic'. In the section following on his opening analysis of the social dangers besetting England he compared two modes of evaluating these dangers. One was to belittle their importance as outweighed by the good in progress which would inevitably rectify them. The difficulty was that such complacency by ignoring the victims of progress perpetuates the evil effects and even aggravates them. The other was to judge the present as a deviation from the absolute good society modelled on earlier times. This could only lead to a fantasy of a perfect past which offers no solutions for contemporary predicaments. When it persists 'long after the reality has ceased' it may afford themes for 'the romancer and the poet', but it cloaks the corrupting elements of outworn social patterns and justifies their continued existence. This objection repudiated his own earlier radicalism. However, equally with the criticism of the first approach it was directed at the same time against the conservatism of the day.[70]

By the time of his death in 1797, the political philosophy of Edmund Burke was rapidly falling out of step with the pace of modern developments. His attack on the French revolutionaries stemmed from a supra-historical conception of society as an equilibrium corresponding to 'the order of the world and with the mode of existence decreed to a permanent body composed of transitory parts'.[71] Assuming the essential soundness of the British social and political order, it hindered the appreciation of the effects that industrialism, commercial expansion and intensive urban growth were having on the traditional ways of life. Such a position could hardly be maintained by later conservatives. Some sought to come to terms with the new order, blurring in the process the distinctions that had marked them off from liberalism. Others interpreted the 'Industrial Revolution' as aberrations from timeless principles, and clung nostalgically to a past to which current issues became progressively irrelevant. Southey's alternative was a historical mode of evaluating the present which allowed him to synthesise elements of both approaches and so escape the *impasse*.

The new view was presented in terms of an organic conception of society. In the form this assumed in the writings of Schelling and Schlegel, as propagated in England by Coleridge, it was based on three assumptions: that society is a corporate body whose parts are interdependent; that it is subject to constant growth and development; and that these are slow and steady. It had much in common with Burke's doctrines, and was essentially conservative in its criticism of the impersonality and divisiveness of the industrial society, and in its stress on the emotional quality of the concrete relationships within family, community and nation. Much of this had been expressed in Southey's youthful writings, but now he was able to combine it with a theory of zig-zag progress with short 'seasons' of change in direction: '... in the political as in the natural body ... [there are] important transitions in the system, which are necessary to its development'.[72] The implication is of two kinds of social change: the one gradual, the other, sudden 'material alteration of manners' comparable to a switch 'from peace to war [or] from war to peace'.[73] He also used the analogy of the passage from childhood to adolescence and thence to maturity.

The 'Inquiry' and subsequent articles show how each kind of change relates to the other, and their points are repeated, often verbatim, in the *Colloquies*. Three dimensions are dealt with: the rate of economic development, the distance between the social classes and the moral assumptions underlying society. A period of rapid economic change is characterised by the erosion of the shared values and beliefs that produce the sense of communality, and by the consequent expansion of social gaps; a period of slow economic change is characterised by the knitting together of shared values and beliefs that produce the sense of communality and by the consequent contraction of social gaps. The thesis is illustrated by a comparative analysis of the two last 'climacterics' England had undergone, and the intervening process between them. The 'greatness and happiness' as well as the misery and social decline of contemporary England resulted from the Reformation and the breakdown of feudal patterns. The ghost of Sir Thomas More, appearing to the modern Mostenios to discuss the similarity between the two periods, describes what led to the Reformation. Over a long period new techniques and objectives of land exploitation, the development of commerce and the access of wealth from the New World rendered traditional codes and structures obsolete. 'A trading spirit gradually superseded the rude but kindlier principle of the feudal system; profit and loss became the rule of conduct; in came calculation, and out went feeling'.[74] The enclosures and division of the ecclesiastical estates among big landowners concerned with their own material interest and increased marketing efficiency forced the villeins to become free labourers who had no choice but to seek their fortune in the towns, and thereby stimulated the growth of manufacture and commerce. To them were added the poor who hitherto had depended on the charity of the paternalistic church. The pace of commercial and industrial expansion steadily increased till 'during the last forty years a tremendous change has been going on ... the manufacturing system has been carried among us to an extent unheard of in any former age or country'.[75] Just as a long process had led to the climax of the Reformation, so the tempo of the machine age was the result of a long period of slow accumulating change after the Reformation; quantity became quality. In 'The Poor' this process was further illustrated by examples taken from the history of Portugal. It was also generalised to indicate a historical pattern:

'... the body politic may be plethoric like the body natural: there is a state of prosperity which, like overfeeding, disposes the system for inflammatory diseases, or makes it break out in blains and blotches'.[76]

The analogy directs attention to the negative social effects of rapid economic change: the upsetting of the healthy equipoise among the parts of the body politic. A rapid increase of national resources does not affect all sections of society to the same degree. The degeneration of spiritual values and vital moral powers that cement society lead to a situation in which the strong, educated and wealthy are quick to exploit the new potentials, whereas the underprivileged pay the price of progress and are reduced yet further. This results in a double trend in the standard of living: the few well-to-do 'for the better, the lowest and most numerous much for the worse'. The situation is aggravated by a sense of discrimination among the deprived, inflamed by ostentatious displays of wealth expressed in new fashions and extravagant behavior. In sum,

> this is no new malady; like causes have in other countries, and in this country in other times, produced similar effects ... the great and rapid increase of national wealth has always been attended by a corresponding pressure of distress ... great advances in civilisation ... can not take place without derangement in the commonwealth.[77]

In the course of time the rate of development slows down, old values and beliefs are modified, new ones emerge to take hold of society, and the healing process of unification begins. True, when the fever has passed certain after-effects may persist. Such were the principle of opposition to government after the Reformation and the debility of religious belief among the lower classes after the religious wars had subsided. Yet society readjusts itself, gaps are reduced, and over the centuries a stable balance is restored. Thus in England, after the convulsions of the Reformation 'the transition [became] ... slow, silent, and unperceived'. The ancient fabric was repaired in some parts and modernised in others. 'Things found their level' and 'the condition of the lower classes underwent little alteration, till the present reign'. Nevertheless progress continues, and in due course it accelerates, leading once more to excesses and their results, as shown by the Industrial Revolution.[78]

However, a re-establishment of the social equipoise on a higher economic level is not automatic. 'Important transitions in the system ... could not be performed without some degree ... of danger', and history provides examples of societies that, instead of passing through transitional periods into higher states of equilibrium, have lapsed into anarchy and tyranny or even disappeared altogether.[79] This gave scope for Southey's fears that England was in danger of decline, although the progress of the human race in the long run was not in doubt. The explanation is to be found in an additional dimension of his historical paradigm. Rapid economic changes and the consequent widening of social gaps are accompanied by an alarming increase of 'disaffection', that is, the tendency of the masses to delegitimise governmental authority; slow economic change and the consequent contraction of social gaps are accompanied by a general legitimisation of governmental authority. The forces of anarchy and of order left to themselves tend therefore to alternate.

As we have seen, periods of rapid economic change undermine the shared idea of the common good. The envy of the have-nots, and the wish of the haves to consolidate their possessions, promote a materialistic and egotistic conception of happiness based on private self-interest. The more numerous deprived are the more dangerous, since being 'deprived as well as ignorant, ... mere animal gratification must be the national end and aim of [their] blind desires'.[80] Their demand for a redistribution of wealth, unconstrained by the appreciation of its wider effects or by concern for others, leads them to challenge the justice of any political system and to nurture a feeling that the will of the people is being ignored by those in power. Such disaffection and atomisation of interests provide ready opportunities for demagogues to offer utopian dreams of immediate material benefits to be achieved through universal and equal participation in politics. They would replace government based on acceptance of self-limitation by another based on the striving of every individual to maximise unrestrictedly his own well-being. Such a government would in effect constitute a reflection of the revolt against limitation and authority itself, for 'the mob who would ... be the electors, would elect none but those who engaged to vote as they were instructed by their constituents'.[81] Such an 'Ochlocracy'[82] spells 'universal anarchy',[83] which could only terminate in an 'iron military tyranny',[84] since every order is preferable to the brute Hobbesian struggle. This relationship between social injustice, disaffection, lawlessness and tyranny is typical of Southey's thought. It brings to mind the analysis of the danger of democracy in Plato's *Republic* (Book VIII) or, to take but one pre-Burkean example which Southey must also have known, in James Usher's *Clio*.[85]

However, Southey's fear of democratic excesses went much further, owing to his distinction between State and Society. This throws light on an extraordinary feature of Southey's historical philosophy. Alongside his dynamic theory of societal development he maintained a static approach to the State. The essence of all societies, he claimed, is order and the sense of community which find expression in systems of government and principles according to which nations are regulated. Unlike the shifts that any developing society inevitably undergoes, political institutions and constitutions are necessarily more formal and depend on a high degree of stability. As embodiments of the permanent elements of social life, they should not be subject to rapid transformations but only to gradual growth and modification. What imposes unity and consistency on the variables of society, thereby preserving its continuity and establishing its identity, is the constitution. It is the 'skin of the body politic in which is the form and the beauty and the life, — or rather it is the life itself.'[86] The more extreme the social change in a period of transition and the deeper the gulfs between members of society, the more essential it is to conserve the constitution as embodied in the existing political order. To undermine that order is to dispense with the sole remaining links that bind the nation together and relate its past to its present. The significance can better be appreciated if we recall, as Southey probably did, Aristotle's distinction between change and extinction. In Aristotle's words, 'underlying the contrary 'poles' of any change' there is a single matter, and the 'being of this matter and the being of 'alteration' stand and fall together';[87] if the matter or common substratum disappears, there is not alteration but cessation. 'The constitution is our Ark of the Covenant', Southey wrote, 'woe to the sacrilegious hand that would profane it, — and woe be to us if we suffer the profanation.'[88]

Southey's fear of a spill-over from social to political disaffection was nourished not only by the historical precedents he cited but by his recognition of the exceptional nature of the changes in his day. Industrialism was 'the greatest of all improvements in society', and 'in no age has [the] improvement [of mankind] proceeded so rapidly'. But it was equally true that, unless its evil effects were nullified, in no age would the deterioration of society proceed so rapidly.[89] This was due to two seemingly contradictory, although actually complementary, facets of the 'manufacturing system': the isolation of the individual and the vastly improved means of communication. The newly urbanised workers, as well as the peasants and small farmers who had been reduced to day labourers, were cut off from the tightly knit, tradition-bound and self-supporting villages, and thrust into an alien, competitive environment. Not only were the familiar patterns of daily life destroyed, but the mediating structures that cushioned them from the harsh realities of the outer world — family, neighbours and village hierarchies — declined or disappeared, leaving them defenceless, depersonalised instruments for the production of wealth. The 'man of the manufacturing system' has been reduced to a 'brute, denuded, pitiable animal', whose intellect became increasingly dispensable as the machine became more perfect. Nor did the curse fall only on the 'hands'. The employers too were becoming dehumanised, for 'he who ... uses his fellow-creatures as bodily machines for producing wealth ... ends in becoming an intellectual one himself, employed in continually increasing what is impossible for him to enjoy'.[90]

Improved means of communication, instead of counteracting these effects by drawing people together, drove them further apart. The mail-coach, steam-engine and multiplication of newspapers had an influence as great as the Reformation or the discovery of the New World, for society had become like a spider's web; the slightest touch on any thread was felt throughout the whole. Increased information led to increased envy by enabling everyone to compare his opportunities and possessions with those of others, and seek to get hold of what the more fortunate enjoyed. Southey was one of the earliest to note that such trends were leading to the simplification and polarisation of English society. The prosperity of 'the middle class' enabled them to acquire the privileges and advantages hitherto reserved for the nobility. Conversely, the poor were not only growing poorer, but increasingly cognisant of their relative deprivation. Consequently, there were now left 'two great divisions of society', each united only by envy or fear.[91]

The 'Inquiry' opens with a description of the two hostile camps which had taken up positions under the flags of Malthus and such revolutionary reformers as Godwin, an antithesis which Southey had already drawn in his review of Malthus's *Essay on Population* which appeared in 1804.[92] The rich, who had succeeded in gaining 'a place at the table of nature', found in Malthus a justification for excluding the poor from the feast. The revolutionaries, on the other hand, proclaimed the right to seize by force what they maintained had in effect been taken from them by force.[93] Southey called a plague on both their houses. He was moved by the distress of the poor, and his loathing of the political economists in general, and of Malthus in particular, knew no bounds,[94] yet he feared the poor since their feelings of injustice made them easy prey for the 'miserable sciolists' and 'literary adventurers' of the 'seditious press' who directed their frustrations against the forces of order. Moreover, from the time of the Reformation, the decline of religion and the expansion of sectarianism had resulted in a 'sort of moral expatriation', and the widespread circulation of anti-government speeches of the Opposition leaders further alienated people from authority.[95] Hostile journalists, dissenting clergymen and Opposition leaders alike spread the teachings of the Jacobins and American radicals, thereby, consciously or unconsciously, supporting the cause of bloody revolution which 'of all evils — of all miseries — of all curses which can befall a civilised country, is the greatest'.[96]

The anti-government press had become, then, a national menace — the most formidable of 'all engines of mischief which were ever yet employed for the destruction of mankind'. It must be suppressed by law. However, this could only be a temporary expedient, for government 'cannot charm away the embarrassments of the rich and the privations of the poor'.[97] Nevertheless, it would gain time for therapeutic treatment designed to bring society through the maladies of transition to stability and health. The particulars have no relevance today; but they indicate Southey's view of the good society. He had three goals in mind: (1) The creation of a new moral ligature to tie together the sectors of society and strengthen the individual's identification with the whole of the people. The encouragement of religious faith and the spreading of knowledge by compulsory national education along the lines of Bell's system would be the chief 'bulwark to the state as well as to the church' and the 'counteracting power' against subversion.[98] (2) The immediate relief of distress by direct governmental actions, such as organising emigration and founding new colonies, forming 'industrial brigades' to be employed in public works, and acquiring tracts of uncultivated land to be settled by disbanded soldiers and the unemployed. Further legislation would abolish child employment, reform the poor laws, establish general savings banks to promote thrift and provision for times of sickness and old age, and so on. (3) Changes in the structure of society to reduce the gaps between the classes and foster trust among them. Since polarisation was the major threat to society, all the reforms, whatever their immediate objectives, were geared to its reduction. The same could be said of the initiation of graded taxes on income to finance reform, for it would create a fairer distribution of wealth. In addition to state action, other reforms would be undertaken by the people, 'everyone according to his station'. This 'full cooperation' itself would modify social attitudes by stimulating mutual trust and interdependence. Instead of enclosing their land, landlords would cultivate it more intensively and use the profit for improved housing for the peasants, who would respond by working harder. Similarly, settling evicted tenants on small plots of unused land to be rented out at nominal rates would be highly 'beneficial both to them and the landlords', and at the same time correct the imbalance of country and city. The grave conditions of the factory workers required greater governmental intervention, but Southey demanded that the managerial classes also play their part in the paternalistic care of the people. Hence his enthusiasm for Robert Owen, to whom he devoted an entire chapter of the *Colloquies*, and whom he described as 'neither more nor less than such a Pantisocrat as I was in the days of my youth'.[99]

Before discussing the implications of Southey's reforms, a word on a few of the points he had in common with a number of early-nineteenth-century socialist critics of capitalism may be useful. Like Saint-Simon and Fourier in France, or Thompson, Gray and Hodgskin in England, Southey was preoccupied with the class division into two polarised groupings: those who owned capital and the means of production and those who owned nothing but their labour power. He too believed that their conflicting interests were set on a collision course by competition, 'the system of perpetual warfare between man and man'.[100] While they all acknowledged the benefits of industrial and technological expansion, they were at one in charging that 'in the midst of the most ample means to create wealth ... [the workers] are in poverty'.[101] Society was in danger of starting on the slippery slope to revolution, of which the major British and French socialists, with the exception of Blanqui, shared Southey's dread. Their alternative was the gradual emergence through persuasion of a new, stable and harmonious order, where 'the right of property shall be founded on principles of justice, and not on those of slavery; [and] *man* shall be held more in honour than the clod he treads on, or the machine he guides'.[102]

The differences, however, were no less marked. For the early socialists, the crisis of contemporary society stemmed from the unprecedented growth of commerce and the means of production which gave rise to a new and more acute form of the class struggle that had always existed in society. Southey, on the other hand, saw the crisis as deriving from the weakening of morality and sense of national cohesion under the pressures of over-rapid economic development, with the effect of breaking up the organic society into antagonistic classes. The class structure was a periodic, not a permanent, phenomenon, although this time it was assuming a more severe form. The early socialists held the state to be the instrument of the 'leviathans who are so anxious to retain their power over us, and who, as legislators ... make the terms which ... oppress us'.[103] Reform, therefore, would not be effected from above. In fact, promises and fine-sounding catch-words, such as 'the rights of man and citizen' were no more than means to befuddle the people.[104] Southey, by contrast, saw the state as the watchdog of the nation conceived as an entity persisting through the vicissitudes of history, and hence above the temporary conflicting interests of the different sectors of society. Consequently, he regarded it as the prime initiating force in reform, whether undertaken directly or by encouragement and example. These differences came to a head over the question of the desirable future order. The socialists held the present crisis to be the final stage of a condition which had existed throughout history, arising from the inevitable disparities between rulers and ruled. Some, like Owen, even held it fortunate for mankind that society had 'now reached the extreme point of error and inconsistency',[105] for the new egalitarian order that must emerge would solve the root problem itself, thereby giving a new direction to history. Southey had no such utopian visions. Transitions, he believed, end in the restoration of the lost moral values and a reconciliation between economic and moral development. As Sir Thomas More states in the *Colloquies*, 'you cannot advance too fast [in industry and technology], provided that the moral culture of the species keeps pace with the increase of its material powers'.[106] Southey, therefore, turned for his model of the new England to the pre-industrial England which had nourished the old values. True, modifications were needed to adapt it to new conditions. But for all his belief in amelioration and his breakaway from romantic feudalism, he nevertheless retained at the core of his social vision an idealised version of the manorial principle. This explains why he saw the new horizontal stratification of society as portending evil, and why his reforms were directed to effect a return to the vertical structure based on mutual concern and responsibility. Paradoxically, his early radicalism looked back to the past, while his new conservatism projected its main principles into a future that accommodated the new industrialism.

The major role assigned to the state in the creation of the good society raises a question of leadership, similar to that faced by the radicals and revolutionaries, since all policies directed to willed change require leaders possessed of special attributes which elevate them above the people. Southey was spared the difficulty of his opponents, which was inherent in the tension between the need for such leadership and the sentiments of moral equality which had given rise to their policies in the first place. Nevertheless, his arguments postulated a leadership representing the general interest and transcending all particular considerations; one familiar with divergent social needs, but immune from and above them. At the same time he was committed to the existing constitution, and regarded the demand for sweeping political reform as the greatest of all dangers. This difficulty was reflected both in his reluctance to tackle the issue, and in his unusual interpretation of the Burkean doctrine of 'virtual representation' when he finally did.

The added qualification of moral leadership meant that hereditary property, the responsibility needed to maintain it and the leisure for culture it afforded could no longer serve as the sole justification for governing. Moreover, landowners could at best represent only a sectional interest in the light of the stupendous growth of the new cities.[107] The solution was to accommodate the commercial and industrial forces to the existing constitution by basing representation on a new criterion. The nearest equivalent to the landed gentry in the great towns were the self-made men of wealth. Their eligibility for inclusion in the leadership could be measured by some quality common to them and the landowners: they were equally above the competitive scramble that was threatening to atomise society. At the same time each was familiar with the problems and needs of the rural and urban populations respectively.[108] The result is an implied condition that entitles men of property to govern. Wealth in itself does not confer this right, but it does release men from such vices as envy and self-interest, and it is this freedom which confers the right. Should the possession of wealth not produce the desired character changes, then the right to rule is invalidated. In the case of the urban leaders Southey ignored the fact that it was usually by virtue of these selfish and aggressive qualities that they had gained their wealth in the first place. As for the landowners, he himself drew attention to the enclosures, eviction of tenants and insistence on the game laws which had greatly contributed to the problems he wished to solve. Nor did the Corn Laws confirm his theory. His very reservations therefore were potential grounds for attacking government. Furthermore, his theories demanded an enterprising leadership and a strong executive, foreign to the basic assumptions of the mixed constitution and the traditional British form of government which he was trying to defend.

Such elements, incompatible with normative conservatism, lend support to the conclusion that Southey was a far less dogmatic and orthodox conservative than many commentators have presented him. In a time of crisis he defended the old constitution and sought to prevent the dissolution of traditional mores and values. However, his response was not that of a frightened reactionary, as Byron, Shelley and other contemporaries suggested; nor can it be claimed that he averted his gaze from the social predicaments of the time. Neither did he enlist metaphysical support for his prognostications and recommendations in the manner of Burke. Rather, his was one of the earliest efforts to update conservatism, eliminate its antiquated elements and transform it into an ideology capable of dealing pragmatically with pressing national problems.

Most of his opinions conform closely to those shared by conservatives after Burke, as enumerated for example by David Y. Allen: abhorrence of violent revolution; dislike of *a priori* theorising about forms of government; the linking of Church and State; aversion to *laissez-faire* economics; commitment to monarchy and aristocracy; and the placing of high value on the 'aristocratic' virtues of temperance, self-sacrifice and *noblesse oblige*.[109] But over and above these, his efforts to restate the principles of conservatism led to a configuration of ideas that were to be formulated with greater frequency as the century progressed. Before taking up the question of the influences and even echoes from his ideas, present at first or second hand in the theories of such figures as Carlyle and Disraeli, we may turn to the points of contact between his historical speculations and those of some of his opponents among the younger generation of romantic writers, and especially Shelley.

Notes

1. K. Curry (ed.), *New Letters of Robert Southey* (New York and London: Columbia University Press, 1965), vol. I, p. 418.
2. E. Dowden (ed.), *The Correspondence of Robert Southey with Caroline Bowels* (Dublin: Dublin University Press, 1881), p. 52.
3. Curry (ed.), *New Letters of Robert Southey*, vol. I, pp. 511.
4. Ibid., p. 81.
5. Ibid., p. 22.
6. Ibid., p. 211.
7. Ibid., p. 314.
8. Ibid., p. 490.
9. W. Wordsworth, *The Prelude*, 1805 version, Bk II, l. 228.
10. Ibid., ll. 468-9.
11. Ibid., Bk I, ll. 490-2.
12. J. Keats, Letter to Reynolds, 3rd May, 1818.
13. J.W. Warter (ed.), *Selections from the Letters of Robert Southey* (London: Longman, Brown, Green, Longmans and Roberts, 1856), vol. I, p. 203.
14. T.W. Copeland (ed.), *The Correspondence of Edmund Burke* (Cambridge: University Press, 1958), vol. VI, p. 268.
15. E. Hodder, *The Life and Work of the Seventh Earl of Shaftesbury* (London: Cassell, 1887), vol. 1, p. 114. See also p. 259: 'I owe much, very much ... to [Southey's] Book of the Church, his Colloquies, and Moral Essays'.
16. Quoted in R. Williams, *Culture and Society 1780-1850* (Harmondsworth: Penguin, 1962), p. 40.
17. Curry (ed.), *New Letters of Robert Southey*, vol. I, p. 63.
18. Ibid., p. 471.
19. Ibid., p. 33.
20. R. Southey, 'Introduction', *Joan of Arc* (London: Longmans, Hurst, Rees, and Drme, 1806), vol. I, p. 11.
21. R. Southey, *Joan of Arc* (Bristol: Bulgain & Rosser, 1796), p. i.
22. Ibid., pp. 110-13.
23. Ibid., p. 113; 1806 version, pp. 213-14.
24. *Joan of Arc*, 1796 version, pp. 110, 114; 1806 version, p. 213.
25. *Joan of Arc*, 1796 version, pp. 110, 113, 115.
26. *Joan of Arc*, 1806 version, pp. 206-11.
27. *Joan of Arc*, 1796 version, p. 380.
28. Ibid., pp. 114-15.
29. Curry (ed.), *New Letters of Robert Southey*, vol. I, p. 40.
30. *Joan of Arc*, 1796 version, p. 353.
31. Curry (ed.), *New Letters of Robert Southey*, p. 28.
32. *Joan of Arc*, 1796 version, p. 409.
33. W. Wordsworth, Preface to the *Lyrical Ballads* (1800).
34. W. Wordsworth, *The Prelude*, 1805 version, Bk I, ll. 355-6.

35. Curry (ed.), *New Letters of Robert Southey*, p. 79. An additional influence on Southey's ideas is probably Count Volney's *Les Ruines ou Meditation sur les Révolutions des Empires*. The early part of the book deals with the 'eternal circle of vicissitudes [which] have sprung from an eternal circle of passions'. As societies grow the original equality of their members is overtaken by the rise of despotic tyrants whose 'spirit of egotism sows the seeds of division and hatred'. By extorting money from the weak they create 'two classes of men essentially opposite and inimical to each other. All the principles of society [are] dissolved. There [is] no longer either a common interest, or public spirit'. The result is revolution. Volney, *The Ruins: or a Survey of the Revolutions of Empires* (London: J. Johnson, 2nd edn, 1975), pp. 66-72 *passim*.
36. Curry (ed.), *New Letters of Robert Southey*, vol. I, p. 389.
37. Ibid., pp. 94, 27.
38. *Joan of Arc*, 1796 version, pp. 378-81.
39. Ibid., p. 408.
40. Ibid., pp. 116-17.
41. Warter (ed.), *Selections from the Letters of Robert Southey*, vol. I, p. 3.
42. Ibid., p. 7.
43. Curry (ed.), *New Letters of Robert Southey*, vol. I, p. 29.
44. S.T. Coleridge and R. Southey, *The Fall of Robespierre* (Cambridge: Benjamin Flower, 1794), pp. 36-7.
45. Curry (ed.), *New Letters of Robert Southey*, vol. I, p. 73.
46. Ibid.
47. Ibid., p. 473.
48. *The Complete Poetical Works of Robert Southey* (New York, Dent, 1880), p. 109.
49. Coleridge and Southey, *The Fall of Robespierre*, especially p. 24.
50. Curry (ed.), *New Letters of Robert Southey*, vol. I, p. 215.
51. R. Southey, *Letters From England*, J. Simmons (ed.) (London: Crescent Press, 1951), pp. 368-9.
52. *Joan of Arc*, 1796 version, pp. 118, 407-9.
53. Ibid., p. 394.
54. R. and C. Southey, *Robin Hood: a Fragment* (London and Edinburgh: William Blackwood & Sons, 1847), pp. 6, 31.
55. Southey, *Letters From England*, p. 197.
56. See Curry (ed.), *New Letters of Robert Southey*, vol. I, p. 313, vol. II, p. 4; BM. MS. adds. 30 f. 177V. For Southey's praise of Pasley's *Essay on the Military Policy and Institutions of the British Empire*, see also BM. MS adds. 30 f. 173r and f. 174r. In R. Southey, *Sir Thomas More: or, Colloquies on the Progress and Prospects of Society* begun two years after Waterloo (London. John Murray, 1829), Sir Thomas More comments on the great fortune that befell England in escaping 'from the danger of peace with a military Tyrant, which would inevitably have led to invasion, when he should have been ready to undertake and accomplish that great object of his ambition', vol. I, p. 49.
57. C.C. Southey (ed.), *The Life and Correspondence of Robert Southey* (London: Longman, Brown, Green, Longmans, 1850), vol. III, p. 303. See also Warter (ed.), *Selections from the Letters of Robert Southey*, vol. II, pp. 206-7, 220.
58. Warter (ed.), *Selections From the Letters of Robert Southey*, p. 296. See also *The Edinburgh Annual Register for 1809* (Edinburgh: James Ballantyne, 1811), vol. II, pp. 228-9.
59. R. Southey, 'Captain Pasley on the Military Policy of Great Britain', *Quarterly Review*, V (June 1811), pp. 407, 413-14.
60. Southey, *Letters From England*, p. 197. See also pp. 147-211.
61. J.S.Mill, *Autobiography* (New York: Columbia University Press, 1944),

p. 123. Cf. e.g. R. Barker, *Political Ideas in Modern Britain* (London: Methuen & Co., 1978), p. 10.

62. Southey, *Sir Thomas More*, vol. I, p. 82.
63. Curry (ed.), *New Letters of Robert Southey*, vol. II, p. 6.
64. *Edinburgh Annual Register*, vol. I, pp. 149-50; Southey (ed.), *Life and Correspondence of Robert Southey*, vol. III, p. 296.
65. Southey (ed.), *Life and Correspondence of Robert Southey*, vol. III, p. 319; R. Southey, 'Bell and Lancaster's System of Education', *Quarterly Review*, vol. VI (October 1811), p. 302; see also Warter (ed.), *Selections From the Letters of Robert Southey*, vol. II, p. 255. For Southey's conception of state and society, see Warter (ed.), *Selection from the Letters of Robert Southey*, pp. 251, 255. Some valuable discussion on the subject will be found in A. Cobben, *Edmund Burke and the Revolt Against the Eighteenth Century* (London: George Allen and Unwin, 2nd ed., 1960).
66. Curry (ed.), *New Letters of Robert Southey*, vol. I, p. 31. Southey, 'Bell and Lancaster's System of Education', p. 302; R. Southey, 'On the Evangelical Sects', *Quarterly Review*, IV (November 1810), p. 510. On Southey's religious ideas after 1811, see G. Cornell, *Robert Southey and his Age* (Oxford: Clarendon Press, 1960), pp. 74-80, 215-20.
67. Southey (ed.), *Life and Correspondence of Robert Southey*, vol. III, pp. 342, 344. See also Warter (ed.), *Selections from the Letters of Robert Southey*, vol. II, pp. 272-4, 277.
68. R. Southey, 'Lives of the French Revolutionaries', *Quarterly Review*, VII (June 1812), pp. 413, 437-8; K.R. Popper, *The Poverty of Historicism* (New York: Harper & Row, 1964), p. 3. Cf. Southey (ed.), *Life and Correspondence of Robert Southey*, vol. IV, p. 88-9; R. Southey, *A Letter to William Smith, M.P.* (London: John Murray, 1817), pp. 27, 30, also republished in R. Southey, *Essays, Moral and Political* (London: John Murray, 1832), vol. II, pp. 3-31; Southey, *Sir Thomas More*, vol. I, pp. 22-38.
69. T. Carlyle, *The Works of Thomas Carlyle in Thirty Volumes*, H.D. Traill (ed.) (London: Chapman and Hall, 1907), vol. XXVII, p. 85.
70. Curry (ed.), *New Letters of Robert Southey*, vol. I, p. 51; R. Southey, 'Inquiry into the Poor Laws', *Quarterly Review*, VIII (December 1812), p. 328.
71. E. Burke, *The Writings and Speeches of Edmund Burke in 12 Volumes* (Boston: Little, Brown & Co., 1901), vol. III, p. 274.
72. Southey, 'Inquiry into the Poor Laws', p. 328, cf. Southey, *Sir Thomas More*, vol. I, p. 199.
73. R. Southey, 'The Poor', *Quarterly Review*, XV (April 1816), p. 190.
74. Southey, *Sir Thomas More*, vol. I, pp. 199, 79.
75. Southey, 'Inquiry into the Poor Laws', pp. 329, 337.
76. Southey, 'The Poor', pp. 190, 193-5. Cf. Southey, *Sir Thomas More*, vol. I, p. 194.
77. Southey, 'Inquiry into the Poor Laws', p. 337; Southey, 'The Poor', pp. 192-4.
78. R. Southey, 'History of Dissenters', *Quarterly Review*, X (October 1813), p. 522; Southey, *Sir Thomas More*, vol. I, p. 99; Southey, 'The Poor', p. 195.
79. Southey, 'Inquiry into the Poor Laws', p. 328, Southey, 'Lives of the French Revolutionaries', p. 438.
80. Southey, 'Inquiry into the Poor Laws', p. 340.
81. R. Southey, 'Parliamentary Reform', *Quarterly Review*, XVI (October 1816), pp. 226-8.
82. Ibid., pp. 255-6.
83. Ibid., p. 272.
84. Ibid., p. 276.
85. BM. MS. add. 30, f. 182v; I.Y. (J. Usher), *Clio* (Dublin: J. Kierman, 4th edn, 1778), especially pp. 218-20. Other parallels in these pages to Southey's

opinions lead one to believe that he must have been familiar with the work.

86. Southey, 'Parliamentary Reform', p. 253; cf. R. Southey, 'Works on England', *Quarterly Review*, XV (July 1816), p. 573.

87. The Work of Aristotle (Chicago: Encyclopaedia Britannica, 1952), vol. I, p. 472.

88. Southey, 'Parliamentary Reform', pp. 552-3; Southey, 'Works on England', p. 561.

89. Warter (ed.), *Selections from the Letters of Robert Southey*, vol. III, pp. 45-6; Southey (ed.), *Life and Correspondence of Robert Southey*, vol. IV, p. 88; Southey, *Sir Thomas More*, vol. 1, p. 108.

90. Southey, 'Inquiries into the Poor Laws', pp. 337-41; Southey, 'The Poor', pp. 195-200; Southey, *Sir Thomas More*, vol. 1, p. 170.

91. Southey, 'The Poor', pp. 191, 195.

92. R. Southey, 'Malthus's *Essay on Population'*, *The Annual Review and History of Literature for 1803*, vol. II (London: T.N. Longman & O. Rees, 1804), pp. 292-5.

93. Southey, 'Inquiry into the Poor Laws', pp. 320-7.

94. Southey, *Sir Thomas More*, vol. II, p. 262.

95. Southey, 'History of Dissenters', p. 138.

96. R. Southey, 'La Roche Jaquelein', *Quarterly Review*, XV (April 1816), p. 2.

97. Southey, 'Parliamentary Reform', pp. 273, 278.

98. Southey (ed.), *Life and Correspondence of Robert Southey*, vol. IV, p. 247; Southey, *A Letter to William Smith, M.P.*, pp. 35-6; Warter (ed.), *Selections from the Letters of Robert Southey*, vol. II, pp. 291-2, 298.

99. Southey, 'The Poor', pp. 215-16; Southey (ed.), *Life and Correspondence of Robert Southey*, vol. IV, p. 195. See also Warter (ed.), *Selections from the Letters of Robert Southey*, vol. III, p. 45; Southey, *A Letter to William Smith, M.P.*, p. 33; Southey, Col. 1, especially, p. 132.

100. J. Grat, 'A Lecture on Human Happiness' (London School of Economics, n.d. (1825)), p. 46.

101. R. Owen, *A New View of Society and Other Writings* (London: Dent, 1949), pp. 247-8.

102. T. Hodgskin, *Labour Defended Against the Chains of Capital* (London: The Labour Publishing Company, 1922), pp. 104-5.

103. Ibid., p. 39.

104. P. Enfantin, *Oeuvres de Saint-Simon et d'Enfantin* (Paris: E. Centu, 1865-78), vol. XLI, p. 186.

105. Owen, *A New View of Society and Other Writings*, p. 248.

106. Southey, *Sir Thomas More*, vol. II, p. 106.

107. The argument as it appeared in the *Quarterly Review* was softened by judicious excisions by the editor, Gifford. The original form was restored in Southey's republication of the article in *Essays, Moral and Political*, especially p. 385.

108. Southey, 'Parliamentary Reform', pp. 255-6. This led Southey to suggest the legalisation of the sale of rotten boroughs to men of wealth. The idea was again deleted by Gifford, editor of the *Quarterly Review*. See *Essays, Moral and Political*, p. 388, and Cornall, *Robert Southey and his Age*, Appendix B, pp. 221-3.

109. D.Y. Allen, 'Modern Conservatism: The Problem of Definition', *The Review of Politics*, 43 (October 1981), pp. 593-4.

3 THE HISTORY SHELLEY NEVER WROTE

I

There is a mixture of both libel and fair comment in Southey's strictures on Godwin as being at the opposite end of the political spectrum to Malthus, the one damned as inspiring reaction, the other revolution. To imply that Godwin's banner served as a rallying point for those who were prepared to attain their ends by force was to deny a central feature of his precepts. As one who believed that the motivating force of human progress is the continued search for truth by the use of reason, he was convinced that only the gradual change of consciousness by means of open discussion and inquiry could induce society to change in the right direction. Revolution through violence precludes the free exchange of opinion and inhibits reason by releasing uncontrolled passions. Consequently, reform should not be initiated by inciting the masses but by enlisting the aid of the enlightened members of society in fostering the intellectual improvement of the people and overcoming the general tendency to be biased in favour of one's own interests. It was precisely on this issue that the London Corresponding Society (LCS) split in 1795, the majority going with Thelwall and the minority accepting Godwin's position. Godwin even saw some justification for governmental action intended to restrain the 'demagoguery' of his former colleagues, though he denounced the repressive nature of the bills proposed by Pitt and Granville with their wide definitions of treason, sedition and unlawful assembly.[1]

However, Southey was correct in seeing the Godwinian antinomy between the dynamic of the evolving human mind and the statis of social codes and institutions as leading to a vision of society far more radical than that of Paine and Thelwall, not to mention that of the Whig reformers of the Foxite school. For Godwin, government was 'a brute engine' which had been the perennial cause of human vice, while law clipped the wings of creativity by raising particular opinions of right behaviour to the status of general truths. The true aim of politics was therefore to strive for the gradual abolition of both. They would be replaced by 'parishes', communities small enough to allow direct democracy, whose sole institution would be a jury to decide on offences against justice and on personal controversies. Moreover, as against the concentration of the LCS and the Foxites on purely political issues such as parliamentary reform, he made radical social and economic demands. One consequence of the opinion that inquiry is the liberating agent of the mind is that the *sine qua non* of freedom is leisure. Hence the hours of labour must be reduced by the elimination of all luxury, the communal possession of property and the equal sharing of work among the members of society.

Southey was also correct in claiming that this Godwinian vision attracted many young idealist rebels. In fact, he himself had provided an example, as had the young Coleridge and, to a more limited extent, the young Wordsworth. Shelley was yet another, later, example. Born of an ancient well-to-do family of landed gentry he showed from early childhood his refusal to submit to what he regarded as tyrannical authority. He revolted against the flogging system of his private school, the fagging system at Eton, the accepted religious doctrines upheld at Oxford, the standards of conduct and taste of his class, and the narrow minded conventionality of his father. All his life an extraordinarily wide reader in many disciplines and many languages, he came across Godwin while still at public school. Not surprisingly, *Political Justice* influenced him enormously, helping him to focus and organise his thoughts on the principles underlying moral and social issues. When Southey and Shelley first met in December 1811, the former felt as though he had been confronted by the ghost of his youth. 'He is just what I was in 1794', he said. Some eight years later Shelley was to remind him that his views, so vehemently attacked by the older man, were close to those Southey himself had expressed in his earlier writings.[2] The diatribes of Southey the reformed rebel against Godwin may therefore shed light on some important similarities and differences in the political theories of the two Romantic poets.

It should be stressed that neither Shelley nor Southey was an abject follower of the philosophical anarchist Godwin but each used major elements of Godwin's doctrines as a basis for a social and political philosophy of his own. The two met on the eve of critical developments in the opinions of each. Southey's 'Inquiry into the Poor Laws', published only a few months later, marks the culmination of a steady process of the divergence from his early theories as expressed in *Joan of Arc* and his breakthrough into his mature conservatism. Shelley was about to embark on the pamphlets relating to the Irish question, *A Declaration of Rights*, and *Queen Mab*, which constituted a significant step in the development of his mature radicalism. Indeed, it could be argued that in many respects Shelley was about to adopt the positions Southey had abandoned.

As against Godwin's belief that man could approach only asymptotically the largely unknown and unknowable axes of truth and the perfect society, the Shelley of 1812 and the Southey of *Joan of Arc* regarded general righteousness, justice and happiness as defined and attainable ideals. Man is 'a link/In the great chain of Nature'[3] who has broken away from its 'Peace, Harmony and Love'[4] to breed unnatural war and tyranny. But his return 'which time is fast maturing,/Will swiftly, surely come'[5] when he will be released from 'the icy chain of custom'.[6] In the spirit of the French philosophers of the Enlightenment, in *Joan of Arc* more particularly Rousseau, and in *Queen Mab* d'Holbach, they applied to the society to come images of the plentitude of nature 'th' eternal energy [that] pervade[s]/The boundless range of nature', as an alternative to the God of 'human error' which sanctifies the old order. Joan's temple of the lonely grove contrasts with 'the high-arch'd roofs' of the Church, while Shelley's spirit of nature 'requir'st no prayers or praises; the caprice/Of man's weak will'.[7] This led both to what a recent critic has termed 'the inspirational paradigm', namely 'the direct communion with a divine presence that exists in nature and humanity', leading to 'an ethical idealism' whose ultimate goal is the realisation of the good society.[8] Joan, learning the truth about man and society during her solitary life in the mountain valleys, set up as a prophet-leader to bring her message to the nation. Similarly Shelley's Alastor was inspired by 'the magnificence and beauty of the external world' which sank 'profoundly into the frame of his conceptions', but he was punished, like Wordsworth's solitary in *Lines left upon a Seat in a Yew-tree*, for his 'self-centred seclusion', instead of communicating his insight to society.[9]

Both Southey and Shelley rejected Godwin's suggested procedure of personal discussions with enlightened individuals, who would in turn spread further the growth of the new spirit, as too slow and inadequate. What was needed was active measures and practical experiments. Joan of Arc was not content with preaching the good life, the Pantisocracy was meant to demonstrate its feasibility, and much of Southey's later development was expressed in detailed down-to-earth reform schemes. Shelley in his Irish pamphlets proposed founding the Association of Philanthropists, a loose federation of intellectual groups which would serve as a reservoir of activists. Their agitation on behalf of Catholic emancipation and for the repeal of the Union Act would prelude demands for more far reaching reforms. A similar awareness of the need for a steady step-by-step process of reform runs through the later 'Proposals for putting Reform to the Vote throughout the Kingdom' in which Shelley outlined plans for ascertaining 'whether the majority of the adult individuals desire or not a complete representation in the legislative assembly'. The fullest list of his proposals appeared in the yet later 'Philosophical View of Reform', where he dealt with such matters as the abolition of the national debt, the disbanding of the standing army and ways of improving the judicial system.

Another feature that marked Southey during the 1790s, especially in his verse, and Shelley after 1812, especially in his prose, was the wish to carry their message to far wider circles than those to which Godwin turned. True, both came to have their moments of doubt. Shelley even wrote a despairing sonnet on 'Political Greatness' in which he lamented that the 'herd' was impervious to art, verse, peace or virtue, and that the masses were knit only 'by force or custom':

> Man who man would be,
> Must rule the empire of himself;
> Must be supreme, establishing his throne
> ... quelling the anarchy
> Of hopes and fears being himself alone.

Such moods, however, were not representative. Southey's *Botany Bay Eclogues*, ballads, satires and Metrical Tales were deliberately written in popular style for wide audiences, and *Joan of Arc*, he hoped, would become part of the legacy of the nation. Shelley's 'Address to the Irish People' was specifically 'intended to familiarise to uneducated apprehensions ideas of liberty',[10] and the 'Declaration of Rights' was written as a broadside to be posted on walls of public buildings. Nor was this a passing phase. As late as 1820 Shelley considered the 'Philosophical View of Reform' to be eminently readable and intended as a 'kind of standard book for the philosophical reformers politically considered'.[11]

The combination of readiness to explore strategies for radical change and appeal to the populace was related in both cases to the ideas of Paine. Shelley's theology goes ill with Southey's dubbing him the priest of liberty and his doctrines as divine truths, but their echoes are audible throughout his works. Perhaps the most obvious example is the 'Declaration of Rights'. Of its thirty-one propositions, the first ten sum up in popular form the principles of legitimate authority expounded in *The Rights of Man*. The following five deal with the right to pursue truth wherever it may lead, and constitute a rendering down of Godwinism. The rest are general moral truths such as 'no man has a right to do an evil thing that good may come' (XVII), or a mixture of principles taken impartially from the two rival philosophers. Thus, the last proposal harnesses Paine's conceptions to Godwin's anarchism: 'The only use of government is to repress the vices of man. If man were today sinless, tomorrow he would have a right to demand that government and all its evils should cease.' Bearing in mind Godwin's attitude to Paine and Thelwall, this influence might be interpreted as showing that the two poets were prepared to adopt a line that logically would lead to revolution. There are indeed signs of ambivalence in each. Southey was in two minds whether Robespierre was a Promethean figure or a dictator who had let loose the jinn of hatred and violence. Shelley conducted in 1812 an epistolary debate with Godwin on the causes of the failure of the French Revolution. Was it the fact of being a revolution, as the older man held, or the absence of intellectuals to guide the liberated forces into the proper channels? Even in 1820 the younger man could hold on to his opinion that revolution, for all the misery it entailed, proved that 'the world is no longer in a temper to decline the challenge' of oppression.[12]

For all that, both Southey and Shelley regarded the use of force with abhorrence. The Maid's debate with Richmond shows that just as tyranny breeds violent rebellion, so violent rebellion leads to tyranny; and a similar idea was put forward in the 'Philosophical View of Reform', where the violence of the revolutionary reaction to tyrannical oppression was described as an example of the same crime that had caused it.[13] In fact, what spurred the two poets was the conviction that to maintain existing conditions was to invite open revolt. Unparalleled industrial and commercial expansion was accompanied by a schism splitting the nation into mutually opposed sections, the minority increasing in wealth and the majority in poverty. The member of a society of savages is happier than the labourer in a modern one, Southey declared.[14] The worker has become a victim of the civilisation he has built by the sweat of his brow, while 'kings nobles and priests fatten on [his] toil and cry out "all is well!"'[15] Shelley compared the society of his day to a sophisticated engine working at the highest pitch which, instead of grinding corn or raising water, grinds the people who operate it.[16] Glossing over the facts that the initiating force of revolt in France came from the bourgeoisie, and that the discontent was not caused by the evils of industrialism, both drew the analogy of England with the years preceding the great French upheaval. The extent of their fear can be gauged by the extremism of their attack on the ideologues of the rival camps that had formed, the *status quo* rich, and the 'to the guillotine!' mob. Malthus was a mischievous reptile which should be crushed; 'A dog which ought to be anatomised alive' (Southey)[17] for spreading 'sophisms ... calculated to lull the oppressors of mankind into a security of everlasting triumph' (Shelley).[18] Southey, as we have seen, was to find that his archangel Godwin was really Lucifer. Shelley, with somewhat greater justification, chose as cheerleader of the new sansculottes Cobbett who had 'polluted a holy ... cause with the principles of legitimate murder':[19]

> The rich are damned, beyond all cure,
> To taunt, and starve, and trample on
> The weak and wretched ...
> Sometimes the poor are dammed indeed
> To take, — not means for being blessed, —
> But Cobbett's snuff, revenge; that weed
> From which the worms that it does feed
> Squeeze less than they before possessed[20]

The only way to avert the catastrophe was by reform. Southey believed that a system along the lines of the Godwin-inspired Pantisocracy 'can alone prevent such convulsions'. Shelley believed that by explaining to the people the causes of their misery, by educating them to appreciate the true values of the good society, and by persistent non-violent opposition to the established order, one could divert the pent-up energy from blind destructiveness into making 'this ugly Hell a Heaven'.[21] Both, in brief, sought to steer a perilous course between the Scylla of despotism and the Charybdis of revolution.

Still the differences between them were acute. As Southey pointed out in an 1820 letter to Shelley, what they had had and still had in common had always been outweighed by more fundamental disagreements:

> I still desire a greater equality in the conditions of men ... [but] you would have found me as strongly opposed in my youth to Atheism and immorality of any kind as I am now, and to that abominable philosophy which teaches self-indulgence instead of self-control.[22]

What lay behind the attack was his unchanging attitudes to the authority of law and the role of religion. This in turn led to the rejection of the principle that individuals had the right to forge their own codes of conduct or make their own laws, the sins which Richmond and 'the Court vermin' equally committed. The Maid therefore accused both sides as ushering in the reverse of a good society — anarchy. Nothing could be further removed from Southey's vision of a return to the pre-industrial pattern of social relationships with their strong local and personal dependencies than Shelley's Godwinian vision of a utopia of universal brotherhood in which man, released from every restraint, becomes an almost disembodied abstraction:

> Sceptreless, free, uncircumscribed, but man
> Equal, unclassed, tribeless, and nationless,
> Exempt from awe, worship, degree, the King
> Over himself[23]

The contrasts were further sharpened as Southey developed. With time, the radical elements which he claimed to have retained became part of a wider framework, supportive of the rest. The result was a radical conservative theory based on a historical conception according to which contemporary England was in one of those transitional epochs that demand incisive action to preserve the constitution and network of political institutions while working for far-reaching social change. Consequently he lent full support to the kind of propaganda that justified repressive governmental action on the grounds that reform meant revolution and Jacobin ferocity. At the same time he condemned Malthus for providing a rationale for social status and adopted the analysis current among British reformists since Arthur Young's first-hand observation of the French Revolution: the violence was the direct consequence of the obstinate refusal of the ruling elite to ameliorate the condition of the people.

Early death prevented Shelley from incorporating his increasing reservations about Godwinism into a comprehensive historical scheme which, like that of Southey, would explain contemporary conditions and provide guidelines for action. However, there is ample evidence that such was his aim. In the preface to *Prometheus Unbound* he announced his intention to analyse the concepts of liberty and of authority and to trace their development in 'a systematical history of what appears to me to be the genuine elements of human society'. In the belief that 'poetry is very subordinate to moral and political science' he projected 'a great work, embodying the discoveries of all ages, and harmonising the contending creeds by which mankind has been ruled'.[24] His later writings develop disparate ideas present in the germ in his earliest works, taking them much further and organising them into a coherent scheme which reached its fullest expression in the 'Defence of Poetry' and the 'Philosophical View of Reform'. These contain sufficient material to allow a reconstruction of the main principles underlying the history he never wrote. It is clear that he was taking further Southey's historical theory by developing the axiological and psychological elements implicit in it into a fully-fledged philosophy.[25] At the same time the cardinal differences between the two men are obvious. Southey accepted a 'Father principle' and saw egotism as the force that distorts natural hierarchy into tyranny and exploitation. Shelley insisted that the hierarchical 'Father principle' itself was the source of tyranny and exploitation. The older poet saw a cyclic return after the transitional phase of crisis to a recurring pattern of the good society, the model of which was the lord-retainer relationship. The younger poet saw each social cataclysm as effecting a surge forward along the line of progress towards an ideal egalitarian and classless society. Such shifts were initiated by individuals such as Socrates, Jesus, Shakespeare and Milton, whom he called 'Poets in the most universal sense of the word'. From these assumptions he developed a philosophy of history assuming a wavelike form of alternating progress and regress, of liberty and authority. In this and the following chapters it is hoped that it can be shown that the influence of these ideas was far more extensive than is commonly assumed, and that they were echoed even in the writings of such conservative thinkers as Carlyle and Disraeli.

II

Perhaps the most important stage in the germination of the history that Shelley never wrote is provided by *Mont Blanc* of 1816, an enigmatic poem foreshadowing the major preoccupations of his mature years. A poem should not be examined merely as a didactic or philosophical treatise. Its diction, imagery and symbolic analogues may point to conceptual meanings beyond the descriptive or rhetorical level. This is especially true of *Mont Blanc*, for its theme, like Einstein's search for a unified formula, is an attempt to fuse the dimensions of time and space, of illusion and reality, of myth and history, of the noumenal and the phenomenal. It offers an example of what Erasmus Darwin described as 'Intuitive Analogy ... [which] is an act of reasoning of which we are unconscious except by its effects in preserving the congruity of our ideas'. However, it is clear that the work constitutes a turning-point from the materialist necessitarianism of Shelley's earlier writings towards the epistemological position of the Lake poets on which his theory of history was to be built. Critics have pointed out the influence of Coleridge, and especially his *Hymn before Sunrise in the Vale of Chamouni*.[26] The opening of *Mont Blanc*, for example, immediately brings to mind Coleridge's experience of the mountain 'blending with my thought/Yea, with my Life and Life's own secret joy'. There are also striking similarities to the famous passage of Wordsworth's trance on crossing the Alps: the river as part of his mind (the 'stream/That flowed into a kindred stream'), the mind that is not 'a mere pensioner/On outward forms' but creates as well as receives, and the yielding of physical sight into a vision that pierces into the heart of things. Shelley could not have read *The Prelude* since it had not yet been published, but such ideas and experiences were not confined to that work, and as Mary Shelley wrote of her husband, 'no man ever admired Wordsworth's poetry more; — he read it perpetually'.[27] A partial list of echoes and suggestive ideas from the preface to *The Excursion* (1814) would include, for instance, the 'individual mind', the 'ideal forms', the conception of the 'Mind of Man' as more awesome than heaven and hell, the fitting of the individual mind to the external world and vice versa and creation as the blending of the two, the human soul of universal earth dreaming of things to come, and the 'Dread Power/Whose gracious favour is the primal source/Of all illumination'.[28]

Mont Blanc presents a powerful pictorial description which serves as a concrete exemplification of the epistemological thesis of the Man, Nature and Society symbiosis. It opens with a statement and ends with a rhetorical question. The first sections deal with the 'unremitting interchange' between the universe of things and the perceiving senses of the individual, the world mind and the individual mind, the ultimate Law and mortal rulers, the Power and power. The mountain peak, unknown and inaccessible, is the ultimate source of Mind and thinghood. From the ice gulphs and ravines that girdle it issue the secret springs of material phenomena which grow into the majestic river of the universe of things which flows through the mind. Out of its obscure caverns human minds contribute their own rills, so that just as the river of things shapes the mind the mind shapes the river. The Power comes down to us 'in likeness of the Arve',[29] which is the name both of the ravine of the mind and the river of things. Proceeding from the general scheme to particulars, material things are no less dependent on intellectual processes than intellectual processes on material things. Hence rainbows are also 'earthy',[30] while waterfalls are equally 'aethereal'.[31] The final lines complete the circle. Is the Power the origin of all thought and matter, and the creator of the human mind, or is the human mind the creator of the Power? The implication is that both are true.

The spatial representation of the epistemological argument also serves as a symbol of the temporal development of humanity. Again the image recalls Wordsworth's:

>   ... peak
> Familiar with forgotten years that show
> Inscribed upon its visionary sides
> The history of many a winter storm
> Or obscure records of the path of fire.[32]

Taken in conjunction with the *Hymn to Intellectual Beauty*, composed at the same period and closely connected with *Mont Blanc*, one can see how the proto-history of Greek myth serves to indicate the earliest culture cycles. The offspring of Kronos-Coelus, the primal god of the 'infinite sky' (identified also with time), and Ge-Rhea, the primal goddess of the 'various world', are the 'giant brood of pines', the Titans or Gigantes, 'children of elder time'.[33] As the eye comes down from the peak it rests on the destructive powers, the glaciers reflecting the 'overhanging heavens', that 'creep/Like snakes that watch their prey', demolishing all in their path.[34] In the theomachy, the battle of successive pantheons for power, each rebellious generation becomes in turn tyrannical and is overcome by a younger generation of gods. One of these battles was to be the theme of *Prometheus Unbound* and another of Keats's *Hyperion*. But the myths of old, as Wordsworth insisted, are not just 'a history of departed things,/Or a mere fiction of what never was'.[35] Rather they convey eternal truths. In the words of Charles Lamb, 'they are transcripts, types — the archetypes are in us, and eternal'.[36] Thus in the descending deserts of Mont Blanc created by the evil forces of authority which issue perpetually from 'the boundaries of the sky',[37] one sees the ruins of successive past cultures where

> Frost and the Sun in scorn of mortal power
> Have piled: dome, pyramid, and pinnacle,
> A city of death[38]

The consuming lust of power starts from the earliest times, 'from yon remotest waste', and continues to the present, 'the limits of the dead and living world'.[39] Surrounding Mont Blanc at a lower level and nearing the present are other 'subject mountains', each exhibiting the same pattern of destruction and symbolising other cultures that have undergone similar processes.

Coming further down to modern times ones sees the rivers formed by the glaciers meeting in 'one majestic River/The breath and blood of distant lands'.[40] Here the poet, musing on the interchange of his own mind with 'the clear universe of things around' seeks 'among the shadows that pass by/Ghosts of all things that are some shade of thee [the mountain]'.[41] His is the latest attempt to grasp the 'secret Strength of things/Which governs thought';[42] the mystery of the 'unseen Power', the eternal force that inhabits the transient forms of life.[43] It is a secret 'not understood/By all'[44] but which only 'the wise, and great, and good/Interpret'.[45] They alone can hear the voices that have the power to 'repeal/Large codes of fraud and woe'[46] and 'free/This world from its dark slavery'.[47] Again we come full circle to the epistemological argument. Each cycle begins with an interpretation of the truth leading to a rebellion against the corrupt codes of previous authorities, but freezes in time into new tyrannies. Just as a new faith leads to new practices, so new practices congeal the living faith into new codes of woe. Another poet is then needed to serve as 'the unacknowledged legislator of the universe'. This last quotation is the final sentence and summary of the 'Defence of Poetry' which is a later prose development and expansion of the ideas present largely in symbolic form in *Mont Blanc* and the *Hymn*, providing, as it were, a blueprint of the history Shelley never wrote.

Like the two poems, the opening sections of the essay deal with the interrelation of the mind and what is outside it. The argument runs that effects flowing from the ineffable cosmic Power, to the degree that they are perceptible by the human senses, are given meaning and order by the two faculties of reason and imagination. Reason is the intellectual or conceptual exploration and analysis of the modes of existence, their categorisation and arrangement into generalised laws by which man is related to his environment. It is partial and quantitative, the 'enumeration of quantities already known'. Imagination, on the other hand, is qualitative, 'the perception of the value of those qualities, both separately and as a whole'. It is the 'creative faculty', producing the harmony of 'the inner faculties of our nature' with 'the external'. Therefore, 'reason is to the imagination as the instrument to the agent, as the body to the spirit'.[48] Such a distinction was something of a commonplace among the romantics. Wordsworth and Coleridge had discussed it in detail especially in relation to their theory of fancy, imagination and creativity. Several decades later, Carlyle adopted the terms 'the mechanic' and 'the dynamic' provinces of the mind for the two faculties, and lamented the decay in his time of the evaluative and creative faculty, namely the imagination. Shelley, however, took the argument a step further. For him imagination is the motivating force of liberty, which he saw as breaking the shackles of authority and releasing our natural originality from the impediments of past prescription and restriction. It operates in three interrelated ways. First, it encourages the mind to encroach on the ineffable unknown by staking out new grounds and 'marking the before unapprehended relation of things'.[49] Secondly, it extends the capacity for communication so that closer relationships develop between new dimensions of experience and the symbolic media of expression. Thirdly, in the social sphere, it generates sensitivity, so that the individual relates empathically to others. The imagination thereby leads to the formulation of new social and moral standards. He therefore regarded the interlocking activities of the creator, the communicator and the social revolutionary as manifestations of the dynamic of creative liberty.

The primary assumptions underlying the thesis are also familiar. Sensory impressions set up corresponding vibrations in the mind, which do not merely copy external phenomena but react to them in a creative mimesis. 'The external and internal impressions' form not a melody but a harmony; they are different but persist in proportional relationships. This harmony is a source of pleasure, which we seek to perpetuate by recalling the sensory stimuli through a medium used symbolically — language, pigment, stone, etc. These in turn become further objects of pleasure. But the 'external world' includes other human beings. 'Man in society', therefore, 'next becomes the object of the passions and pleasures of man; an additional class of emotions produces an augmented treasure of expression.'[50] The pleasure in the media is thus extended even more strongly to the social sensations, and constitutes a further stage in the going out of our own selves already present in an elementary form in the very nature of perception.

Perception and the pleasure derived from it imply order, for by means of it man finds meaningfulness in the welter of stimuli impinging on his mind. It becomes a function of the expression of human reactions, and in turn is felt as desirable. Different facets of what we conceive as reality have their own characteristics which in turn condition the distinct orders of impression, which in turn condition the distinct orders or rhythms of expression or 'mimetic representation'. Every branch of stimuli has for the time and place its own normative form. The poet in the universal sense is he who is most sensitive to the deeper relationships between all three levels: the sense data, the *Gestalten* and value systems we create out of them, and the order or rhythm of expression. All creators of such order are poets in this sense, whether they are artists, philosophers or law-givers. They constantly extend further the awareness of the mysterious relationships of the three dimensions of time and 'perpetuate their apprehension'. Whereas the ordinary man uses words or signs as equivalents of single separable concepts, the poet sees and formulates new and more complex structures, connections and relations. He creates new combinations forming new associations and new orders, reducing isolated particulars to 'integral unity'. As in *Mont Blanc* and the *Hymn*, the process of extending and perfecting our apprehension of the dimensions of order in the universe and of their relations was seen in the 'Defence' as of direct social importance. Man's behaviour in society is conditioned by his understanding of himself and his world. The poet, in creating and perfecting the structures of thinking and feeling, creates thereby the norms and moral basis of social conduct. Thus poets 'are not only the authors of language and of music, of the dance, and architecture, and statuary, and painting; they are the institutors of law and the founders of civil society'.[51] Social behaviour, therefore, cannot be justified by appeal to absolute, divine injunctions or to precedent. Rather it derives from the apprehension of the shifting relations between existence, perception and expression in a specific time and place. In this respect social morality is relative.

There is nevertheless a higher order of the ultimate 'Power' which, though incomprehensible to man, unfolds itself by degrees through the intuition of poets at successive periods. History is not random, and poets are prophets who advance humanity according to the 'indestructible order of the universe'; for the poet 'not only beholds intensely the present as it is, and discovers those laws according to which present things ought to be ordered, but he beholds the future in the present, and his thoughts are the germs of the flower and the fruit of latest time'.[52] Shelley, however, did not accept the view that progress is steady and continuous. As the principle of theomachy in *Mont Blanc* indicates, the pattern of historical development is wavelike, a series of crests and troughs.

Crests in the development of societies as initiated by successive poets represent the divine pattern as far as human beings can intuit it. The force that produces the high points of historical development is the human analogy of the 'Divine Creative Power'. Shelley called it 'Love'. Like other romantic poets he based his interpretation of Love to a large degree on the Christian doctrine of charity in its etymological sense, on Plato's 'Symposium' (which he translated), and on the Roman doctrine of *Venus Creatrix*. It probably owed something also to Godwin's famous notion of 'universal benevolence'. In his early 'Essay of Love' it is described as 'the bond and the sanction which connects everything which exists'.⁵³ In the 'Defence' it is defined as a 'going out of our own nature, and an identification of ourselves with ... thought, action, or person, not our own'.⁵⁴ It is the principle that links existence and perception, and is creative since it enters into fruitful communion, or 'Oneness', with all that is outside the self, and since it prevents us from getting so used to things outside ourselves that we can no longer react fully to them. Liberty of thought, behaviour and expression allows the imagination to respond to the creative activity of the universe. The evolution of man resolves itself then into an ever widening and opening out of human sensitivity. It embraces man's sense of identity with his fellow man as revealed in social order and relationships. Above all, through its emphasis on consideration for others, it demands toleration based on the idea that all norms are relative and subject to modification.

The extension of knowledge into the *terra incognita* of existence, the creation of new patterns of communication and the increase of awareness of new aspects of society must proceed without stop, the old becoming in time mere formulae. What stood before for a complex relationship is worn down to cliché. It is then that 'new poets should arise to create afresh the associations which have been thus disorganised [otherwise] language will be dead to all the nobler purposes of human intercourse'. Habituation, by constant repetition of the cliché, intervenes between the self and the non-self. This blunting of response and appeal to outworn formulations is the mark of authority. It is not other-centred but self-centred, and the retention of power beyond its vitality span spells egotism. For Shelley this shutting oneself off from the cosmic Power has a negative ethical significance, for 'a man, to be greatly good, must imagine intensely and comprehensively; he must put himself in the place of another and many others'.⁵⁵ In this sense Love, as the power diametrically opposed to self-centredness and egotism, is a moral regenerator of humanity.

The eternal struggle between the cliché as the vehicle of past-oriented authority and Love which is the vehicle of future-oriented liberty recalls forcefully what Abraham Moles called the 'banal-original dialectic' of redundancy in information theory.⁵⁶ In proportion as the communication consists of 'information items' already rendered familiar by established codes and precedents, the 'redundancy' and degree of triteness increases. It is the new and unfamiliar that add to the amount of information, though it may be at the cost of easy intelligibility. Unexpected stimuli promote activity; routine responses lead to passivity. Most communication must therefore take some position between the polar extremes of the esoteric and the cliché, shifting with growing familiarity towards the latter end of the scale.

To point up Shelley's thesis it is worth noting its similarity to Carlyle's well-known theory of the Hero which will be examined more closely in the next chapter. Already in 1831, nearly ten years before the 'Defence' was posthumously published, Carlyle defined Love in *Sartor Resartus* as that which 'connects my *Me* with all *Thees*', and creates the 'Union of the Like-Unlike'. It is a moral force that unites society so that 'even the pitifulest mortal person' is not 'indifferent to us'. Through 'the conducting medium of fantasy' the 'Universe is majestically unveiling, the everywhere Heaven revealing itself on Earth'. Those who formulate most sensitively this sentiment and transmit it most clearly to ordinary mortals so as to 'excite them to self activity' are the Heroes. They are the 'inspired (speaking and acting) Texts of that divine *Book of Revelation*, whereof a Chapter is completed from epoch to epoch, and by some named *History*'. Like Shelley's poet 'who develops new and wonderful applications of the eternal truth', and replaces by new symbols and metaphors the old which have lost their vitality, Carlyle's Hero 'Prometheus-like can shape symbols and bring new fire from Heaven'.[57]

Both thinkers conceived man as the arena in which two opposing qualities wrestle for supremacy. The same struggle creates the dynamic of social history which is the essence of historical evolution. Like Carlyle's Devil and God coexisting in his archetypal Diogenes Teufelsdröckh, Love and Egotism — the liberating going-out of the self and the tyrannical restrictions of self-centredness — strive for mastery in Shelley's conception of man. This Manichaean principle is stated explicitly in *The Revolt of Islam*, the reworking of his earlier *Leon and Cythna, or the Revolution of the Golden City: a Vision of the Nineteenth Century*:

> Two powers o'er mortal things dominion hold
> Ruling the world with divided lot
> Immortal, all-pervading, manifold
> Twin Genii, equal Gods[58]

Likewise, in *Prometheus Unbound* the evil Furies, as they torment the good Prometheus, tell him:

We will be dread thought beneath thy brain
And foul desire round thine astonished heart,
And blood within thy labyrinthine veins[59]

Both writers maintained that whereas the poet in the universal sense, or in Carlyle's terms the 'Promethean Hero', is the agent of Love, egotism has a covenant with the 'icy chains of custom' and habit. Both shared Wordsworth's lament in 'Intimations of Immortality', that 'custom lie upon thee with a weight,/Heavy as frost, and deep almost as life'.

Where the two differed was in their conception of the way these opposing qualities operate in historical terms. Carlyle, largely basing himself on Southey, regarded egotism as the power that causes man to demand excessive liberty, in the sense of freedom from restraint and obligations to other members of society. It substitutes a world of alienated individuals, related to one another by the abstract cash-nexus, for a hierarchical world where a man is identified by his personal position in a scale in which each is related to every other by bonds of mutual rights and obligations. Shelley, by contrast, insisted that exploitation and the depersonalised reduction of labour to its monetary value resulted from insufficient liberty caused by the egotistic urge of the few to dominate the many. It substitutes a world where isolated individuals have in common only fear and hatred, instilled by institutionalised power, for a world where people are linked by the bonds of social love and concern. In *Queen Mab* he claimed that 'Kings, priests and statesmen', indeed all institutions and institutionalism, are 'like subtle poison through the bloodless veins/Of desolate society'.[60] In spite of the remarkable development and deepening of his thought during his short career, this idea remained with little change. Though in the 'Defence' poetry even assumed the form of law-making or institution-creating, he retained to the very end his abhorrence of priests, Kings and aristocrats.[61] Even in his latest works he saw the dynamic of history as the eternal war between the Promethean spirit of liberty and the Jupiter spirit actuated by the desire to dominate and fetter.

The final victory of the good in each battle of the unending war was not in doubt. In *Prometheus Unbound*, Demogorgon, Jupiter's son and the spirit of historical inevitability who can only fulfil his mission when called upon by Love, put an end to his father's reign just as Jupiter put an end to the reign of Saturn. But in the final speech of the play he warns that the virtues which bar 'the pit over Destruction's strength' may be called upon to act again, whenever Eternity frees 'the serpent that would clasp her with his length to reassume/An empire o'er the disentangled doom'.[62] Repeatedly Shelley insisted that the revival of poetry in any of its forms 'has ever preceded or accompanied a great and free development of the national will'. Each triumph marks the release of another group of people from oppression and exploitation. However, after each crest of poetical creativity there follows the downward slope when lesser men apply the victorious principles until they are in danger of hardening into dogma, and a widening gap develops between the letter and the spirit. Then compromises are arrived at between those who have gained their liberty and the remaining forces of tyranny, at the expense of those who are still in bondage. 'The liberators ... in turn become their [the people's] tyrants'.[63]

These compromises are described in the 'Essay on Christianity' as 'so many trophies erected in the enemy's land, to mark the limits of the victorious progress of truth and justice'. In the 'Philosophical View of Reform' the image is repeated: 'maxims so solemnly recorded remain as trophies of our difficult and incomplete victory, planted in the enemy's land'. Trying to make permanent the *modus vivendi* with the enemy, they spell the corruption of society. 'Poetry is ever accompanied with pleasure' and there can be no pleasure where people do not 'open themselves to receive the wisdom which is mingled with its delight'. 'The end of social corruption is to destroy all sensibility to pleasure; and, therefore it is corruption. It begins at the imagination and the intellect as at the core.'[64] Whereas in the early stages in his writing career Shelley believed in the approach of the 'Golden Age' when all evil would finally disappear, in brief, a secular millenium, later he saw no end to historical progress.[65] After the crest comes the trough. It is important to emphasise that he saw the alternations of crests and troughs as by no means regular. The crests are far from equidistant in time, and the waves are not of equal height or depth. Furthermore, there is a complex of activities involved in the ascent towards the crest or the descent from it. Literary, philosophical, social, political and similar activities cannot, as Shelley repeatedly noted, be synchronised with any exactitude. Commonly, a high crest is followed by a series of decreasing crests declining to the trough, and thereafter by lesser ascending crests increasing to the highest point. But always there is 'a reflex in the tide of human things which bears the shipwrecked hopes of man into a secure haven after the storms are passed'.[66] One principle obtains throughout history; even in the steepest down-slopes, 'The wingéd seeds [of poetry] lie cold and low/Each like a corpse within its grave',[67] until their revival in the next upward move. Poetry is thus always 'the faculty which contains within itself the seeds at once of its own and of social renovation'.[68]

III

A similarity that thrusts itself upon the attention is that of the Shelleyan dialectic of history and the ideas present in the poetry of his friend and fellow-radical, John Keats. That the latter proposed for himself a scheme of development as a poet which would culminate in a theory of society is already evident from his early *Sleep and Poetry*. Aware of his adolescent delight in sensual joys, voluptuous tales and romances, he asks whether he can ever wean himself from them. He feels that he 'must pass them for a nobler life' when he will confront the 'agonies, the strife/Of human hearts'. This will allow him to 'sort/Out the dark mysteries of human soul/To clear conceiving'. It is then that he will be able to achieve the 'vast idea' which is 'the end and aim of Poesy' to 'soothe the cares, and lift the thoughts of man'.[69] As with Shelley, the echoes from Book I of Wordsworth's 'The Recluse' prefaced to *The Excursion* are clear. What must have struck him was the older poet's declaration that the mysterious 'Mind of Man' was the main region of his song,[70] that he must not avert his gaze from 'the solitary anguish' of humanity and the 'storm of sorrow' that it suffers, and that with this insight poetry may shed 'benignant influence' on society, expressing 'the image of a better time'. Again like Shelley he combined the Wordsworthian elements into a theory of history, the blueprint of which he was to offer in the two unfinished versions of his epic *Hyperion*. But whereas Shelley started with a vision of a realised utopia, and only later came to appreciate the impossibility of a social formula forever immune from the deadening effects of habit and custom, Keats began with a total disbelief in perfectibility. Earthly paradise, he wrote in a journal-letter to his brother in America, is impossible since 'the nature of the world will not admit of it'. Man improves by degrees both in mind and in 'bodily accommodations and comforts' but 'at ech stage, at each ascent there are waiting for him a fresh set of annoyances — he is mortal and there is still a heaven with its stars above his head'.[71] In *Hyperion* this view was elaborated in the speech of Oceanus, the 'sophist and sage' god of the sea, before the assembled gods of the defeated pantheon of Saturn. It is the eternal truth of 'Nature's law', he tells them, that every generation of gods must become exhausted and sterile and face 'the pain of truth' that it will be dispossessed by a younger, more advanced generation:[72]

> ... on our heels a fresh perfection treads
> A power more strong in beauty, born of us
> And fated to excell us[73]

but in due course it too will be superseded by another race of gods.

In *The Fall of Hyperion* the law of unending progress is inserted as a vision of the poet himself in his own age. The work opens with a general preamble closely following Wordsworth's theory in the Preface to the *Lyrical Ballads* that all men are creators, the poet differing from others only in degree by virtue of his powers of communication. Like the hero of *The Prelude*, he is more than an individual but assumes the stature of a representative of his generation. In his dream the poet drinks a toast to the past and the present, to 'all the mortals of the world/And all the dead whose names are in our lips', and thereupon within his dream falls into a slumber. From this he emerges into a yet deeper vision, to be followed later by a vision within the vision which is of the theomachy. The intention of these four levels of dream or vision is to enter even more deeply into the levels of the mind, till the mythic or archetypal theomachy. After the magic draught pledging the continuity of time we have a description of the poet in relation to his generation. He awakes into the infinitely large sanctuary of Moneta (Mnemosyme in the epic's earlier version), the mother of the muses, goddess of memory and prophetess of the future. Approaching the steps of the shrine he hears the goddess's voice commanding him under the threat of death to ascend the 'immortal steps' to the altar. He begins the 'prodigious toil' of moving towards them, but a chill paralyses him so that he can barely move. On the verge of death he manages to touch the lowest stair. At once life returns to his iced limbs and he reaches the veiled shadow of the goddess.[74]

The following passage[75] provides the key to understanding the message of the epic. The goddess reveals to the poet that he has been saved from death because he had the power to escape the paralysis of the 'thoughtless' who are content with conditions as they are. He is one of 'those to whom the miseries of the world/ Are misery, and will not let them rest'. But there are surely others, he replies, who 'like slaves to poor humanity/Labour for mortal good', whereas he alone has reached the shrine. Her answer is that these are not visionaries but men of action who work to alleviate immediate misery. As a dreamer he is weaker than they, for he does nothing directly and concretely to remedy 'the giant agony of the world'. However, being acutely sensitive to the unhappiness of others he suffers so intensely that his whole life is poisoned. His compensation is the ability to complement the men of action by sharing with them his understanding of the 'eternal law' that underlies the evolution of society, thereby helping to guide their efforts. The poet is then granted the privilege of beholding the scenes in the 'globed brain' of the goddess,

>   ... whereon there grew
> A power within me of enormous ken
> To see as a god sees, and take the depth
> Of things.

At this point the epic takes up the narrative of the change of pantheons described in the first *Hyperion*.

'Whom the gods love die young', and Keats, like Shelley, did not live to produce a complete history. At his death he was barely 25, and for the last year or more of his life was virtually too ill to compose. Had he lived longer perhaps he would have applied his theory of social development to the politics of his day. But that too was a history he never wrote. Shelley did not reach the age of 30, but he at least was able to draw on his ideas in his analysis of historical processes as relevant to his own day, in such prose works as the 'Essay on the Revival of Literature', the 'Essay on Christianity' and the Preface to *Leon and Cythna*. The analysis is further elaborated in the 'Defence of Poetry' and yet more fully in the 'Philosophical View of Reform'. However, in the 'Defence' it is admittedly digressive from the main theme which is the theory of poetry as the mainspring of liberty, and is largely confined to earlier historical periods. In the 'Philosophical View' it is for the most part related to later periods, since in this work his concern was essentially with the present and the future. Combining both, therefore, one can see the pattern of the 'systematical history' he planned to write.

The high points of human achievement in the history of the Western world were the age of Homer, the age of Pericles, the Renaissance, the Reformation, and, as Shelley confidently anticipated, the immediate future of the Europe of his own day. The first period provided 'the elements of that social system which is the column upon which all succeeding civilisation has reposed'. The century preceding the death of Socrates was pre-eminent in the arts, philosophy and 'the forms of civil life', although 'Athenian society was deformed by many imperfections', such as slavery and the degradation of women.[76] These were gradually erased 'from the habits and institutions of modern Europe by the poetry existing in chivalry and Christianity' and later by the 'modern Europeans'. The time of the Renaissance and the Reformation witnessed not only a great galaxy of writers and thinkers: it also saw the challenging of the supremacy of the degenerate Catholic Church, the peasants' revolts against the despotism of the wealthy and the founding of the Swiss and Dutch republics. In England the same liberating movement manifested itself in the passing away of the strain of conquest.[77]

Between these high points of spiritual and social liberation Shelley noted two periods during which spiritual and social tyranny all but stifled the creative impulse of civilisation. The great age of Rome, though it largely imitated Greek art and culture, nevertheless retained enough of the vital spirit of creativity to make its contribution to civilisation through its powerful sense of order. 'The true poetry of Rome lived in its institutions.' The decline and fall of the Roman empire marked the beginning of the period commonly known as the Dark Ages. However, the sparks of poetry, creativity and freedom, were not wholly extinguished. The embers were kept alive by 'the mythology and institutions of the Celts', and by 'the poetry in the doctrines of Jesus', though the 'system of liberty and equality ... preached by that Great Reformer were perverted to support oppression' by the Church. Jesus had even anticipated the idea of egalitarianism, but the system he established necessarily failed 'because it is a system that must result from rather than precede the moral improvement of human kind'. The embers burst out in brief flame during the eleventh century and later in Florence, where 'freedom had one citadel wherein it could find refuge from a world which was its enemy'.[78]

A second great period of darkness followed the Reformation and the Renaissance, and was associated in England with the Stuart dynasty. Cromwell tried to stem the ebb, but his Protectorate was short-lived owing to 'the selfish passions and compromising interests of man'. Shelley did not see the Bill of Rights of 1688 as a 'Glorious Revolution'. It was no more than another compromise 'between the spirit of truth and the spirit of imposture, between the spirit of freedom and the spirit of tyranny'. Nevertheless, corruption and tyranny failed to quench the vital spark in the writing of Milton. During the eighteenth century the onward march of progress was slowly and hesitantly resumed. The political philosophy of Locke and his followers, and 'a crowd of writers in France', though far from reaching the heights of their predecessors, illustrated 'with more or less success the principles of human nature as applied in political society'. Contemporaneously there was a remarkable advance in the 'mechanical sciences' and commerce. But their effect was limited by the 'inartificial forms' of government and society. Instead of contributing to the spiritual and material well-being of the people as a whole, they widened the gap between the strata of society. It was to the credit of the political philosophers that people became aware of their condition and understood what was happening. The outcome was the American Revolt and the French Revolution. The former succeeded in material and political terms, but failed spiritually because of its acceptance of utility as the standard of value. The latter, after its initial successes, led to a yet steeper decline because of its excesses. After 'the great tyrant' Napoleon came the Bourbons who, Shelley maintained, were repeating the pattern of the Restoration of 1660. Both periods came after a revolution which saw the execution of a despotic monarch by leaders of high ideals. Both failed because the people were animated by passions which debased those ideals. 'But in both cases abuses were abolished which never since have dared to show their face.' The final outcome, both in England and in France, was again a compromise between the true spirit of liberty and the political institutions of the day.[79]

After the French Revolution, political philosophy was further restricted to the doctrine of utility. In the 'Defence' Shelley opened his criticism of his own times with an attack on this approach. He distinguished between two concepts of pleasure and two concepts of utility. The first kind of pleasure is 'durable, universal, and permanent'. This, as we have seen, results from the progressive 'going out of the self' inherent in the nature of perception, and develops from the child and the savage to the most sophisticated forms of society. The other kind of pleasure is the 'transitory and particular', deriving from the 'here-and-now' satisfaction of the self. Utility may either 'express the means of producing the former or the latter'. In the former, 'whatever strengthens and purifies the affections, enlarges the imagination, and adds spirit to sense, is useful'. In the latter, utility is only 'that which banishes the importunity of the wants of our animal nature'. No one can deny the importance of the 'promoters of utility in this limited sense' in the conduct of 'common life', so long as they confine themselves 'to the inferior powers of our nature'. However, Shelley maintained that many of them had taken animal life as the highest value, and thereby 'debased the eternal truths charactered upon the imaginations of men'.[80] In effect, he was anticipating J.S. Mill's criticism of Utilitarianism, that it was quantitative, whereas true happiness is qualitative. In his *Autobiography*, Mill conceded that Carlyle had levelled the same criticism before him, though he was not then aware of the fact. Both, then, were preceded by Shelley, though neither could have known the 'Defence' or the 'Philosophic View'.[81] Shelley, like Carlyle, saw the philosophy of 'Utility' as a dangerous compromise which had extended the extremes of luxury and want by encouraging the egotism of the powerful at the expense of the helpless and poor. Love, or the 'going out of the self', had given way to exploitation and the idolisation of the self by the 'unmitigated exercise of the calculating faculty'.[82] Carlyle would have endorsed Shelley's summary of the situation: 'poetry and the principle of self, of which money is the visible incarnation, are the God and Mammon of the world'.[83] He too bewailed the weakening of Love, the creative faculty, and the strengthening of the spirit of self-centredness. Similarly he regarded egotism as the quality that had given rise to the new aristocracy-of-money that lacked the responsibility of the old landowners. This new aristocracy, Shelley maintained, consisted of the middle classes who had once proclaimed the principle of liberty and egalitarianism against the hereditary land-owning aristocracy, but had been seduced by their opponents to share in the despoiling of the nation. Their elevation led these 'advocates of equality' even to accept the pernicious doctrine of Malthus which would throw the entire burden of the state upon the lower classes, 'merely because their opponents have insolently announced it'.[84] The result, as Southey, Carlyle and in due course Disraeli were also to insist, was the splitting of the people into two classes, the rich who were becoming richer and the poor who were becoming poorer, to a degree that revolution became imminent. But whereas Southey, Carlyle and Disraeli believed that revolution could and should be prevented, Shelley saw revolution as inevitable and desirable, though his hope was that it would be achieved without bloodshed. While they hoped to revive the responsible paternalism of the old system, he was convinced of the inevitability of a free classless egalitarianism. The spirit of revolution already reviving in Spain, Italy, Greece and the Caribbean already indicated that a new wave was building up to a crest which would tower over all the changes and developments that had occurred since the last great wave of the Renaissance. It was heralded by 'such philosophers and poets as surpass beyond comparison any who have appeared since the last national struggle for civil and religious liberty'.[85] In his verse and prose Shelley repeatedly called it 'a new birth', literally 'a Renaissance'.

Perhaps no poem of Shelley's expresses in such concentrated form the difference between these two streams that issued from the same Romantic source as the *Ode to the West Wind.* Written on receiving news of the Peterloo massacre, it develops the imagery of his letter to Peacock: '... these are, as it were, the distant thunders of the terrible storm which is approaching. The tyrants here, as in the French Revolution, have just shed blood'.[86] The iconoclastic wind of autumn sweeps away the vestiges of the old order and drives the seeds into the earth covered by the dead leaves, where they lie till they are quickened into new birth by the sister wind of spring. The revolution of the seasons serves to symbolise that of society. The dead leaves that preserve the seeds through the winter are 'yellow, and black, and pale, and hectic red', the colours of the four humours whose balance constitutes human temperaments, as well as of the four races of mankind. Likewise, the first five stanzas are devoted each to the four elements — air, earth, fire and water — and to the fifth, or quintessential, element of the human soul. The wind of change bringing the approaching storm with its lightning, black rain, fire and hail, arouses the Mediterranean (Spain, Italy and Greece) from its summer dream of past glories and whips up the level Atlantic (the revolutions in the Carribbean) till the old orders, 'the sapless foliage of the ocean', grow 'gray with fear'. The pattern of life, death and resurrection is symbolised in the imagery and the structure of the Ode. The locks of the approaching storm are like 'the bright hair uplifted from the head of some fierce Maenad', the followers of Bacchus who brought culture from the east, was annually killed and was brought back to life by their frenzied cries. It should be noted that the imagery of the last stanza refers back to that of the first, while the use of the terza rima is one of interlocking rings and, rare in English, was the form of Dante's *Divina Commedia*.

The last two stanzas narrow down to the poet himself. From the days when Shelley rebelled against the flogging system at Eton he tried to put in practice his ideas of liberty. His exile from England and ill-health compelled him to confine his activity to his writing. Yet he always saw himself as a Prometheus 'chained and bound' or a Christ who had fallen upon 'the thorns of life'. He was, in his constant premonitions of early death, ready to offer himself, like the leaders of primitive societies, as a sacrifice to maintan the life of the people. Playing on the associations of the word 'wind', in Latin the 'spirit' or 'breath' which is the root of 'inspire' and of 'anima' (from which the French 'âme' and the English 'animate' are derived), he called on the breath of autumn:

> ... Be thou, Spirit fierce,
> My spirit! Be thou me, impetuous one!
> Drive my dead thoughts over the universe
> Like withered leaves to quicken a new birth!

Shelley did not live to accomplish his purpose of producing a systematic history of human liberty. Nor did his hopes of revolution in England materialise. But the Chartists, the late-nineteenth-century radicals, socialists and even conservatives like Disraeli were responsive to his 'trumpet of a prophecy'. In the final analysis, his wish in the *Ode to the West Wind* was granted, for the spirit of change did 'scatter as from an unextinguished hearth ashes and sparks' his 'words among mankind'.

Notes

1. See J.P. Clark, 'On Anarchism in an Unreal World. Kramnick's view of Godwin and the Anarchists', *American Political Science Review*, 69 (March 1975), pp. 163-7.

2. E. Dowden (ed.), *The Correspondence of Robert Southey with Caroline Bowels* (Dublin: Dublin University Press, 1881), pp. 262, 265.
3. P.B. Shelley, *Queen Mab*, Act II, ll. 107-8.
4. Ibid., Act III, ll. 196.
5. Ibid. ll. 236-7.
6. Ibid., Act I, l. 127.
7. R. Southey, *Joan of Arc* (Bristol; Bulgain & Rosser, 1796), pp. 110-11; Shelley, *Queen Mab*, Act VI, ll. 198-200.
8. M.H. Scrivener, *Radical Shelley* (Princeton: Princeton University Press, 1982), p. 78.
9. P.B. Shelley, *Alastor, or the Spirit of Solitude*, Preface.
10. F.L. Jones (ed.), *The Letters of Percy Bysshe Shelley* (Oxford: Clarendon, 1964), vol. I, pp. 232-3.
11. Ibid., vol. II, p. 201.
12. D.L. Clark (ed.), *Shelley's Prose, or the Trumpet of a Prophecy* (Alburquerque: University of New Mexico Press, 1954), p. 236.
13. Ibid. p. 235.
14. R. Southey, *Letters from England*, J. Simmons (ed.) (London: Crescent Press, 1951), p. 147.
15. K. Curry (ed.), *New Letters of Robert Southey* (New York and London: Columbia University Press, 1965), vol. I, p. 70.
16. Clark (ed.), *Shelley's Prose*, pp. 233-4.
17. Curry (ed.), *New Letters of Robert Southey*, vol. 1, pp. 327, 351.
18. P.B. Shelley, *Leon and Cythna, or the Revolution of the Golden City: a Vision of the Nineteenth Century*, Preface.
19. P.B. Shelley, *Peter Bell the Third*, footnote to line 652.
20. Ibid. ll. 232-41.
21. Shelley, *Peter Bell the Third*, l. 244. See also P.B. Shelley, *The Mask of Anarchy*, Act LXXIV passim.
22. Dowden (ed.), *The Correspondence of Robert Southey with Caroline Bowels*, p. 365.
23. P.B. Shelley, *Prometheus Unbound*, Act III, scene 4, ll. 194-7.
24. Jones (ed.), *The Letters of Shelley*, vol. II, p. 491.
25. Volney's *Ruins*, to which reference has been made in relation to Southey, may also have contributed something to the similarities between the historical ideas of Southey and Shelley. The latter quoted the work extensively. See J.W. Beach, *The Concept of Nature in Nineteenth Century English Poetry* (New York: Pageant, 1956), pp. 214, 216, 221, 225 and H.W. Piper, *The Active Universe* (London: Athlone Press, 1962), p. 170. It is worth noting that in Mary Shelley's *Frankenstein*, written under the constant encouragement of her husband, much of the monster's education before he was forced into evil was derived from his reading of *Ruins*.
26. See H. Bloom, *Shelley's Mythmaking* (New Haven: Yale University Press, 1959), pp. 11-13; C.E. Robinson, *Shelley and Byron, the Snake and the Eagle Wreathed in Flight* (Baltimore: Johns Hopkins Press, 1976), pp. 35-7; V. Khazoum, 'Mont Blanc', HSL (*Hebrew Studies in Literature*), XI (special issue, 1982), pp. 225-44.
27. Shelley, *Peter Bell the Third*, note by M. Shelley.
28. P.B. Shelley, *Mont Blanc*, ll. 9, 43, 14, 63-71, 84-5, 100-2.
29. Ibid., l. 15.
30. Ibid., l. 25.
31. Ibid., l. 26.
32. W. Wordsworth, *The Excursion*, Bk I, ll. 275-9.
33. Shelley, *Mont Blanc*, ll. 60, 21-2; P.B. Shelley, *Hymn to Intellectual Beauty*, l. 3.

34. Shelley, *Mont Blanc*, ll. 65, 99-100.
35. W. Wordsworth, 'The Recluse'.
36. C. Lamb, 'Witches and Other Night Fears'.
37. Shelley, *Mont Blanc*, l. 108.
38. Ibid., ll. 103-5.
39. Ibid., ll. 112-13.
40. Ibid., ll. 123-4.
41. Ibid., ll. 45-6.
42. Ibid., ll. 138-9.
43. Shelley, *Hymn to Intellectual Beauty*, ll. 1-2.
44. Shelley, *Mont Blanc*, ll. 81-2.
44. Ibid., ll. 83-4.
46. Ibid., ll. 80-1.
47. Shelley, *Hymn to Intellectual Beauty*, ll. 69-70.
48. Clark (ed.), *Shelley's Prose*, p. 277.
49. Ibid., p. 278.
50. Ibid.
51. Ibid., p. 179.
52. Ibid.
53. Ibid., p. 170.
54. Ibid., pp. 282-3.
55. Ibid., pp. 178, 283, 208.
56. A. Moles, *Information Theory and Aesthetic Perception* (Urbana, Chicago and London: University of Illinois Press, 1968), p. 124.
57. T. Carlyle, *The Works of Thomas Carlyle in Thirty Volumes*, H.D. Traill (ed.) (London: Chapman and Hall, 1907), vol. I, pp. 52-3, 107, 153-4, 21, 179.
58. P.B. Shelley, *The Revolt of Islam*, Canto I, ll. 347-50.
59. Shelley, *Prometheus Unbound*, Act I, ll. 488-90.
60. Shelley, *Queen Mab*, Act IV, ll. 104, 106-7.
61. Clark (ed.), *Shelley's Prose*, p. 279.
62. Shelley, *Prometheus Unbound*, Act IV, ll. 565-8.
63. Clark (ed.), *Shelley's Prose*, pp. 297, 261.
64. Ibid., pp. 213, 232, 281, 286.
65. See for example Shelley's attack on 'the false view of the Golden Age' in Clark (ed.), *Shelley's Prose*, p. 211.
66. Ibid., p. 316.
67. P.B. Shelley, *Ode to the West Wind*.
68. Clark (ed.), *Shelley's Prose*, p. 287.
69. J. Keats, *Sleep and Poetry*, ll. 122-5, 288-9, 246-7.
70. See H.E. Rollins, *The Letters of John Keats* (Cambridge, Mass: Harvard University Press, 1958), vol. I, p. 279. See also pp. 117-18.
71. Ibid., vol. II, p. 101.
72. J. Keats, *Hyperion*, Book I, ll, 230-1.
73. Ibid., ll. 212-14.
74. J. Keats, *The Fall of Hyperion*, Canto I, ll. 1-135.
75. Ibid., ll. 144-62. 302-5.
76. Clark (ed.), *Shelley's Prose*, pp. 282-3.
77. Ibid., p. 232.
78. Ibid., pp. 287, 230, 212, 231.
79. Ibid., pp. 232-3, 236.
80. Ibid., pp. 291-2.
81. See J.S. Mill, *Autobiography* (New York: Columbia University Press, 1944), p. 100; cf. Carlyle, *Works*, vol. XXVII, p. 67, vol. I, p. 153.
82. Clark (ed.), *Shelley's Prose*, pp. 292-3.

83. Ibid., p. 245.
84. Ibid., p. 248.
85. P.B. Shelley, *Hellas*, Preface; Clark (ed.), *Shelley's Prose*, pp. 296-7.
86. Jones (ed.), *The Letters of Shelley*, vol. II, p. 119.

4 THOMAS CARLYLE'S 'MARRIAGE OF HEAVEN AND HELL'

I

In a review of Disraeli's political novel *Sybil*, Lord John Manners, one of the co-founders of the Young England movement, proclaimed that the work merited a place alongside Carlyle's *Past and Present*. The two, he argued, bore a common message which was the essence of the new conservatism.[1] The historian Froude, the biographer of both Disraeli and Carlyle, went further to maintain that 'Disraeli had studied Carlyle ... had taken his teaching to heart, and in his own way meant to act upon it.'[2] Strangely enough, towards the end of the century somewhat similar assertions were made by the leaders of the new Independent Labour Party. The profound influence of Carlyle and his followers, wrote Keir Hardie, saved British socialism from foundering on the rocks of materialism.[3] And Blatchford, in a rare moment of agreement with the leader of the party, stated that 'the new religion which is socialism' is indebted less to Marx than to Carlyle and Darwin.[4]

In a large measure, the explanation of such genealogical claims by right and left alike lies in Carlyle's place in the romantic tradition. Though born in the same year as Keats (1795) and a mere three years after Shelley, he died some sixty years after both, and his earliest publications date from about the time of their death and that of Byron too. If chronologically he belongs to the second generation of great romantics, in terms of his productivity he belongs therefore to the third. But the matter is more than one of time. His writings elaborated and brought into sharper focus the radical and the conservative elements, often co-existing, in the political theories that have been traced in the previous chapters. Carlyle was familiar with the writings of Wordsworth and had made a close study of the writings of Coleridge, but he 'never considerably reverenced' the one and 'never excessively esteemed' the other. Wordsworth's views, he maintained, were largely derived at second hand from Coleridge, and the latter had drawn on the immense 'German fund' of 'unfathomabilities'.[5] Notwithstanding his uncomplimentary comments on the two, their influence on him was greater than he was ready to acknowledge. His central thesis of symbolism, terms such as 'Soul Politic' and 'Body Politic', and even semi-quotations[6] show his debt to Coleridge, while his theory of *Homo Faber* bears a striking similarity to Wordsworth's doctrine of Man the Creator. However, of the Lake poets the greater impression on him was made by Robert Southey. As a youth, he recalled in 1867, he had accepted blindly the common denunciation of the Poet Laureate as a 'renegade', but on coming to read *Joan of Arc* and the epics he was completely won over by the blend of tenderness, love of God and man, and the 'clang of chivalrous valour' that he found in them. Thereafter

> I always looked out for his Books, new or old, as for a thing of value; and, in particular, read his Articles in the *Quarterly*... in spite of my Radicalism, I found very much in these Toryisms, which was greatly according to my heart.

Acknowledging his debt to Southey's general principles, he 'strove to base them on a better ground than his'.[7] The outcome of these efforts was the development of an interpretation of capitalist society strongly reminiscent of the doctrines of Carlyle's younger contemporary, Karl Marx. This is far from claiming that Marx was a romantic or Carlyle a Marxist. Indeed, the aim of the comparison offered in this chapter between the two critics of capitalism, the one a major influence on British, the other a major influence on continental, political ideas, is to show up the unique qualities bequeathed by the romantics to British socialism and conservatism.

The examination of Carlyle's thought in this chapter will focus on the social and political works written during the period of his greatest flowering, from 'Signs of the times' (1829) to *Latter Day Pamphlets* (1850). In these he presented a world view that remained essentially unchanged and can be discerned even after 1880, when his outlook became increasingly reactionary and misanthropic. To quote St John Packe, 'His mentality was not progressive, and the whole of what he had to say was included fully and often several times over in any one of his major works.'[8] However, it was not presented systematically in linear logical form, but was involved in mystical and symbolic doctrines, expressed in a style the extravagance of which was in part intended to shake the reader out of conventional predilections and prejudices. In all the voluminous corpus of the works, the fullest and most influential exposition is provided in *Sartor Resartus*. The unusual organisation of this seminal experimental thesis novel reveals the way Carlyle conceived his thesis. It consists of three books. The first indicates the inset framework and introduces the protagonist, Professor Diogenes Teufelsdröckh. Interspersed are interpretations of the Professor's philosophy and the theoretical assumptions on which it was based: his conception of Man and Maker and his philosophy of 'Clothes'. The second book is devoted to a theory of the Hero and social change, exemplified by the biography of the protagonist which is also a broad outline of the author's own life. The third book takes up the issues facing contemporary England, points to the nature of the good society, and climaxes by warning that revolution will ensue unless correct steps are taken towards achieving it. An organisational procedure similar to that of the three parts will be followed in this chapter, though the material will not be restricted to the novel. We shall start by discussing the theories underlying Carlyle's philosophy of history. We shall then turn to his outline in *Sartor Resartus* of the stages of his own career and their universalisation to form a model of social evolution, and thence to the way it was to be applied in the *French Revolution*. Finally, we shall look into Carlyle's application of this historical model to the capitalist society and into his suggestions for remedying current evils.

II

Any consideration of Carlyle's ideas in relation to those of Marx must start with the confluence of German and English romantic thought and the indebtedness of each to German idealism. The impact of this movement on the two has been adequately treated elsewhere. However, while Carlyle's position in the romantic pantheon is established, less well known is the early romantic influence on Marx, who studied for a short time under A.W. Schlegel and even wrote romantic verse.[9] Moreover, just as Carlyle was deeply interested in the literature of Germany, so Marx even before his sojourn in London was already following what was happening and being debated in England.

Carlyle's exposure to post-Kantian German idealism dates from the early 1820s, by which time he had mastered the language sufficiently to read widely in the philosophy, criticism and fiction of the new German renaissance. Charles F. Harrold has shown that his understanding of the theories of the German philosophers was shallow and haphazard.[10] But then Carlyle, like Wordsworth and Southey, and unlike Coleridge and Shelley, could not be termed a philosopher in the strict sense, although he did develop a consistent philosophical view of life. Nevertheless, his reading in Kant and Fichte served to reinforce ideas that he found in the German imaginative writers, above all Goethe, whom he called his 'spiritual father' and whose works he described as the 'Gospel of Gospels'.[11] From them he absorbed what he later called 'Natural Supernaturalism', the conception of the universe as consisting of two distinct yet interrelated orders, the spiritual and the material. Changing matter is the symbolic medium of the Absolute, 'a garment woven and ever a-weaving in the Loom of Time',[12] art is the interpretation of the hieroglyphics of nature, and artists are a 'perpetual priesthood' who, like the heroes of Greek mythology, half-gods, half-men, intuit the spiritual shining through the material.[13] Their function is to communicate truth to ordinary men and bring them to act in accordance with the forces of the spiritual world. We have seen that similar views were current in England. His increasing familiarity with the works of the first generation of romantics probably reinforced the German influence, as well as his doctrine of Hero-worship, which was basically an extension of such views to wider spheres.

Engels, reviewing *Past and Present*, fastened on this hieratic approach as the main distinguishing element between the backward-looking religious vaticism of Carlyle and the forward-looking anti-mysticism of Feuerbach. The two, he claimed, were at one in maintaining that 'as faith gradually weakened [and] religion crumbled in the face of civilisation', man was 'bound to despair of truth, reason and nature'. Where they differed was on the remedy. Feuerbach argued that man had projected his human attributes onto the phantom of an other-wordly God. The alternative to the self-centredness stemming from the loss of faith was therefore 'giving back to man the substance he has lost through religion; not as divine but as human substance'. Carlyle, on the other hand, followed his romantic predecessors in asserting that man should return to the belief in supreme forces which humanity must obey and whose imperatives it must realise. Whereas Feuerbach saw history as the process of man's self-fulfilment, Carlyle and the romantics saw it as the process of the dictates of a transcendent essence. Engels following Feuerbach looked therefore to a future when a new social order would allow man to 'organise the world in a truly human manner according to the demands of his own nature'. Carlyle, by contrast, looked back to an age of faith and strove to regain the continuum between God and man through the intermediaries of Heroes.[14] Marx, of course, owed much to Feuerbach. However, the idealist concept of the relationship between creativity in man and in the universe contributed much to the similarities between his theories and those of Carlyle.

If sensory data are regarded as illusory, the mind's relation to the hidden unknown may be understood in two ways. It could be conceived merely in terms of its effort to apprehend it. Alternatively, Kant and his followers regarded man's highest power as his ability to shape his spiritual reality and thereby share in the self-realisation of the universal spirit. As we have seen, this was a doctrine held by the great English romantics, as in Wordsworth's identification of man the creator and the creative Power of the Universe. Indeed, M.H. Abrams saw it as dominant in English critical theory from about 1800.[15] However, the English differed from the German idealists in one central respect. The latter considered the reality shaped by man as existing only in his consciousness. The former held that there is a something 'out there' which exists independently of us, and sought a middle way between idealism and materialism. They concluded therefore that human creativity is not confined to mental activity, but also manifests itself in our shaping of the world outside us, and that between the two there is an 'unremitting interchange'.

Carlyle's notebooks show that some years before writing *Sartor Resartus* he was still wrestling with the problem of reconciling idealism with the existence of an objective world. 'Which is right', he asked, pure idealism or pure materialism?[16] By the time he wrote the work he finally made up his mind. In words that seem to echo Wordsworth's 'half perceive and half create' and Coleridge's 'we receive but what we give' he wrote that mankind both 'reflects and creates nature'.[17] Marx, as has been noted, arrived at his own point of view through a similar process of rejecting materialism and idealism as mutually exclusive. He agreed with Feuerbach that the external world has an objective existence and that 'man too is an object "of the senses"'. At the same time he accepted Hegel's view that reality is shaped by consciousness. Divorcing activity from the idealist's metaphysical basis, he conceived consciousness as operating on a world of actual physical particulars. Reality, which the materialists conceived only in the form of the object of contemplation, thereby became human, both in the sense of being shaped by human conscious activity and in the sense of that which in turn shapes human consciousness and activity.[18] In brief, Marx, too, arrived at the English romantic view that man, as Wordsworth put it, 'Doth ... create, creator and receiver both, /Working but in alliance with the works/Which [he] beholds'.

From the turn of the nineteenth century the English romantics were confronted with a revolution in the traditional ways of life, caused by dramatic industrial and commercial developments. But despite their strong interest in social and political issues they did not develop a theory of work as a consummation of the relationship between man and his environment. Instead, they directed the doctrine of the 'primary and secondary imagination' mainly to art and psychology. Coleridge, it is true, marvelled that 'everywhere might be seen roads, railways, docks, canals, made, making and projected',[19] and Southey, as has been seen, claimed that industrialism was 'the greatest of all improvements'. But their attention was concentrated rather on the ill effects of industry: the artificiality of urban life, the degradation of the poor in the midst of wealth, and, above all, the destruction of the spirit of communality. It was Carlyle who first applied their epistemological approach, bringing it to the logical conclusion of a social theory which anticipates Marx in many ways.

In his doctrine, Carlyle, and probably Marx too, were influenced by Fichte's conception of 'industry'. However, Fichte meant by it only the externalisation of the mind's activity through such media as art or philosophy. To this Carlyle and Marx added a physical dimension, the altering of the phenomenal world, and they made it the cardinal feature of their concept of man. Where earlier thinkers tended to view the distinguishing characteristic of mankind as the possession of reason, they argued that evolving man in an evolving world, in the evolution of which he not only participates but to which he contributes, must be judged in terms of his activity. Furthermore, they argued that although it may be possible to describe human beings in non-historical terms, it is impossible to explain man's behaviour in a temporal vacuum.

Both followed the traditional philosophic strategy of arriving at the *differentiae specificae* of man by contrasting him with other living creatures. Animals introduce changes in their environments to fulfil their physical needs, but there is a world of difference between, say, a beaver building a dam and an engineer. The one acts by inherited instinct and is identifiable with its activity. The other plans his means to achieve a preconceived objective, and therefore is teleologically constituted and time-oriented. Carlyle used the examples of the spider and the oyster, Marx of the spider and the bee. Spiders spin, bees and oysters build their homes, but man acts out of prior intention. He 'Raises his structure in the imagination before he erects it in reality. At the end of every labour process, we get a result that already existed in the imagination of the labourer at its commencement.'[20] What distinguishes his activity, then, is his freedom of choice. Carlyle's blacksmith 'by brain and sinew preaches forth one little textlet from the Gospel of Freedom, the Gospel of Man's Force'.[21] Marx described labour as a process in which 'man of his own accord starts, regulates, and controls the material reactions between himself and nature'.[22]

The clearest indication of this distinction is man's capacity to devise and employ tools. Both Carlyle and Marx defined man as a tool-making animal. Whereas Marx directly quoted Benjamin Franklin, the originator of the phrase, Carlyle described man as a 'tool using animal' before he came across the American's words. In his journal he wrote under the date January, 1832, that he found Boswell had quoted two or three times Franklin's definition. 'Teufelsdröckh therefore has so far been anticipated. *Vivant qui ante nos nostra dixerunt!*'[23] Carlyle and Marx agreed, however, that other animals seem to use tools. Carlyle conceded that 'the spider himself has a spinning-jenny, and warping-mill, the power-loom within his head'; Marx admitted that animals use instruments 'in the germ'. But man employs for the process his brain, itself a 'wonder making tool'. Echoing Saint-Simon, Carlyle was fond of describing the world as a work-shop and the human head as 'the best room in it, that where your tools lie most convenient'. Indeed, he could refer to a mechanical invention such as the steam engine as an 'IDEA'. Similarly, Marx wrote that nature does not build machines. These are 'organs of the human brain created by human hands; the power of knowledge, objectified'.[24]

With such instruments man not only alters but controls nature. For Carlyle, he is the force that integrates and recreates the phenomenal world. The blacksmith uses 'iron Force and coal Force and the far stranger Force of Man', so that forging a horse shoe serves as 'a nerve centre, in the great vital system of

Immensity'.²⁵ In effect, as Marx put it, he 'reproduces the whole of nature' so that 'it appears as *his* work and *his* reality'.²⁶ Human tools are also unique in that they are evolutionary. Their products serve as means for producing other, more developed products. Carlyle extended this idea to include not only man's manipulation of natural phenomena but of himself: '... For not mankind only, but all that mankind does or beholds, is in continual growth, regenesis, and self-perfecting vitality.'²⁷ Marx likewise asserted that man's nature, in the sense of his powers and the objects through which they are manifested, changes with his activity: '... by acting on the external world and changing it, he at the same time changes his own nature. He develops his slumbering powers and compels them to act in obedience to his sway.'²⁸ Both therefore viewed man as at once initiator and product of a dynamic process. Marx would have approved of Carlyle's statement that 'Opinion is at all times doubly related to Action, first as cause then as effect.'²⁹ Carlyle would have approved of Marx's formulation that 'the production of ideas, of conceptions, of consciousness is at first directly interwoven with material activity'.³⁰ From this common stand, however, they proceeded in different directions.

Carlyle's theory was basically mystical. In this 'ever living ever working universe' man is committed to the principle of unceasing creativity and must affirm life through his activity; hence the injunction: 'Produce, Produce, in God's name!' This makes him a partaker of the cosmic forces. In Wordsworth's words, 'with Godlike powers [he] Informs, Creates [and] ... daily spreads abroad his being'. But Carlyle adopted also the traditional view of man as fallen. Competing with the principle of Love which unites the 'I' with the 'not I' through creative activity is the principle of Egotism which tempts human beings to create a world in which they are the centre while what is outside them exists only to satisfy their appetites. In short, 'a Devil dwells in man, as well as a Divinity'. Contempt for the individual 'wherein Devilish passions ... lodge' is coupled with the reverence for 'the visible Manifestation and Impersonation of the Divinity'. Being finite and time-bound he can more easily react to the satanic than the divine which is infinite and eternal. To counteract this propensity he must build out of his limited perceptions limited conceptions of a world infused with the Godhead. These conceptions are symbols, in the sense that they reflect, however inadequately, abstract universal truths revealed to us through concrete phenomena. But symbol systems, 'Ideas' or

'Clothes' as Carlyle called them, are not merely representations; they also serve to reduce the eternal and infinite creative force to temporal and local dimensions. The general injunction to create is thereby translated into particular deeds which enable us to establish on-going control over our realities in ever-growing harmony with the unceasing creativity of the cosmos.[31]

Such a putting into effect implies the limited durability of 'Ideas'. As the phenomenal world is changed by human activity, the symbol system becomes progressively outmoded, parts become obsolete and cease to serve as stimuli for further action, and open-ended progress is impeded by cliché-ridden stereotypes. The more effectively the 'Idea' achieves its end of motivating people 'to do', the more redundant it becomes. Man therefore must constantly modify it to accord with the changing reality. Nevertheless, there comes a point when piecemeal reforms cannot catch up with the deterioration of the whole and a new Idea must take shape. The need for periodic rejuvenation led Carlyle to regard the successive representations of the cosmic force as a rising spiral. Using the metaphor 'clothes' for symbol systems, this is expressed in the very title of *Sartor Resartus*, the tailor retailored. Man covers himself with a 'Clothes-Thatch'. But

> ... day after day [he] must thatch [himself] anew; day after day ... some film of it, frayed away by tear and wear must be brushed-off ... till by degrees the whole has been brushed thither, and [he] get[s] new material to grind down.[32]

In *Past and Present* the process is presented as a 'Law of Nature' by which 'Ideas have fatal limits and lot: their appointed periods of youth, of maturity or perfection, of decline, nothing born but to die'.[33]

The similarities between this doctrine and that of the earlier romantics are obvious. One is reminded of Wordsworth's custom and creativity opposition, Keats' succession of cultural cycles, and even more strongly of Shelley's theory of communication which we called, using Moles' term, the banal-original dialectic. Where Carlyle departs from most of his predecessors is in his emphasis on the co-existence of two theories: the cyclic theory of a constant recurrence of temporal symbols for the eternal force, and a linear theory of progression in the direction of its realisation in material terms through human endeavour. Such an approach bears some resemblance to Southey's, but it receives an added dimension through the conception of man as *Homo Faber* and as a tool-using animal. This led Carlyle to the conclusion that the index of overall human progress is the degree to which man can shape and control his environment: '... if we consider the interval between the first wooden dibble ... and [the] Liverpool steam-carriages, ... we shall note what progress [man] had made'.[34]

As against this collocation of two historical models, cyclic and linear, and two dimensions, mystical and pragmatic, Marx's position was more materialistic. The premise of 'human existence', he wrote, is the necessity to satisfy 'earthly', or 'materialistic' needs. Whereas animal needs are fixed, human needs are subject to evolutionary developments. Since man is not only conditioned by his environment but shapes it, his needs are determined by the world outside at the same time as they are modified and generated by his willed activity. Man is a bundle of potentialities which depend on what is outside himself for their realisation. 'The action of satisfying and the instrument for satisfaction' of 'the first need ... leads to new needs' including moral and spiritual ones.[35] Whereas in Carlyle the relation of the material and spiritual is a two-way process of cause and effect, with Marx each single act in the process of human development involves the simultaneous interfusion of idea and sense, of object and subject. This links up with Carlyle's view of progress as motivated by an eternal force revealing itself in different guises at different times, as against Marx's conception of the sequential satisfaction of needs and the production of new ones which occur 'every day and every hour, today as well as thousands of years ago'.

All this led Carlyle and Marx to the opinion, common since the Greek philosophers, that man must be considered as essentially a social being. They distinguished between two senses in which the word 'man' can be used: as a specific biological species possessing fixed physical characteristics, and as a creature possessing mental faculties developing in time. Considered in isolation, man can be conceived only in the first, biological sense. In the second sense he can be conceived only as one of a group. In Carlyle's words, 'it is in society that man first feels what he is; first becomes what he can be ... the solitary man were but a small portion of himself'. Similarly, Marx held that only in society has man's '*natural* existence become his human existence ... the individual *is* the *social being*'.[36] Both drew on the attacks launched by German and

English romantic conservatives against the contract theories held by eighteenth- and early-nineteenth-century radicals, often justifying their antagonism to such individualist doctrines by appealing to common sources. The concepts of the individual as inseparable from his social context and of society as the integral totality of all its components had been clearly put by Burke, whose *Reflections on the French Revolution* was translated into German in 1798. Conversely, the organic conception of society as 'the totality of human affairs, their union into a living whole'[37] maintained by the German romantics was widely disseminated in England, largely through the agency of Coleridge. The resulting view found lucid expression in Carlyle's definition of society as 'the vital articulation of many individuals into a collective individual'.[38] Marx gave these ideas a revolutionary content: the alteration of any important aspect of society demands the alteration of the whole. The two, moreover, followed up the developmental implications of the organic metaphor. As Levine noted, 'recognising the legacy of the past as a factor necessarily conditioning the present is what distinguished Romanticism and Marxism from radical individualism'.[39]

In line with his philosophy of clothes Carlyle applied his theory of communication to the analysis of social evolution. Ideally, man should evolve in harmony with the ever-active universe. However, human progress proceeds in jerks, periodically disrupting the harmony. Society is 'the embodiment ... of an Idea': a system of interrelations into which the individual enters in the fulfilment of the purposes inherent in the Idea as a temporalisation of the eternal injunction 'produce! produce!' Accordingly, all society's 'tendencies of endeavour, specialities of custom, its laws, policies and whole procedure ... are prescribed by an idea, and flow naturally from it'.[40] The passage of the Idea along the esoteric-cliché continuum must therefore have a social impact. During the process of fulfilment society is characterised by harmonious relations based on shared purposes, values, modes and codes of behaviour. As the Idea becomes obsolete and is repatched, the orders of society that derive from it will also grow obsolete and need repatching. Once it becomes totally unviable, however, the concept of society as a whole is lost and there is no cohesive force to bind its elements into an organic unity. The principle of satanic egotism then takes over. It is each man for himself and the devil take the hindmost: 'Men [are] no longer social but Gregarious;

which latter state also could not continue, but must gradually issue in universal selfish discord, hatred, savage isolation, and dispersion.'[41] The entire symbol system and consequently the entire social order must then be replaced. Thus we have two kinds of social change that alternate in every society: that which proceeds slowly and continuously, by way of reform within an established framework of society, and the more rapid social change of limited duration, which has the effect of replacing the old framework by a new one. This transition from one framework to another is illustrated in *Sartor Resartus* by three metaphors: the snake renewing its skin, the phoenix rising anew from its ashes, and the moulting eagle which breaks his old beak and grows a new one. In each case the changes are from an old to a new form, from sickness to strength, or from death to rebirth.[42]

Marx too maintained that in its evolution society passes through phases, each conditioned by preceding stages and working itself out to its logical conclusions. Human needs and the modes of production developed to satisfy them necessitate what he called 'relations of production': the distribution of work, ownership of the means of production and division of the products. These are determined by conscious activity involved in satisfying needs, but in turn they condition consciousness which provides justifications, explanations and legitimisations of different modes of activity and corresponding social relations. Like Carlyle he held that the good society would be an expression of perfect human harmony, but since all societies are still at the state of functioning according to the principle of 'division', production depends on the co-operation of antagonistic social elements each working for its own materialistic ends. As new needs arise and new modes of production are developed, vested class interests seek to freeze the relations of production and prevent them from keeping pace with the changes.

> At a certain stage of their development, the material productive forces of society come in conflict with the existing relations of production ... from forms of development of the productive forces these relations turn into their fetters. Then begins an epoch of social revolution.[43]

Carlyle and Marx agreed, then, that production is necessarily a social process. Carlyle called society the skin and flesh without which the 'Muscles of Industry were inert';[44] according to Marx, 'the mode of cooperation is itself a "productive force"'.[45] Both also agreed that when the forms and codes of society fail to play their part in promoting production, the time is ripe for drastic social change. Each from his own perspective arrived at the conclusion that such conditions arose in their time. Carlyle saw the cause in that the rapid advance of industry and technology had resulted in the obsolescence of the Idea, and 'the Soul Politic having departed ... what can follow but that the Body Politic be decently interred, to avoid putrescence'.[46] Marx's explanation was that the growing perfection of the means of production, and the consequent generation of increasing wealth, had led to the spiritual impoverishment of the producers of that wealth: 'The *devaluation* of the world of men is in direct proportion to the *increasing value* of the world of things'.[47]

At this point we shall suspend our comparison of the two writers to examine more closely Carlyle's theory of history in *Sartor Resartus* and the *French Revolution*. We shall then be able to resume more adequately our analysis of the war by him and Marx with the capitalist society of their time.

III

Carlyle's principles of social progress are usually described as strongly resembling those put forward by Saint-Simon. Carlyle himself announced in his first letter to Saint-Simon's disciple, d'Eichtal, that 'in [the] Books of your society ... I find little or nothing to dissent from'.[48] Shine, followed by many others, concluded that Carlyle had indeed taken his ideas from the French socialists, and was loath to acknowledge the debt.[49] However, since Carlyle began to read the works of the Saint-Simonians only in 1830, *after* he had published 'Signs of the Times' where his theory first appears, the imputation is unfounded. Wellek has rightly pointed out that he could have got such views from other sources, and his style and the echoes suggest more than one.[50] Our argument has been that the foundations of his doctrine are much deeper than commonly appreciated, belonging to the same geological formation as that of the great English and German romantics. The similarities to Saint-Simonism referred to in the letter to d'Eichtal may, therefore, lead one to a different conclusion. They explain why the Saint-Simonians found his 'Signs of the Time' so congenial that they sent him their publications and took pains to meet him in England. They also explain why Carlyle in turn became interested in Saint-Simonism after reading the material they sent him, some time after he had written in his notebook that Saint-Simonism is 'a political theory ... of which I had hitherto never heard, and which seems to mean very little if anything'.[51] What is more significant is that from the time he did become affected by Saint-Simonian doctrines, he began to develop his own original view of the historical process. In particular this applies to the theories of the Hero, and of revolution as distorted social change. These were given prominence in *Sartor Resartus* and later provided him with a theoretical framework for his interpretation of the French Revolution.

The starting point of Carlyle's theory of Heroes is the interdependence of private and public conceptions of reality. Collective symbols are initiated by individuals and adopted by wider communities. Conversely, collective symbols condition every individual through education and personal contact. The Hero, or original symbol-maker, arises to replace moribund symbol systems, and is the one who blazes new trails for society to follow. He is endowed with the power to divine the reality behind the symbols, and with an ineluctible sense of mission to pass on his message, like that which Jeremiah 'felt burning in his bones', or like the fire which burnt, yet did not consume, the burning bush.[52] He is both a leader of men and an intermediary between them and the creative force of the universe: a 'Pontiff of the world ... who, Prometheus-like can shape symbols and bring new fire from Heaven to fix it there'.[53]

Like the Faustian Hero, coming from medieval legend through Marlowe to Goethe and thence to Byron and other writers, the Promethean Hero was a favourite symbol of the romantics. Shelley, as we have seen, used his character to symbolise the new society that he hoped would be born out of the death of the old. Carlyle chose the figure of Prometheus who had stolen the fire from heaven for the benefit of mankind to show the Hero's type of activity. The stealing of fire can be described as building a bridge between the spiritual and the physical worlds. It can also be taken as bridging two ways of regarding history: the history of man as the changer of nature, and the history of the phenomenal world as it is changed at the hands of man: 'Great Men are the inspired ... texts of that divine book of Revelations, whereof a chapter is completed from epoch to epoch, and by some named History.'[54]

The prototype of such a figure is Diogenes Teufelsdröckh, the hero and Hero of *Sartor Resartus*. The work is widely accepted as a disguised autobiography and at the same time an 'autobiographie de la pénsee de Carlyle'.[55] But even after the centenary of his death, there still remain a number of lacunae and debatable interpretations. To give but a few examples, the identity of Blumine, Teufelsdröckh's unfaithful beloved, is a riddle,[56] the division of his life into the signs of the Zodiac is generally ignored, and his disappearance at the end has been dismissed as a crude device to end the narrative, or a reference to the author's coming to London to publish it. Such problems, however, can be solved once one appreciates that there is a further dimension to the novel, hitherto ignored. It constitutes a philosophy of history in the guise of fiction, and its hero is a personified theory of history rather than a flesh-and-blood protagonist.

Diogenes was the famous Greek pursuer of truth, and literally means the offspring of God. Teufelsdröckh is the German for assafoetida, an evil-smelling medicinal drug, and literally means devils' dung. As the 'son of God' the Hero is the reformer of society's thought and behaviour, and being ahead of his time he is condemned by others as the vilest of all things. Though he is the major figure in the novel, we are allowed to know very little about him as a person. He is less an identifiable human being than an abstract idea in human form. He has neither parents, wife nor children, and his appearance in the world is affected by unknown agencies. His sole function in life is to struggle against 'Darkness' and 'Stupidity'.[57] His life is compared to that of the Wandering Jew, and his travels are 'anecdotes, oftenest without date or place or time'.[58] His profession is that of Professor of Things in General in the University of Nowhere (Utopia in Greek). His books are published by the firm of 'Silence', and his author's fees are the love for the world.[59] We first meet him at a time of 'fearful Unbelief', a temporary resident in the city of 'I don't know where', in the upper storey of 'the highest house ... which rose sheer up above the contiguous roofs'.[60] There he served as the link between the city below and the heavens above, a connection of the divine and the earthly that is explained by his theory of clothes, which 'excited us to self activity'.[61] After publishing his doctrine he disappears from the city, only to reappear from time to time in other places. Having completed the mission of communicating his 'Idea' he is lost sight of, but like Jesus or King Arthur, he will appear again on earth to usher in a new Idea suited to a new age. The narrative of his life falls into six periods, which the pseudo-editor has pieced together from six bundles of scattered notes and written scraps. Each is marked by a sign of the Zodiac, corresponding to the end of summer (beginning of September) till the first promise of spring at the end of February; from the approaching end of one cycle to the re-birth of another. The nature of the extant biographical information available to the pseudo-editor frees Carlyle from the obligation of presenting the hero's life in unbroken continuity, and enables him to concentrate on the high points. At the same time it corresponds to six distinct phases of progress paralleling stages in his own development.

Carlyle was born of peasant stock and brought up in an obscure little Scottish market town serving a farming community. Economically underdeveloped, rural Scotland of the time shared with the remoter parts of England a tradition of voluntary local cooperation among the classes. With the Speenhamland system not in force there, and capitalism making only slow progress, this was expressed chiefly in concern for the weaker sections of society. The spirit is illustrated in James Carlyle's report to his son on the actions taken by the local lairds and farmers, who banded together to devise means for alleviating the lot of the labourers during the economic crisis after the Napoleonic wars.[62] Though Carlyle spent more than half his life in London, he always looked back to the Scottish countryside of his youth with its values and way of life as where he truly belonged. This applied no less to his parents' home. His reminiscences of his father, written upon his death some months after the completion of *Sartor Resartus*, show him to have been a man of deep religious belief and uncompromising integrity, whose 'great maxim of Philosophy ... gathered by the teaching of nature alone [was] that man was created to work'. He was, Carlyle wrote, 'among the last of the true men which ... the old system produced'.[63] The first phase of Teufelsdröckh's life is likewise spent in the obscure farming village of Entepfuhl (the duck pond in German). His origins, like those of Jesus and Arthur, are wrapped in mystery, and he is brought up by foster parents, the Futterals (long overcoat in German). There he receives his first suit of clothes sewn out of seamless cloth that covers him from neck to ankle. In the context of the philosophy of clothes, it symbolises a complete and unified Idea, handed to him by his foster father. Futteral is referred to variously as King, Priest, Prophet and Father. From his tales of old, and those of the old men of the village, the child acquires 'incalculable knowledge'.[64] The house metonymically represents society as a whole, and the village, named after a common natural feature to be found in most villages, 'stood in the middle ... of a World ... Any road, this simple Entepfuhl road, will lead you to the end of the World'.[65]

The Entepfuhl period covers two signs of the Zodiac. The first, Libra, is the 'idyllic' period of Teufelsdröckh's infancy. Though society has passed its peak and lives on its memories, it still retains something of the glory of the good old days ('The old Theorem of the Universe', Carlyle wrote of his father, 'was sufficient for him, and he worked well in it.'[66]). The second sign, Scorpio, covers the period of school and the Gymnasium (after the parish school Carlyle entered the Amman Academy). The schoolmaster is 'a good soul', but 'downbeat', who can teach little. The Gymnasium is already situated at a distance from the village, and the boy is among strangers. His teachers are 'hide-bound pedants without knowledge of man's nature', totally out of touch with the needs of the day.[67] At this time Futteral dies, and Teufelsdröckh learns that he was not his father. The process of disintegration accelerates and the distance between him and society rapidly widens.

In the third stage, Sagittarius (November), the scene changes to the university in the 'corrupt city', and the discrepancy reaches its climax. (In 1809 Carlyle entered the University of Edinburgh, 'the Athens of the North', which several decades earlier had seen some of the brightest intellectual luminaries of the Scottish Enlightenment, Hume, Smith and Blair, to name but a few. Though its lustre had diminished, it was still a citadel of the new thought. The spirit of rational analysis, critical empiricism and distrust of tradition was vastly different from that which the boy had hitherto known.) Teufelsdröckh's university is like an aging society at the stage of 'impotent skepticism': 'Our era is the Era of Unbelief'. After a period of anguished questioning of the university's values, he comes to the conclusion that it, its teachers and the values it teaches are transitional, a trick of Nature to keep society going till some new truth emerges. Instead of following the prescribed routine order of the profession of law he breaks out of the ordained sequence in quest of the truth that surely must exist somewhere (in 1817 Carlyle abandoned his studies for the ministry, and later also threw up his plan of studying law). The dislocation of

Teufelsdröckh's projected career and expectancies is symbolised by the next sign, Pisces (February), which is out of sequence. Henceforth the biography is that of an individual who has broken away from organised society and is totally alienated from it. He wanders all over the world looking for some existing truth (in 1818 Carlyle gave up his work as a teacher and took to odd tutoring jobs, miscellaneous journalism and translation). Driven by an irresistible inner urge Teufelsdröckh moves from place to place, from one pattern of belief to another, only to find that there is no healing.

Capricorn returns to the order of the Zodiac, December, the turn of the year, and marks his illusion and disillusion. The phase describes his infatuation for the beautiful Blumine, the ideal he has been looking for, and which he fondly believes presages the rebirth, the spring (her name suggests Flora, the goddess of flowers). But his passion does not last; he soon realises that her love is false and his dream untrue. The beautiful world he had created turns out to be a mirage, and he finds himself 'alone with the night'.[68] The month is the depth of winter, not spring; the world is not a unity but 'a shivered Universe'.[69] Henceforth he has done with the outer forms of truth. He has reached the nadir and must look for the truth from within.

The final stage, like Dante's *Divina Commedia*, falls into three parts, the 'Everlasting No', the 'Centre of Indifference' and the 'Everlasting Yea'. In the Inferno of the 'Everlasting No', he sinks into himself in self-defence against a world which is a desert inhabited by wild beasts and abandoned temples crumbling in decay. (After leaving his teaching post, Carlyle sank into a spiritual, intellectual and economic nadir which seriously affected his health. Only in the 1820s did he begin to pull out of the crisis of loss of meaning and direction in life.) Teufelsdröckh refuses to acquiesce in this living death and continues to search for the inner truth. He tries in vain to find answers to the questions he puts to himself. His frustration arouses in him anger at the belief in self-love as a doctrine of life. The Purgatorio, or 'Centre of Indifference', begins with the struggle between egotism and altruism, between self-centredness and the desire to change the world, for mastery over him. Though he succeeds in casting out the 'devil' within him, his questions remain unanswered. He is in a state of exhaustion, incapable of distinguishing any truth at all. He falls asleep, his strength is restored, and he wakens into the final stage, the Paradise of the 'Everlasting Yea'. (Carlyle later used to describe his recovery as proceeding from a moment of revelation, or 'Baphometic Fire-Baptism'. This was probably the culmination of a longer healing process in which the reading of Goethe's *Wilhelm Meister* played no small part.) Teufelsdröckh finds himself on a high peak from which he can discern every detail in the whole world, and thereby gains understanding of the nature of things. In this moment of mystic illumination he finds the eternal truth: 'Love not Pleasure; love God: This is the EVERLASTING YEA ... wherein whoso walks and works, it is well with him.'[70]

Here ends what the pseudo-editor has been able to make out of the scraps and jumbled notes. Henceforth the events in Teufelsdröckh's life cannot be separated from the growth of society. He sets out as 'Professor of Things in General', to teach the truth he has found, and in consequence society itself awakens out of its torpor. The gap between the Hero and society is bridged, for now he has become its spiritual guide. The editor does not have the material of the next sign Aries (March), which is the first sign of the Zodiac, marking the rebirth of the year in spring. After achieving his purpose of regenerating one society Teufelsdröckh disappears, but the pseudo-editor insists that he will reappear to save another society in distress, perhaps this time in England ('your son is a missionary', Carlyle wrote to his mother from London, '[out to] save the British heathen, an innumerable class, whom he would do something to convert'[71]).

The mythological pattern of the Quest and Test, almost amounting to a formula, is clear. Carlyle's younger friend Tennyson was to apply it in his epic on the Arthurian cycle, *Idylls of the King*, and it was taken up again in this century by T.S. Eliot in *The Waste Land*, which with its desolation and its ruin has the same symbolic significance in terms of the death and rebirth of a culture pattern. In Tennyson we have the Hero's search for the ideal to save his society which is in great danger of death. Arthur appears as he finally disappears at the winter equinox, and the twelve books represent the twelve months of the year. Even the theme of the Hero's faithless beloved has points in common in two works. In both these myths the Hero is the representative of his society. And similarly, as 'the tailor retailored', Teufelsdröckh, who had made himself a new set of clothes to replace the outworn one, has done the same for his society.

After describing the life of his protagonist, Carlyle turns to a further analogy of society with religion:

> Every conceivable Society, past or present, may well be considered as ... a Church, in one or other of these three predicaments: an audibly preaching and prophesying Church, which is the best; second, a Church that struggles to preach and prophesy, but cannot as yet, till its Pentecost come; and third and worse, a Church gone dumb with old age, or which only mumbles delirium prior to dissolution.[72]

In this passage the stages of society are presented in order of value: the peak of achievement, what led up to it and the descent from it. One may also see a threefold division within the period of transition, between the collapse of an old social order and the establishment of a new. The first phase is the final breaking up of the old order, the third phase is the first beginning of the new order, and between the two lies the negative equilibrium, the time in which 'old truths have fallen nigh dumb; the new lay yet hidden, not trying to speak'.[73]

The parallel with *The Prelude* is clear. From the vantage point of one who had progressed from the simple happiness of childhood, through the City of Destruction, and had finally reached the peace of spiritual maturity, Wordsworth contemplated the problems of society. Hearing again in memory 'Humanity in fields and groves/Pipe solitary anguish' he proclaimed his goal of 'arousing the senses from the sleep of death'. Similarly, Teufelsdröckh, having won his 'spiritual majority',[74] turns back to bring home to society the nature of its condition, and to offer from his own experience a way out of the dangers besetting it. His message is that parallel to the three-stage scheme of rapid change, as exemplified in his own psychological crisis, society has now entered on the first stage of total rejection and the whittling away of the old order which has been reduced to mere meaningless forms, 'empty Masks, full of beetles and spiders, yet glaring out ... from their glass eyes, with a ghastly affectation of life'.[75] He therefore preaches the need for a new religion, a new seamless garment to replace the patched tatters of the old society. And there is no time to spare. the Phoenix is ready for rebirth out of the ashes of the past. But if the opportunity is missed, if those whom the older order serves try to stem the tide of history and fight to retain their no-longer-justified privileges, then the forces generated under pressure will explode and a new equilibrium will be established through revolution.[76]

According to Teufelsdröckh's scheme, revolution is the force that breaks down the obstacles that barricade the path towards a new order of society. Once started, its headlong rush cannot be stopped till it has run its course, leaving society in a negative state of pause. This ends only when a new Idea arises, assuming its new organic social forms. In an interesting anticipation of psycho-history, Carlyle compares the spread of revolution to the hydrophobia of rabid hounds who turn on the huntsmen and tear them to pieces. As he wrote in his journal shortly before *Sartor Resartus*, 'a madman lies within every sane man'.[77] Repression by those who enjoy undeserved authority lets loose this madness, and once unleashed the disease is contagious. It issues in blind destruction, and the normal modification of conditions wildly accelerates, so that there ensues a period of over-rapid change whose pace is not reduced till the new order is built on the debris of the old.

In *Sartor Resartus* Carlyle already had in mind the application of his thesis to the French Revolution and rise of Napoleon, as indicated by his warning that the sudden flaring of the Phoenix's funeral pyre may consume millions, 'among them such as a Napoleon'.[78] Elsewhere in the work he described the Emperor as a Hero, 'one of the completest Ideologists [or] at least Ideopraxists', a 'Divine Missionary, though unconscious of it', who preached through the cannon's throat 'that great doctrine ... The Tools to him that can handle them, which is our ultimate Political Evangel'.[79] In the same year he wrote to his brother concerning the Bristol riots that 'a second edition of the French Revolution is distinctly within the range of chances'.[80] In the year he began collecting material for his projected *French Revolution* (1832) he referred again in 'Characteristics' to the 'wholly insane attempt' of the rulers of a moribund society 'to chain the Future under the Past' by 'eternal Creeds, eternal Forms of Government and the like'.[81] In the *French Revolution*, written and rewritten till its publication in 1837, he developed yet further his psycho-historical theory:

> ... a background of wrath, which can be stirred up to the murderous infernal pitch, does lie in every man ... which indeed is but another phase of the more general fact, that everyone of us is a *self*... How can you be a self and not have ten-

dencies to self-defence![82]

He also formulated his ideas on the nature of revolution in the precise terms of a definition:

> A revolution ... is a speedier change ... open violent Rebellion, and victory of disimprisoned Anarchy against corrupt worn-out Authority: Anarchy breaks prison, bursts-up from the infinite deep, and rages uncontrollable ... enveloping a world, in phases after phases of fever-frenzy, till the frenzy burns itself out ... and its mad forces [are] made to work towards their object as sane and regulated ones.[83]

His adherence in this definition to the general ideas enunciated metaphorically in *Sartor Resartus* may explain some of the problems he faced when he came to exemplify it by the facts. The first relates to violence: what is the line of demarcation separating criminal violence or riot from revolutionary violence? According to the definition, revolution is distinguished by its being a large-scale mass movement whose aim is destruction of the total social order. This, however, ignores the changes that a revolution may undergo as it progresses. Carlyle pointed out in the *French Revolution* that the intentions and the outcome may be very different, and purposes, directions and means are modified in the course of revolution as it works itself out. As he noted, the Revolution began as a result of the decisions of the National Assembly deputies who wanted anything but the total destruction of the existing social order. Furthermore, he defined a revolution by its successful outcome. But does a revolution that fails to sweep away the idols of the past thereby cease to be a revolution? Could the same results not be achieved by less abnormal social change? Carlyle was not unaware of the problems that confronted him, as for example the standards by which the rates of change are to be measured. As he put it,

> ... all things are in revolution; in change from moment to moment. Revolution means speedier change. Whereupon one has still to ask: How speedy? At what degree of speed does revolution begin and end; cease to be ordinary mutation and again become such?

His answer, however, is an evasion: 'it is a thing that will depend on definition more or less arbitrary'.[84]

The very structure of *French Revolution* reinforces the impression that his interpretation of the historical facts originated in the theory promulgated in *Sartor Resartus*. The work falls into three major sections. The introduction deals with the causes of the Revolution. He begins by a short summary of his theory of symbols and his analogy of the stages of society with the human phases of birth, growth, decline and death. He then proceeds to describe the development of the last stages of the *ancien régime* by a narration of the life of Louis XV, where the king stands metonymically for the whole social order. The story opens with a brief passage concerning the King's early years. He is presented as a bold and widely beloved ruler, who serves as the rallying point of the whole nation, both in times of peace and in war. There follows a long chronological leap to the description of the same King 30 years later: a sickly old man, selfish, mad, who holds on to life under the belief that he will never die. This time-loop achieves a *chiaroscuro* contrast and is intended to evoke an emotional response. Using the same image as in *Sartor Resartus* Carlyle shows how religion, once pure and noble, has become a mere mask. The aristocracy has ceased to guide, and the whole government appears in the eyes of the people as a 'mistake of Nature'. After the death of the King a series of governments, each more ineffectual than the previous one, vainly try to make the dry bones live. The failure of their attempts only hastens the process of decay. As a last resort the General Assembly is convoked, and this marks the beginning of the Revolution: 'A superannuated system of society, decrepit with toils ... dotage and senility, is now to die ... with death-throes and birth-throes'.[85] The adoption of even such an effective framework explains why Carlyle totally ignored such historical influences as the American Revolution, let alone forces that had been operating long before Louis XV, and had grown increasingly acute during the gap Carlyle left in the description of his reign.

After this lengthy introduction comes the main body of the work, dealing with the events of the Revolution itself. It falls into four phases, each following a similar pattern of development. In each, another layer of 'clothing' is torn off, until the naked body of society is revealed *sans culottes*, literally and figuratively. In each phase a group of revolutionaries rises against the authority which is trying to arrest the process of further change. The rebels either compel the governing body to continue the process of change or take over the reins of power themselves. In due course they themselves

Thomas Carlyle's 'Marriage of Heaven and Hell' 135

try to arrest the forces of change. The collapse of the fourth and most radical group of revolutionaries and the execution of Robespierre marks the demolishing of the last remnants of the old order and therefore of the revolution itself.

But there is a remarkable discrepancy between the chronological duration of the different phases and the space devoted to them. *French Revolution* was published in three volumes, each sub-divided into chapters. The introduction and the first stage of the Revolution, the period of the General Assembly, covering about 38 months, are dealt with in no less than the first two volumes. The narration is detailed and full of minute particulars. The third volume, covering about the same length of time, covers the last three phases of the Revolution and the finale. The detail is considerably reduced and the selection far more rigorous. The second phase of the Revolution, the reign of the *Girondins*, covering some 12 months, is presented in the first four books of the volume. Next come the *Jacobins*, lasting about 13 months described in only two books, and the reign of Robespierre up to his death and the rise of Napoleon, followed by a general conclusion to the whole work which is hurried over in one short book. The tempo of presentation increases to an extraordinary degree as the record races towards its end. This technique has been noted and discussed in relation to fiction, Fielding's *Tom Jones* for instance, where the author's chapter headings explicitly reveal the ever-shortening duration to be covered.[86] But Carlyle was dealing with history, packed with actual events, and not with an imaginary life which an author can manipulate in accordance with principles of suspense, reader-interest or aesthetic structure. He was selecting and telescoping events, irrespective of the time they covered in reality, to accord with his own definition of the continued acceleration of the pace of change that marks a revolution.

If we think of the introductory chapters as an extended prologue to the main body of the work, the conclusion may be regarded as an extended epilogue. It is composed of two sections. The first continues the historical sequence of events after the revolutionary process is completed, ending dramatically with Napoleon's order to his guns to open fire.[87] The reader is left in suspense. Enough, however, is hinted as to suggest that the Hero has appeared on the scene, and that he will build a new society on the ruins of the old. The rise of Napoleon is not presented as a continuation or development of the French Revolution, but as a new isolated historical phenomenon, a *deus ex machina*. To reinforce the thesis that the revolution wipes the slate clean to allow a totally new society to arise, Carlyle conveniently ignored the fact that institutions, processes, changes and innovations that grew or developed during the Revolution and sometimes even before it, were taken over and often further modified during the period of Napoleon. This contrasts strongly with the profusion of detail regarding earlier institutions destroyed by the Revolution, and new revolutionary institutions destroyed between one phase and the next.

The second section of this epilogue sums up the lessons of the French Revolution, generalises its effects and sets it up as a paradigm of all revolutions and as a warning all rulers to take note in time of such movements as those of the French *sans-culotte* and the 'Irish sans-potato':[88]

> If the gods of this lower world will sit on their glittering thrones, indolent as Epicurus' gods, with the living chaos weltering uncared for at their feet ... then the dark chaos ... will rise; — has risen, and, O Heavens, has it not tanned their skins into breeches for itself?[89]

Here we have the value judgment which initiated Carlyle's entire thesis.

In *French Revolution* then, Carlyle was presenting historical evidence to prove the thesis he had put forward under the guise of fictional biography in *Sartor Resartus*. He invented no facts, nor did he confuse legend and history in the manner of the early chroniclers. But he consciously selected and manipulated his evidence and adopted such devices as passing general comments on the court, press or church which, by passing over their specific French reference, could be taken to apply to England in order to evoke the powerful emotions of fear among his readers; he tailored the material of the revolution in France to fit his own society and provide a warning for the future.

Proceeding from the generalisations to their particular applications, we can now turn to the evidence Carlyle adduced to prove that Britain was approaching a point of no return and to the means he suggested to avoid catastrophe. This leads us back to the comparison with Marx.

IV

The sense of the passing of an age and of impending doom was shared by the German and English conservative romantics, whose vision of the whole man in an organic society was in collision with the codes and values of their day. The crisis, they believed, was the outcome of the discrepancy that had developed between increasing moral degeneration and improving means of production. The new industrial culture was replacing spiritual values and all that binds people together by the ethics of the market-place with its materialistic outlook and emphasis on private interest and rational calculation. Novalis lamented that rationalism and science, oblivious to the deep springs of human conduct, substituted the strident monotony of the mill for the varied harmonies of creation. Fichte insisted that 'man should work, but not as a beast of burden', and dwelt on the soullessness of an age where 'the property of a *nation*' was judged by that of 'a few individuals whose greatest prosperity is often the most striking indication as well as the true cause of the greatest misery of the nation'. Müller attacked Adam Smith for ignoring the spiritual aspects of work and reducing the state to a 'mere factory' concerned solely with the product, and pointed to the alienation of man from his labours in a society based on self-seeking.[90] To this the English romantics added an acute awareness of the class schisms developing in the capitalist order and the consequent dangers of revolution. Wordsworth mourned the 'solitary anguish' of the peasants and the 'storm/Of sorrow, barricaded evermore/Within the walls of cities'. Coleridge warned that 'the most ... ruinous houses equally with those in best repair are included in the same brief after an extensive fire'. Southey, as we have seen, developed systematically the social theory implicit in the writings of his fellow-poets in the *Quarterly Review* articles which so impressed Carlyle as full of 'things rare and worthy'.[91] However, for all their similarities, the German and the British romantics differed widely in several respects. The former for the most part put the blame on technological progress and sought the way out by a return to the norms and forms of the pre-industrial past. The latter for the most part sought solutions in incorporating rejuvenated organic social unity and moral values into the dynamics of industrial development rather than in a return to the static nature of the old agriculturally based society.

Broadly speaking, this latter approach was the approach

adopted by Carlyle and Marx. Their common conception of *Homo Faber* led them equally to regard the new industrial world as the manifestation of man's creative power. In the words of the Communist Manifesto, its builders were 'the first to show what man's activity can bring about. [They] accomplished wonders far surpassing Egyptian pyramids, Roman aqueducts, and Gothic cathedrals'. Carlyle went even further to welcome the machine as a religious, no less than material, accomplishment. Industry for him was 'the voice of God'; the sound of Manchester's thousand mills 'sublime as Niagara or more so'; Arkwright, Brindley and Watt were comparable in greatness to Shakespeare, Bacon and Sidney, or to Goethe and Odin, for they were saints, leading mankind in a fulfilment of the Divine purpose.[92] Carlyle and Marx likewise shared the view that capitalism had torn the delicate web of dependencies and responsibilities in society and stripped it of the rituals, myths and traditions which had cloaked the structures of authority. Henceforth men were no longer bound by the ties of personal and concrete relationships. Instead, the dependence became universal and abstract, mediated by commodities, chief of which was money. Carlyle pictured society as an 'over-crowded lodging-house where each, isolated ... turns against his neighbour, clutches what he can get, and cries "Mine"! ... [where] Friendship, Communion, has become an incredible tradition'.[93] From 1838 he used a new term he had coined to express this new link: the cash-nexus. Marx defined money as the 'chemical power of society',[94] and the Communist Manifesto stated that

> ... the bourgeoisie ... has put an end to all feudal, patriotic, idyllic relations. It has pitilessly torn assunder the motley feudal ties that bound man to his 'natural superiors', and has left remaining no other nexus between man and man than naked self-interest, that callous cash payment!

However, the two writers differed from the romantics of both nations on one major issue. The crux of the attack by the romantics on the capitalist order was the problem of poverty, especially among the urban workers. Carlyle's and Marx's theory of Man the Creator led them to shift the centre of gravity from poverty in itself to the alienation of the individual from his labour. This they interpreted not merely as estrangement from the activity of work, but also from nature, from the worker's fellow-beings, and finally from himself.

The similarities to the English romantics as well as the differences can best be pointed up by bringing Southey's socio-economic theory into our comparison. A brief recapitulation of the main points of his historical argument highlights the debt owed him by Carlyle. Society, he claimed, develops through periods of rapid economic growth characterised by the collapse of the community of values and by the widening of social gaps, alternating with periods of slow assimilation characterised by the restoration of a community of values and the narrowing of social gaps. In the former the spirit of egotism takes over. The upper classes are quick to exploit the new potentials, while the underpriviledged suffer 'a corresponding pressure of distress' ending in their threatening authority. In the latter the corporate spirit takes over and social unity is re-established. The pattern then repeats at a higher level. His analysis of his day as a fateful period of social and spiritual crisis was essentially sociological. The newly urbanised workers and the small farmers reduced to day-labourers were cut off from their tightly knit and self-supporting communities and thrust, isolated and defenceless, into an alien, competitive environment. The 'brute, denuded, pitiable ... man of the manufacturing system' took no pride in his work and had little profit from it. But the exploiters were no less degraded, for they became slavers of greed and the forces of the market.

Carlyle, trying to base this analysis on 'more fundamental principles', took the psychological effects of the Industrial Revolution as the starting point of his criticism. The wearing down of the Idea leaves the world of the senses as mere indifferent matter. Men have 'parted company with the inner Facts of this Universe and follow the transient outer Appearances', recoiling upon themselves in egotism. The universe has become 'a warehouse' and the only activating principle that of hunger, 'be it the hunger of the poor Day-drudge who stills it with eighteen pence a day, or the ambitious place hunter who can nowise still it with so little'.[95] The consequence was that the products of labour are no longer regarded as evidence of self-realisation, the worker's union with the universe, but as mere means of satisfying appetites external to his work. Money has become the target, and production the penalty one has to pay to get it. The worker has become a 'white Negro' or 'drudge', compelled to work to satisfy the needs of bare subsistence. The more time he devotes to make products for others the less self-fulfilled he feels. 'The lamp of his soul' goes out, 'no ray of heavenly ... Knowledge' visits him, and only 'Fear and Indignation bear him company'.[96] But his employer too is debased. He is a 'Dandy', devoted to accumulating wealth, symbolised by his clothes. Both suffer from the same distortion, save that the one resents it while the other embraces it in a 'willing sacrifice of the Immortal to the Perishable'. Indeed, the 'Dandy' is 'clothes' embodied, what the show of wealth makes him, a man whose 'existence consists in the wearing of clothes'.[97] In *Past and Present* Carlyle pictured the economic crisis of the forties as the nemesis of the curse of Midas. Exploitation leads to overproduction. The workers are punished for producing by a reduction in wages, and finally unemployment. The rich, already poor in spirit, now with 'the very guineas threatening to vanish, feel ... poor indeed'.[98] The world has become topsy-turvy. 'Things, if it be not mere cotton and iron things, are growing disobedient to man',[99] and money has become 'the frightfullest of masters'.[100]

Marx's theory of alienation deals with the same elements and in a similar fashion. He too argued that in a capitalist order the worker is alienated from his products. They are not made in order to satisfy his needs or his natural propensity to create, nor does he use them to develop further his creativity. All that he 'produces for himself is *wages*', and his products 'resolve themselves for him into a definite quantity of the means of subsistence'.[101] The more products he makes the lower their price and hence the lower his wages; the more he gives of himself the more he is diminished in himself and the poorer his 'inner' world. The product confronts him as something outside, hostile, determining how he will live. Since man is alienated from nature and the products of his work, labour itself is no longer self-realisation but 'self-sacrifice [and] penance'.[102] Those who can afford it avoid work. The poor who must work feel coerced into slavery. Like Southey and Carlyle, Marx claimed that the same alienation afflicts the propertied class. Driven by the necessity to accumulate capital and not by the need to fulfil itself, it nevertheless 'feels at ease and strengthened in its self-estrangement, it recognises estrangement as *its own power* and has in it the semblance of a human existence'.[103] Like Carlyle's 'Dandy', the Capitalist is money embodied, 'Money's properties are the possessor's properties and essential powers'; what he is is what the market forces make him.[104]

Carlyle and Marx were at one in claiming that the alienation of man from nature, labour and products means that he is alienated from the characteristics of his species and reduced to what he has in common with the animal. In *Past and Present* and other works, Carlyle lamented the degeneration of the English into 'mere building beavers, spinning arachnes, much more the predatory vultures and vulpine species'.[105] Marx argued that contemporary man felt human when he performed his animal functions, and animal-like when he worked; alienation of labour 'first estranges the life of the species and individual life, and secondly makes individual life in its abstract form the purpose of the life of the species, likewise in its abstract and estranged form'.[106] They further agreed that all these forms of estrangement lead to estrangement from others. As Marx put it,

> ... when man confronts himself, he confronts other men. What applies to [his] ... relation to his work, to the product of his labour and to himself, also holds true of man's relation to other men, and to the other man's labour and object of labour.[107]

'Man's inhumanity to man' evoked in both the comparison of the worker with the horse. But whereas Marx stated that horse and worker alike 'receive just as much as will enable them to work',[108] Carlyle was more extreme. Man as compared to the horse is 'a more cunningly-devised article even as an Engine', and his true market value should be 'from fifty to a hundred horses'. Yet in any market a horse commands a high price, whereas man is 'worth nothing to the world'.[109] Following Owen's telling aphorism he claimed that the freedom of the rich to use their power is the freedom of the poor to die of starvation.[110]

The dynamics of such relations, so Southey followed by Carlyle and Marx believed, must lead to the simplification and polarisation of society. Southey saw this process largely as a result of the revolution in the means of communication and locomotion. Local differences in wealth had always existed in times of rapid economic change, but industry and commerce now worked on a national scale; 'capitalists become like pikes in a fish-pond, who devour the weaker fish; and it is but too certain that the poverty of one part of the people seems to increase in the same ratio as the riches of another'. Nuanced gradations of society are thus replaced by 'two great divisions' confronting each other in envy and fear.[111] Carlyle classified them as 'Dandies' and 'Drudges', each 'recruiting itself from the intermediate ranks, till there be none left to enlist on either side'.[112] Marx likewise observed how 'society as a whole was more and more splitting up into great hostile camps'.[113] All three asserted that such a development left to itself could have only one outcome: revolution. Southey warned against an imminent '*bellum servile*'. Carlyle saw the opposed classes as two whirlpools that had 'broken-out on opposite quarters of the firm land', each corroding its banks, till there is only 'a mere film of land between them; this too is washed away, and then we have the true Hell of Waters'.[114] Marx had a similar picture: 'the antagonism between the proletariat and the bourgeoisie is a struggle ... which carried to its highest expression is a total revolution' culminating in 'brutal *contradiction*, the shock of body against body, as its final denouement'.[115]

Both Carlyle and Marx would have endorsed Southey's definition of his time as preluding an 'important transition in the system which [is] necessary to its development'. Likewise, they would have shared his belief that the final outcome would be a new harmonious and moral order. Here again, however, the similarity ceases. Their conception of social evolution led Southey and Carlyle to regard morals as the lever to social progress. Alienation, they insisted, is a characteristic symptom of periods of transition, a psychological malaise following on the disappearance of a shared Idea that had united society. Revolution, therefore, was not a cure. Even if Carlyle saw it as an iconoclastic force, sweeping away outworn forms and ideas where conditions had degenerated beyond the point of no return, the price was general suffering, hatred and further division. Marx, on the other hand, did not see alienation as a periodic phenomenon nor yet as an ailment peculiar to modern man, but rather a necessary concomitant of private ownership throughout history:

> The revolution is necessary, therefore, not only because the *ruling* class cannot be overthrown in any other way, but because the class overthrowing it can only in a revolution succeed in ridding itself of all the muck of ages and become fitted to found society anew.[116]

The abolition of private property would eliminate the primary form of alienation. But since 'economic alienation belongs to actual life', including both the material and non-material, this would release man from his fetters in both spheres. Society would turn into a classless association where man, freed from the estrangement that had dogged him throughout history, would 'return ... from religion, family, state, etc., to his *human*, i.e. *social existence*'.[117]

What Marx described as 'the muck of ages' Southey and Carlyle saw as the repository of the great tradition established in the heyday of the pre-industrial golden age. This was directly related to their view of the cyclic pattern of history, where each return is at a higher level. Thus an agricultural society has a landed aristocracy to represent the Idea and govern the peasants and craftsmen in accordance with it. An industrial society must shift the weight to the Captains of Industry which will represent the Idea and govern the urban factory workers in accordance with it. But in either case the pattern is an idealised abstraction of the lord of the manor and retainer relationship. It assumes different appearances according to the needs of the society in question, and these constitute what Carlyle called the 'Body politic' as distinct from the 'Soul politic'.[118] Such a pattern might easily lead to distortion if the angle of vision from which one views the rising spiral reveals the retrograde or the upward direction exclusively. This explains why the two writers have so often been judged either as progressive or reactionary. It also explains a seeming ambivalence in their own attitude. We have noted that Southey's historical thesis stemed from his rejection of medievalism as suited only for poetry and fiction. Carlyle's condemnation of his day was likewise based on what he considered to be its slavish adherence to the outworn 'clothes' of the past.[119] But he drove the medievalist poets, and novelists too, from his Republic as peddlers in the nostalgic fantasies of a confused age that was seeking to escape its problems. For similar reasons he attacked the Oxford Movement as 'Galvanic Puseyism' and 'dancing of the sheeted dead'.[120] At the same time we have seen how Southey's reform schemes were directed to revive a social system strongly reminiscent of the pre-industrial one, while *Past and Present* is built on the contrast between life in contemporary and medieval England, to the great advantage of the latter. Both projected into their vision of the future a dream of a past which would be revived by therapeutic reform, material and spiritual. To unite the people through shared values and a sense of common destiny was the function of

Southey's national church and Carlyle's Hero. More immediately, they demanded the rectifying of social abuses. Both appealed to the landed aristocracy to enlist for the improvement of the national welfare, by renewing the direct contact with the people as their natural leaders. As Carlyle wrote, their lives must cease to centre round the preservation of game and shooting parties; they must return to what true Aristocracy is: 'a Corporation of the Best, of the Bravest'. Furthermore, he included the Captains of Industry as the rising aristocracy of the new civilisation of the machine, calling on them likewise to take over the patriarchal responsibilities of the feudal lords of the manor. The two kinds of aristocracy, the one purified and restored, the other newly created, should fuse to form a single, new kind, an 'aristocracy of talent'. Only then, 'by degrees, we shall again have a Society with something of Heroism in it ... instead of Mammon-Feudalism with unsold cotton-shirts and Preservation of the Game, noble just Industrialism and Government by the Wisest'.[121]

No less important was their demand for a supra-personal state transcending all time-bound manifestations of society, which would initiate reforms to alleviate immediate grievances, encourage future economic growth and repair the web of relationships torn by capitalism. Southey echoed the popular cry for universal education and industrial legislation, and adopted Coleridge's plea for taxes on income to finance reform and reduce inequality. To these he added founding colonies, using state land for resettling evicted tenants and demobilised soldiers and the formation of work brigades to be employed in national enterprises. Carlyle took over and further developed these demands. In *Chartism* (1839) he argued forcibly for the establishment of new ministries, with 'secretar[ies], with adjuncts, with funds, forces ... and ever-increasing apparatus' to deal with emigration and education. He also supported and called for the extension of state inspection of labour conditions and commissions of inquiry into the state of the poor and working classes. In *Past and Present* (1843) he advocated setting up a ministry of health and far-reaching legislation to cover the relations between masters and men. But it was his final scheme in *Latter Day Pamphlets* (1850) for the founding of national industrial brigades to be employed in state enterprises that best reveals the nature and scope of his vision. The resemblance to Southey's project as well as to the writings of Blanc and the 1848 *Ateliers Nationaux* is clearly not a coincidence. However, he went further in that he saw state involvement in the economy as an Archimedean fulcrum to move the entire society. The advantage of sure employment under fair conditions would, he claimed, attract not only the unemployed but others who would wish to escape the drudgery and uncertainties of private employment. Competition for labour would compel industrialists more effectively than any legislation to seek ways to attach other workers themselves through such benefits as permanent employment, higher wages, educational, recreational and health schemes, and pensions, thus forming anew the old personal ties binding masters and men. This would be an education both for the awakened worker and the understanding employer. Such competition would not be of the *laissez-faire* type, but rather a vying to better the life of the English. 'Thus will ... all private captains of industry be forced to ... incessantly cooperate with the State and its public captains; they regimenting in their way, the State in its way, with ever widening field; till there be no unregimented worker'.[122] Like Shelley and Southey before him, Carlyle held an axiological theory in which social relations and the interpretations given them are conditioned by ethical values, and these in turn are conditioned by the ways in which they are propagated. Marx, on the other hand, held a materialistic theory according to which the forces of production and the concomitant social relations into which people enter when engaged in production determine in the final instance the nature and weight of ethical values, political and judicial institutions, and cultural patterns. Carlyle, like Southey, saw social history as essentially the record of alternating expansions and contractions of class differences reflecting cyclic processes of the wearing down and rejuvenation of symbol systems for inculcating values. What he sought was to bridge the gaps, through the promotion of community consciousness based on shared values and interests. Marx saw social history as essentially the record of class struggle determined by man's developing needs and their satisfaction. He held that working-class consciousness under capitalism would lead to revolution and the subsequent elimination of all social differences. Again like Southey, Carlyle advocated a State that would transcend sectional division and check unbridled capitalism. Marx considered the State to be an administrative, political and ideological apparatus geared to the reproduction and reinforcement of capitalist social relations. Such an apparatus, he insisted, would have no place in a classless society. Finally, Carlyle, like the earlier romantics, recognised the need to build a new social order where greater distributive justice would prevail. Nevertheless, he was content to maintain the traditional division of labour between directors and workers. Marx, by way of contrast, insisted that the new order would reveal itself in essence in the changing of relations of production and the disappearance of differences between intellectual and manual labour. One may turn to two slogans, from *Past and Present* and from the *Critique of the Gotha programme*, as expressing *in petto* the two visions: Carlyle's capitalism reformed and Marx's capitalism overthrown: 'A fair day's wages for a fair day's work' *vis-à-vis* 'From each according to his ability, to each according to his needs'.

Notes

1. Anon. (J. Manners), 'Review of *Sybil, or The Two Nations*', *The Oxford and Cambridge Review*, I (July 1845), pp. 1-11.
2. J.A. Froude, *Lord Beaconsfield* (London: Sampson Low, Maeston, Searle and Rivington, 1890), p. 84.
3. *Labour Leader*, January 1893.
4. R. Blatchford, *The New Religion* (*Clarion* pamphlet no. 20, 1895), p.3.
5. T. Carlyle *Reminiscences*, C.E. Norton (ed.) (London: Dent, 1972), pp. 57, 293, 358.
6. E.g. Carlyle's description of the French Revolution: 'Europe rose like a frenzied giant, shook all that poisonous magician trumpery to right and left, trampling it stormfully under foot; and declared aloud that there was strength in him, not for life only, but for a new and infinitely wider life', T. Carlyle, *The Works of Thomas Carlyle in Thirty Volumes*, H.D. Traill (ed.) (London: Chapman and Hall, 1907), vol. XXIX, p. 152; cf. Coleridge's *France: an Ode*:

> France in wrath her giant-limbs upreared,
> And with that oath, which smote air, earth and sea,
> Stamped her strong foot and said she would be free.

7. Carlyle, *Reminiscences*, p. 344.
8. M. St John Packe, *The Life of John Stuart Mill* (London: Macmillan, 1954), p. 158.
9. See P. Wessell Jr, 'Marx's Romantic Poetry and the Crisis of Romantic Lyricism', *Studies in Romanticism*, XVI (Autumn 1977), pp. 509-34.
10. C.F. Harrold, *Carlyle and German Thought 1819-1834* (New Haven: Yale University Press, 1934).
11. A. Carlyle (ed.), *Letters of Thomas Carlyle to John Stuart Mill, John Sterling and Robert Browning* (New York: Haskell House, 1970), p. 211; C.R. Sanders, R.J. Fielding (eds.), *The Collected Letters of Thomas and Jane Welsh Carlyle* (Durham: Duke University Press, 1970), vol. IV, p. 182.
12. Carlyle, *Works*, vol. I, p. 163.
13. Ibid., vol. XXVI, p. 58.
14. K. Marx, F. Engels, *Collected Works* (New York: International Publishers, 1978), vol. V, pp. 462-4.

Thomas Carlyle's 'Marriage of Heaven and Hell' 147

15. M.H. Abrams, *The Mirror and the Lamp* (New York: Oxford University Press, 1953), pp. 21-2.
16. T. Carlyle, *Two Notebooks*, C.E. Norton (ed.) (New York: Grolier Club, 1898), p. 102.
17. Carlyle, *Works*, vol. I, p. 196.
18. Marx, Engels, *Works*, vol. V, pp. 40-1, 3.
19. S.T. Coleridge, *Lay Sermon Directed to the Higher and Middle Classes* (London: Bell and Daldy, 1917), p. 397.
20. K. Marx, *Capital*, trans. S. Moore and E. Aveling, ed. F. Engels (Moscow: Progress Publishers, 1967), p. 179.
21. Carlyle, *Works*, vol. I, p. 76.
22. Marx, Engels, *Works*, vol. III, pp. 276-7.
23. Carlyle, *Two Notebooks*, p. 248.
24. Carlyle, *Works*, vol. I, pp. 95-6; Marx, Engels, *Works* vol. III, pp. 276-81; Carlyle (ed.), *Letters of Thomas Carlyle*, p. 5. See also Carlyle, *Works*, vol. I, pp. 31, 72, 78, 158. Cf. 'Le Système Industriel', *Oeuvres de Saint-Simon et d'Enfantin*, vol. IV, especially pp. 91-2; K. Marx, *Grundrisse*, D. McLellan (ed.) (New York: Harper Torchbooks, 1973), p. 116.
25. Carlyle, *Works*, vol. I, p. 56.
26. Marx, Engels, *Works*, vol III, pp. 276-7.
27. Carlyle, *Works*, vol. I, p. 31.
28. Marx, *Capital*, vol. I, p. 177.
29. Carlyle, *Works*, vol. XXVII, p. 70.
30. Marx, Engels, *Works*, vol. V, p. 36.
31. Carlyle, *Works*, vol. I, pp. 157, 154, 91, 31.
32. Ibid., p. 174.
33. Carlyle, *Works*, vol. X, p. 57.
34. Ibid., vol. I, pp. 32-3.
35. Marx, Engels, *Works*, vol. V, pp. 41-2.
36. Carlyle, *Works*, vol. XXVIII, pp. 10-12; Marx, Engels, *Works*, vol. III, p. 217.
37. H.S. Reisse (ed.), *The Political Thought of the German Romantics 1793-1815* (New York: Macmillan, 1955), p. 157.
38. Carlyle, *Works*, vol. XXVIII, p. 12.
39. M. Levin, 'Marxism and Romanticism: Marx's Debt to German Conservatism', *Political Studies*, XXII (December 1974), p. 408.
40. Carlyle, *Works*, vol. XXVIII, p. 12.
41. Ibid., vol. I, p. 172.
42. Ibid., p. 128.
43. Marx, Engels, *Works*, vol. V, p. 43; K. Marx, F. Engels, *Selected Works in One Volume* (London: Lawrence and Wishart, 1968), p. 182. It is noteworthy that Mill, before he met Carlyle, had developed a similar theory of 'the natural order of human progress' based on the Saint-Simonian division of history into organic and critical periods with intervening eras of transition. The present was such an era, and he looked forward to a new age which would combine the universal and permanent moral principles of the one with the freedom of individual action of the other. Seemingly he was not aware of Southey's earlier enunciation of similar patterns. See J.S. Mill, *Autobiography* (New York: Columbia University Press, 1944), pp. 115-17.
44. Carlyle, *Works*, vol. I, p. 172.
45. Marx, Engels, *Works*, vol. V, p. 43.
46. Carlyle, *Works*, vol. I, p. 186.
47. Marx, Engels, *Works*, vol. III, p. 272.
48. 'Carlyle's Letters to the Socialists of 1830', *The New Quarterly*, I (January 1909), p. 280.

49. H. Shine, *Carlyle and the Saint-Simonians* (Baltimore: John Hopkins, 1941), p. 20. See also, among others, D.B. Cofer, *Saint-Simonism in the Radicalism of Thomas Carlyle* (Austin: von Boeckmann Jones, 1931), p. 33; L.M. Young, *Thomas Carlyle and the Art of History* (Philadelphia: University of Pennsylvania Press, 1939).

50. R. Wellek, 'Carlyle and the Philosophy of History', *Philological Quarterly*, XXIII (January, 1944), p. 65.

51. Carlyle, *Two Notebooks*, p. 113, see also p. 158.

52. Carlyle, *Works*, vol. V, pp. 24, 45-6, 81; vol. X, p. 127.

53. Ibid., vol. I, p. 179.

54. Ibid., vol. I, p. 142.

55. V. Basch, *Carlyle: L'Homme et l'Oeuvre* (Paris: Gallimard, 1938), p. 124.

56. Careful research has failed to turn up any evidence of such a person or situation in Carlyle's life. See G.B. Tennyson, *Sartor called Resartus* (New Jersey: Princeton University Press, 1965), pp. 192-3. Cazamian alone ventured on an explanation, that Carlyle was servilely following a literary tradition. Since *Sartor Resartus* flouted all literary conventions, he regarded the episode as 'a moment of weakness exceptional in the entire book'. L. Cazamian, *Carlyle*, trans. F.K. Brown (New York: Macmillan, 1932), p. 114.

57. Carlyle, *Works*, vol. I, p. 13.

58. Ibid., p. 15.

59. Ibid., p. 20.

60. Ibid., p. 25.

61. Ibid., p. 44.

62. J.A. Froude, *Thomas Carlyle: A History of the First Forty Years of his Life, 1795-1835* (London: Longmans, Green and Co. 1882), vol. I, p. 45.

63. Carlyle, *Reminiscences*, pp. 4-5.

64. Carlyle, *Works*, vol. I, p. 76.

65. Ibid., pp. 71-2.

66. Carlyle, *Reminiscences*, p. 4.

67. Carlyle, *Works*, vol. I, pp. 83-4.

68. Ibid., p. 119.

69. Ibid, p. 123.

70. Ibid., pp. 153-4.

71. Sanders and Fielding (eds.) *The Collected Letters of Thomas and Jane Welsh Carlyle*, p. 180.

72. Carlyle, *Works*, vol. I, p. 171.

73. Ibid., vol. V, p. 117.

74. Ibid., vol. I, pp. 149-50.

75. Ibid., p. 228.

76. Ibid., p. 189.

77. Carlyle, *Two Notebooks*, p. 243.

78. Carlyle, *Works*, vol. I, p. 189.

79. Ibid., p. 151.

80. Froude, *Thomas Carlyle*, vol. II, p. 221.

81. Carlyle, *Works*, vol. XXIX, p. 37.

82. Ibid., vol. II, p. 214.

83. Ibid., pp. 211-12.

84. Ibid., vol. II, p. 211.

85. Ibid., p. 133.

86. Adam A. Mendilow, *Time and the Novel* (New York: Humanities Press, 1972), pp.63-84.

87. Carlyle, *Works*, vol. IV, p. 313.

88. Ibid., p. 321.
89. Ibid., p. 323.
90. Reiss, *The Political Thought of the German Romantics*, pp. 91-2, 145-50.
91. Carlyle, *Reminiscences*, p. 344.
92. Carlyle, *Works*, vol. X, pp. 43, 193, 293; vol XXIX, pp. 181-2.
93. Ibid., vol. I, p. 185.
94. Marx, Engels, *Works* vol. III, p. 324.
95. Carlyle, *Works*, vol. X, p. 5; vol. XXVIII, pp. 30-1.
96. Ibid., vol. I, pp. 182-223.
97. Ibid., p. 218.
98. Ibid., vol X, p. 5.
99. Ibid., p. 6.
100. Ibid., p. 217.
101. Marx, *Selected Works in One Volume*, p. 75.
102. Marx, Engels, *Works*, vol. III, pp. 274-5.
103. Ibid., p. 324.
104. Ibid., vol. IV, p. 324.
105. Carlyle, *Works*, vol. X, pp. 145, 184, 187; vol. XXVIII, 325.
106. Marx, Engels, *Works*, vol. III, p. 276.
107. Ibid., p. 277.
108. Ibid., p. 241.
109. Carlyle, *Works*, vol. I, p. 183.
110. Ibid., vol. X, p. 212; cf. R. Owen, *A New View of Society and other Writings* (London: Dent, 1949), p. 143.
111. R. Southey, *Sir Thomas More: or, Colloquies on the Progress and Prospects of Society* (London: John Murray, 1829), vol. I, p. 193.
112. Carlyle, *Works*, vol. I, p. 228.
113. Marx, Engels, *Works*, vol. VI, p. 485.
114. Carlyle, *Works*, vol. I, p. 228.
115. Marx, Engels, *Works*, vol. VI, p. 212.
116. Ibid., vol. V, p. 53.
117. Ibid., vol. III, p. 297.
118. Carlyle, *Works*, vol. XXIX, p. 56.
119. Ibid., p.60.
120. Froude, *Lord Beaconsfield*, p. 95.
121. Carlyle, *Works*, vol. XXIX, p. 160; vol. X, Bk IV, Chap. IV.
122. Ibid., vol. XX, p. 148.

5 THREE SHADES OF TORY RADICALISM

I

God bless the King, I mean the Faith's Defender;
God Bless — no harm in blessing — the Pretender;
But who Pretender is, or who is King,
God bless us all — that's quite another thing.

John Byrom, an ardent Jacobite, writer of religious verse and admirer of William Law, encompassed in his epigram three of the pillars of eighteenth-century Toryism: the Crown, the Church and the sense of national communality. A fourth was the attachment to the land and the traditional structures of rural society which befitted a party largely representing the country squire and parson. One may speculate that had the Conservatives adhered blindly to these principles after the Reform Act of 1832 they would have been swamped by the tide of change or, at best, reduced to a minority party of protest. One alternative was to trim the sails to the 'liberal' wind by compromising with the largely urban middle-class which had been given the vote, and attracting its support for a tacit defence pact against the challenge of the lower classes. The Tamworth Manifesto was a signpost in this direction, as was the repeal of the Corn Laws, both associated with Robert Peel — himself born of a family of middle-class industrialists. In the long run such an approach taken broadly was inevitable, even though Peel had to resign because of his liberal tendencies. In fact, later Conservative electoral successes would have been unthinkable without the ability to win over large numbers of the bourgeoisie. But no small part in shaping the party's destiny and ideology was played by the effects of a different alternative, which sought to confront the 'selfishness' of the well-to-do industrialist, and shop-keepers, and of the Whigs as 'party of a sect', by what was in effect a coalition of discontented industrial 'hands' and aristocratic land-owners.

Such a line of action fitted in well with traditional doctrines, drawing on them to infuse something of the spirit of the manorial system into industrialism. The fundamental lack of sympathy with the ethos of industrial capitalism, sometimes accompanied by an aversion to industry itself, made Tories more prone than Liberals to advocate factory reforms that would curb the pursuit of Mammon and protect its victims. In contrast to the impersonality and unconcern that marked the 'cash nexus', the hierarchic conception of society based on inherited wealth and position prescribed property as entailing duties and *noblesse oblige* as a condition of power. It therefore lent force to the assertion that industrialists must show paternalist interest in the welfare of their employees. Additional weight to such demands was provided by the doctrine of the organic society. The interest of the whole overrode that of individuals and particular groups. Self-restraint and a sense of national responsibility were required to counteract the divisiveness created by the separation of the people into 'haves' and 'have-nots' and to restore the cohesiveness essential for the perpetuation of the nation. In spite of the Tory proclivity to the decentralisation of authority, such arguments offered justification for the use of legislative powers implemented by the Administration to put into effect the necessary reforms. Church and Crown were thus called upon to fulfil their obligations as guardians of the nation. Paradoxically, central authority was invoked to restore the social links that would turn industrial plants and agricultural estates into organic, semi-autonomous communities, thus reviving a partly-imagined past in the context of the modern age.

The propagation of such doctrines goes far to explain the success of the Tory party after the second Reform Act of 1867 in enlisting under its banner a significant proportion of the working-class electorate.[1] But the new trends were already distinguishable during the second quarter of the century, long before the Earl of Malmesbury introduced the idea of 'Conservative Democracy' (1853)[2] or Randolph Churchill coined the term 'Tory Democracy'. Michael Thomas Sadler, chairman of the commons committee for factory legislation and promoter of large-scale improvement schemes for the peasantry, led the High Tory revolt against Wellington and Peel in the early 1830s. Joseph Rayner Stephens agitated for reform and ended by joining the Chartists. Richard Oastler, 'the Factory King' and a leading fighter against the New Poor Law and child labour, not only sympathised with Chartism but went so far as to assert that 'right will only be granted to an armed host of freemen'.[3] The most influential of them all, however, was Lord Ashley, whose life-long dedication to the cause of the poor and the exploited made his name a household word, and who probably more than anyone else became associated with nineteenth-century factory legislation.

As has been noted earlier, Ashley drew much of his inspiration from Robert Southey, and wrote that he was a diligent follower of Southey's pioneering message. Indeed, Southey's historical outlook led him to see the principles of the pre-industrial order as relevant to the new age, and his aspiration to have them replace the moral, economic and social principles that underlay capitalism, express the same attitudes and opinions that activated Tory radicalism. Such a structure of ideas grew out of the wrestling of men like himself and Coleridge with the questions of social justice and political stability that issued from pondering the lessons of the French Revolution at the time of strain during the Napoleonic Wars. But it was not only the first romantic that contributed to the emergence of the trend. Rather, it was Carlyle who did most to disseminate the philosophy of his predecessors and adapt it to the rapidly changing conditions of a later day. The following section seeks to illustrate the influence of the romantic tradition, largely as transmitted through Carlyle, on three conservatives active in his own time each of whom presented a different shade of Tory radicalism. Disraeli, Kingsley and Ruskin were, each in his own way, proponents of the Carlylean moral interpretation of society, the view of man as an essentially creative being and the cyclic theory of social change. They also shared his diagnosis of spiritual crisis leading to social polarisation and the threat of revolution, his rejection of class consciousness for community consciousness, his call for a new order based on greater distributive justice and a reconciliation of decentralised community structures and personal relationships, and his conception of the state as a centralised authority representing the nation as a single whole. However, they differed from one another as well as from their mentor not only in the relative weight they attached to each facet of this configuration but in their concentration of different aspects of the theory of value, respectively the social, the religious and the aesthetic, thereby indicating the potential scope of its application to social analysis.

II

One of the very earliest political pieces written by Disraeli was a small pamphlet, expounding his views after two abortive attempts to enter the Commons as M.P. for High Wycombe. Under the title 'Who is he?' it purported to be his answer to a question which he attributed, probably fictitiously, to Lord Grey. At his death, nearly half a century later, after a corruscating parliamentary career, the critics continued to ask themselves and one another the same question: 'What was he?' 'The lawgiver' of modern Toryism, answered a conservative admirer;[4] one who 'invented nothing, strained at nothing' but resolutely and unequivocally carried on the policies set by his predecessors, wrote another.[5] Conversely, he was attacked for being 'a politician with a constant hatred of nothing except consistency',[6] a 'perfect will-o'-the-wisp, flittering about from one opinion to another'.[7] And *The Standard* in its obituary notice had its own interpretation of the ambiguity: 'Conservatives could claim him just as little as either the Radicals or the Whigs'.[8]

To a greater or lesser degree, such contrasting evaluations are to be expected when summing up the record of an important politician, active for many years both in opposition and in government, during a period that witnessed so many changes. Disraeli's own words in 1834, in defence of Peel's readiness to institute reforms despite his previous stand against the great Reform Act, express the problem succinctly. Statesmen, he proclaimed, should be sensitive to the shifting circumstances of the age. Their

> conduct and opinions ... at different periods of their career must not be too curiously contrasted in a free and aspiring country. The people have their passions, and it is even the duty of public men occasionally to adopt sentiments with which they do not sympathise because the people must have leaders.[9]

However, his was perhaps an extreme example. A chameleon figure, with as many colours as his famous waistcoats, the sequence and development of his ideas proceeded in jerks, closely involved as they were with the hopes and frustrations of one who by his own admission was 'devoured by ambition [he] did not see any means of gratifying'.[10] Thus, shortly before the above-quoted speech he still sought nomination as Radical candidate for Aylesbury. The speech was delivered when he stood for Parliament as an Independent in High Wycombe. Several weeks later he became a regular member of the Tory party, in which he was to play a central role in ousting Peel himself. And this is only one example. Nevertheless, an examination that takes into consideration Disraeli's own analysis of the difficulties of assessing the course of a statesman, reveals, if one overlooks the details of the hustle and bustle of day-to-day politics, a consistent direction in the development of his thought which reached its clearest form in the Young England trilogy.

The three political novels, stated a leading biographer, are quite different from anything Disraeli wrote before. 'A wide gulf separates them from his silver fork novels and historical romances.' It is not merely a matter of genre; there is no connection between the views expressed in them and those in the rest of his fiction.[11] The argument may be open to debate, but even those who have reservations tend to gloss over a quality traceable in virtually all his writings, whether prose or verse, narrative or discursive.[12] In his maturer years Disraeli spent little time in reading belles-lettres. This perhaps throws into greater prominence the importance of those writers he had admired in his earlier reading years, and especially Byron, Southey and Shelley. The first attracted him less for his ideas than for his flamboyant personality and 'pure unalloyed sagacity'; essentially he was 'greater ... as a man than as a writer'.[13] Southey, on the other hand, evoked Disraeli's respect and interest as a historian and defender of earlier political structures. In Disraeli's first novel, *Vivian Grey*, Southey is introduced under the transparent disguise of the foremost essayist of the *Quarterly Review*. Under his own name in the chapter on literature and politics he is described as a man of 'splendid talents', 'the most poetical of prose writers' and a political thinker whose historical and poetical writings 'are alike political pamphlets'. He is, furthermore, the most philosophical of partisans and the most influential exponent of Tory ideology.[14]

Shelley aroused Disraeli's admiration equally as a man, poet and social thinker. In the novel closing his pre-parliamentary period, *Venetia* (1837), the poet appears with Byron as one of the major protagonists. It is clear that Disraeli was familiar with his published writings such as the *Revolt of Islam* and *Queen Mab* from which he quoted freely. He even had access to texts that had not yet appeared in print. The quotation from the 'Discourse on the Manners of the Ancients' (published in 1840) he probably got from Medwin's *Shelley Papers*; that from the 'Defence', 'Poets are the unacknoweldged legislators of the world', with a slight inaccuracy in the wording, presumably from Byron's valet, Tita Falcieri, who served in the Disraeli household.[15] His verdict, echoing that of Byron, was that Shelley had been vilely misjudged by prejudiced bigots for 'there breath[ed] not his equal among men'. This young and gifted radical philosopher had 'called into creation that society of immaculate purity and unbounded enjoyment which he believed was the natural inheritance of unshackled man'.[16]

Buridan's ass, faced with two equal and equidistant bundles of hay, died of starvation. Disraeli, unable as yet to choose between two opposite sources of inspiration located in the past and in the future, in effect deferred the solution to a great leader who would one day arise. In the *Revolutionary Epic* (1834) he introduced the figure of Demogorgon from *Prometheus Unbound* as arbiter in a debate between the spirit of the Past and that of the Future, a situation resembling that of the 'herald of eternity' and the debate between Christ and Satan from the prologue to *Hellas*. The spirit of the Past extols the organic society where the many are bound by 'Loyalty' born of 'Obedience' to their leaders, all sharing a 'joyous creed that made a Heaven of Earth', and attacks the new revolutionary break with the past till 'on all alike/Tramples the hoof of Anarchy, that steed/That hath no rider'. The spirit of the Future, bolstering his argument with the help of unacknowledged borrowings from *Prometheus Unbound, Alastor, Hellas* and *Queen Mab*, attacks despotism and superstition which course like poison through the veins of society. They derive from selfishness, excessive wealth, the exploitation of the many and a selection of other vices hallowed by 'Custom/That consecrates a lie'. He anticipates their purging and the coming of a utopian 'Age of Human Nature'. Demogorgon's judgment is that man is eternal, and eternity knows neither past nor present. 'In Man alone the fate of Man is placed', and the solution will be found on the rise of a man of destiny, who will unite the best qualities represented by the two antagonists.[17]

Another solution was suggested in *Venetia*, where Disraeli prolonged Herbert's (explicitly identified as Shelley) life to allow him to recant some of his extreme radical utopianism. One of the least convincing scenes is where the poet's separated wife and their daughter reach Arquâ and spend the night in the house Petrarch had lived in. The landlord is away, but the local inhabitants are full of admiration and gratitude for the paternal benevolence that renders him the ideal of aristocratic virtue. Later they meet fortuitously with Shelley who, it transpires, is no other than the generous patron they had heard so much of. In due course a reconciliation ensues, the wife returns to him, and he perfects the ideology foreshadowed by his activities as a landlord. Without foregoing his ideals of progress his abstract metaphysics yield to the realism of human contacts. He still believes that 'the mist of familiarity obscures from us the miracle of our being' and renders us insensitive to our fellow men. The standard of excellence still remains that pictured by Cervantes: 'a great and benevolent philosopher' in quest of beauty and justice, accompanied by Sancho Panza, a 'complete personification of the world, selfish and cunning, and yet overawed by the genius alive to all the material interests in existence, yet sighing after the ideal'. But now he feels 'how dependent we are in this world on our natural ties, and how limited, with all his arrogance, is the sphere of man'.[18]

Such a meeting of Toryism and Radicalism was not confined to Disraeli's prose fiction and verse epic. It may have contributed something to the political volatility of his career before joining the Tory party. His shifts from radicalism via radicalism-with-Tory-leanings and Toryism-with-radical-leanings again to radicalism and finally to conservatism were certainly connected less with principle than with parliamentary place-hunting, circumstance and relations with friends and opponents. None the less, it is noteworthy that in *What is He*, written to justify these changes, he looked forward to 'Great Spirits' who may yet arrive to guide the world between the conflicting forces of revolution and tradition, and he called upon the Tories and the Radicals to 'coalesce ... [in] a National Party'.[19] Moreover, there can be little doubt that his early reading contributed a good deal to the historical and constitutional theory, first presented in the political writings of 1835, and repeated time and again throughout his works.

The *Peers and People* articles (August-September 1835) were written at the request of Lord Lyndhurst, the most insistent advocate of amending the Commons' Municipal Corporations Bill. The *Vindication of the English Constitution* appeared at the end of the year as a letter to him, and *Whigs and Whiggism* is in effect a resumé of it. The immediate purpose of all three was the defence of the House of Lords against the ire of the reformists. The argument was grounded on the principle of preserving an equilibrium between the estates of the realm, the upper house consisting of the lords temporal and spiritual, the lower representing the more numerous commoners. The monarch alone is responsible 'through his Ministers' to the entire nation, and therefore any upsetting of the balance between them invites class tyranny.[20] However, the thesis was presented within the framework of a Tory answer to the Whig interpretation of history and to the threat posed by Utilitarianism, philosophical Radicalism and *laissez-faire* Liberalism.

Its first premise was the Southeyan differentiation between the rhythms of change undergone by a constitution and the society which it regulates. Civil policy is built on conventions which give permanent form to reciprocal rights and obligations, thereby inspiring the whole with a sense of organic unity and a distinctive character as of a family or an individual. Man is 'the child of the State, and born with filial duties. To disobey the State therefore [is] a crime; to rebel against it, treason; to overturn it, parricide'.[21] The constitution, representing the personality of the state, is therefore the product of slow development and 'the creation of ages' demanding respect and reverence; 'the perpetuity of a State could [not] be otherwise preserved'.[22] Yet this does not imply that society must remain static. In fact, English history shows that constitutional stability is a stimulus for dynamic social development. The basis of the former is that 'property shall be the qualification for power'[23] and duties. Since all aspire to property and power, stability has 'promoted civilisation and ... [an] almost unbroken tide of progressive amelioration [which have] made us the freest, the wealthiest, and the most refined society of modern ages'.[24] Already the country's commercial supremacy is unchallenged, its industry supplies the world and its agriculture is the most advanced in Christendom. 'Every half century develops some new and vast resource of public wealth, which brings into national notice a new and powerful class',[25] and this without any of the upheavals that have menaced or destroyed other states, built on the quicksands of shifting constitutions.[26]

Another familiar premise was that the constitution is always subject to threat. History witnesses a constant conflict between two elemental forces: altruism, national unity and the reaffirmation of lasting principles are identifiable with Toryism, while egotism and exploitation tending to the erosion of shared values characterise Whiggism. As the embodiment of the 'anti-national spirit' exhibiting itself in petty schemes of personal aggrandisement, the Whig party was always 'at war with the English Constitution', seeking to centralise power in its hands by reducing the influence of the Crown and depriving the bulk of the population of their rights. Being indifferent to the demands of higher principle they have 'only one object — the establishment of an oligarchy'. The welfare of the people and the continuation of progress hinged therefore on which of the two forces gained the upper hand.[27]

Disraeli also shared with the romantics the view that the danger posed by the forces of egotism tends to reach its height whenever rapid change brings about the rise of new social groups. Before the constitution has time to adapt to the situation the Whigs fan discontent and present themselves as a party of reform. Their policy is 'ever to smuggle in laws for the increase and consolidation of the power of their party under the specious guise of advancing the cause of popular amelioration'.[28] The same devious tactics had been employed by the Parliamentarians during the reign of Charles I.[29] Now the constitution was being assailed by a 'whole gang of pseudo-Reformers and political economists ... and all the other base and unsavoury fungi that have been generated ... in the hotbed of Whig agitation'. The Reform Act of 1832, passed by a treasonable compact with the Irish Papists, was a means of 'swamping' the Commons with groups of middle class voters whom the Whigs hoped to manipulate. Having already 'captured' the Crown, they were now laying siege to the House of Lords and planning to reduce the influence of the Tory gentry in the municipal corporations, thus giving free reign to their despotic rule.[30]

Notwithstanding the severity of the current crisis, Disraeli concluded on a note of optimism. The genius of the English Constitution is such, he affirmed, that the more violently it is assailed, it 'ever becomes more firm and vigorous'.[31] Already the people were beginning to wake up to the danger and to close ranks round their natural leaders, the Peers of the Realm.[32] Moreover, transitions cannot last indefinitely. Even the tradesmen and manufacturers who had profited from the Whig Act would in the nature of things become the defenders of the constitution. 'When passions have a little subsided, the industrious ten-pounder ... proud to have obtained the first step of aristocracy, will be the last man to assist in destroying the other gradations of the scale which he or his posterity may yet ascend'.[33] Tories, Disraeli reminded his readers, 'are not opposed to measures of political amelioration', although their conception of reform was not as a means to achieve power for themselves. They had therefore opposed the Whig Reform Act, but had urged measure after measure 'infinitely more democratic' than 'that cunning oligarchical device'.[34] This would assure that the Radicals, that 'honest and considerable party', would eventually join forces with them to ensure that 'the good old times would soon return'.[35]

Some two years before entering Parliament Disraeli, then, seeking to give the party a new impetus by basing it on wider public support, had already envisaged a reinvigorated brand of Toryism. His hopes and expectations of his role may be gauged by his description of himself as a follower of St John Bolingbroke. Combining 'all the wisdom which can be derived from literature and a comprehensive experience of human affairs', Queen Anne's Secretary of State 'opposed the Whigs from principle' but also recoiled from Toryism as it then was, thereby incurring 'at the outset of his career ... the commonplace imputation of insincerity and inconsistency'.[36] On joining the Tory party he found it in disarray, following the accession of George I and the failure of the Jacobite rising. He applied his unorthodox doctrines to set it up anew as the popular party of the nation, favouring the Crown and a strong administration to replace the earlier cliques of aristocrats clinging to the theory of the Divine Right of Kings.

A modern critic has dismissed this analysis as 'pure myth' and the debt of the *Vindication* to Bolingbroke 'as much imagined as real'.[37] This may well apply to the writings of 1835 and thereafter it becomes even more pronounced. Bolingbroke was a legitimist whose concern lay in the checks and balances of the mixed constitution as laid down in 1688. Disraeli, on the other hand, directed the main thrust of his Tory-radical argument into the channel of national welfare. The seeds were discernible earlier, and in the *Vindication* he already attacked the Poor Law Bill as an insidious indication of Whig malice towards the well-being of the common people. By July 1839, in what he called his 'capital speech on chartism'[38] where he urged that the National Petition be considered, the trend became more pronounced. He agreed with most of the House that general suffrage was no panacea for social ills. Yet he 'sympathised with the Chartists ... a great body of his countrymen ... [that] laboured under great grievances'. Far from being incited by sedition-mongers, they were 'a very remarkable social movement' of protest against 'a monarchy of the middle classes' that promised the workers no relief other than a degrading

New Poor Law. To ignore the justice of their claims was to invite insurrection.[39] About a year later he again warned of the dangers of violence stemming from social neglect and asserted that 'a union between the Conservative party and the Radical masses offers the only means by which we can preserve the Empire ... united they form the nation'.[40] But the crystallisation of such views was not complete till the early 1840s, with his growing dissatisfaction with the Peel government, the deepening economic crisis and his finding himself 'without effort the leader of a party chiefly of the youth and new members'.[41] It was then that the impact of Carlyle on him made itself felt.

On the face of it, such an influence is incongruous. Disraeli was proud of his Jewish descent, whereas Carlyle despised the Jews as 'an impotent race, who had never distinguished themselves in their entire history by any estimable quality' save money-grubbing and the crucifixion of 'any man [who] appeared among them [with] something to tell worth their attention'.[42] Furthermore, Disraeli led the successful revolt against Peel over the repeal of the Corn Laws, whereas Carlyle saw them as a 'strangling band of famine [around] ... our necks'[43] and came to appreciate Peel as a politician of conscience, capable of regenerating English society. Part of the explanation may lie in Disraeli's taking Carlyle's meteoric rise in national esteem and influence as a model for himself just as he had done with Bolingbroke. Years later he wrote that in his novels he had Carlyle in mind as one who had 'succeeded, after long neglect and constant protest against his principles', in making the world read and admire him.[44] In such works as *French Revolution, Sartor Resartus* and especially *Past and Present* Disraeli found ideas which fitted in with those he had absorbed from his reading of Southey and Shelley, but applied to the very time and conditions with which he himself was concerned. Finally, he found in Carlyle's writings a ready-made synthesis of those principles which he too was striving to harmonise. This allowed him to clarify and sharpen his perceptions and to emphasise elements which were already present in less-developed form in his earlier thought.

Of the period when Disraeli was working out the ideas formulated in the Young England trilogy, it was said that 'none of the abler young men escaped being ... Carlyle bitten'.[45] Some went so far as to warn of the danger of Carlyleanism becoming a religion that 'superseded the soul-saving truths of the Gospel of Christ'.[46] This might substantiate the view expressed by biographers that the similarities between the ideas in the trilogy and the ideas in Carlyle's works cannot be adduced as proof that Disraeli had drawn on them through actual reading. Nor does the turning of the Young England group to the Sage of Chelsea for advice prove their first-hand knowledge of his work. Even the appearance in the trilogy of typically Carlylean aphorisms, terms and turns of speech can only illustrate the truth of Mason's testimony that phrases from Carlyle's books 'were affecting public speech'.[47] However, one cannot explain how, without a close reading, Disraeli could have written under the *nom de plume* 'Coeur-de-Lion' articles so reminiscent of the Master's themes, style and diction that, to Disraeli's great annoyance, they were widely attributed to Carlyle.[48] The fact that they were written in January 1838 shows furthermore that Disraeli had been carefully following Carlyle's literary career right from the time he achieved fame with *French Revolution*.

The unity of the Young England trilogy is provided not merely by the reappearance of the leading characters, but by a common philosophy of which the point of departure is a historical thesis including, but going beyond, that touched on in the *Vindication*. An important summing-up appears in a discussion between several of the major protagonists of the three novels on the eve of Tancred's departure to the Holy Land to rekindle the fire of the true faith in the absence of which society has sunk into selfishness and division. The human race, they agreed, constantly advances, and history is the record of 'the progressive development of the faculties of man'. Yet the march forward is not in a straight line but spirals upwards. Every cycle has its dominant race which absorbs the achievements of its predecessors and proceeds to realise its own potential. Thereafter it declines to be replaced by another. Parallel processes take place within each cycle. Two human forces constantly battle for supremacy, one giving preference to the progress of the whole over the individual, the other of the individual over the whole. Periodically, the first becomes exhausted, and after a time of transition the second gains the upper hand, till a new revitalising spirit restores the 'community of purpose that constitutes society'. Each generation must adjust to changing circumstances the shared values and the principles of reciprocal relations which it inherits, the initiators of which are unique individuals, the 'personification of [their] race ... its perfection and choice exemplar[s]'.[49]

The doctrine is elaborated by Sidonia, the apotheosis of ancient Hebrew wisdom, the Jews being the sole race whose values are perpetually valid. All men are made in God's image, he argues, but the Hero is closer to Divinity than others. Human greatness is less by virtue of intellect than of imagination. But whereas that of ordinary mortals is restricted by time and space, that of the Hero is comprehensive. By inspiring society with his vision he instils the spirit of the Divine in its members and unites them around common values. However, time dulls the freshness of response, the vision fades and principles are reduced to routine ritual. Egotism then takes over and human energy degenerates into self-interest: 'Man is made to adore and obey; but if you will not command him, if you give him nothing to worship, he will fashion his own divinities and find a chieftain in his own passion.' Reciprocal ties give way to 'reciprocal hostilities' and 'the various classes ... [become] arrayed against each other'. Sidonia's conclusion is therefore that class struggle is a cyclic phenomenon which is not directly attributable to economic factors. Rather, it is generated by the collapse of social principles that had previously held in check any tendency to widen gaps between the sectors of the people, and that had prompted 'the wise statesman' to 'watch, to regulate, to ameliorate [and] to modify' any destructive effects of material progress.[50]

As early as 1835, Disraeli maintained that the English constitution rests on the primary assumption that property entails duties. In the 1840s he still held that it was this principle that persisted through change and gave continuity and direction to social progress. His location of its origin in the feudal system not only conformed with the tastes of his colleagues in the Young England movement but was in harmony with the cult of medievalism that had become so prominent for the late eighteenth century. An important element in the appeal of the chivalrous knight was the protection he offered to those in need and his sense of responsibility to his dependents, on whose loyalty he could therefore rely. There were, however, significant modifications in Disraeli's version. The traditional relationship of the lord to his retainers was no longer to be a matter of *noblesse oblige* or philanthropy, but a legal obligation towards those whose labour had produced his wealth. This lay at the root of Disraeli's doctrine, earlier promulgated by Carlyle, that it was the duty of the Crown acting through the administration to enforce its fulfilment, and that the responsibility of the 'wise Statesman' was to see to its proper application in accordance with the conditions of the time. A clear expression, one of the several, comes in a speech describing the historical source of what Disraeli called the 'territorial constitution':

> When the conqueror carved out parts of the land, and introduced the feudal system, he said to the recipient, 'You shall have that estate, but you shall do something for it: You shall feed the poor; you shall endow the church; you shall ... execute justice and maintain the truth to the poor for nothing'.[51]

One senses the influence of Southey and of Carlyle's *Past and Present* in a surprising theory advanced in *Sybil* in defiance of the common Tory antipathy to the Papists. The model of right rule was the early Catholic monasteries, where the monks felt themselves custodians of the spiritual and economic welfare of the peasants, and held the Church estates for the benefit of the community as a whole. The appropriation of their property at the Reformation was an example of the destructive impulse to allow self-interest to override conscience and to promote individuals above society. The new land-owning nobility, ancestors of the Whigs, had won their excessive wealth at the expense of the people, thereby creating social problems that were to be the bane of England for centuries, especially in the towns to which the dispossessed poor flocked.[52] The heirs of the spoilers of ecclesiastical wealth were therefore not entitled automatically to power, unless it was earned in the manner of the original owners. Heredity, Disraeli held, in itself confers no rights. The proud claims of the Earl of Marney, for example, rested upon a false foundation since the original title and wealth were granted by Henry VIII to one of his servants in appreciation of his gift of valuable Church loot. His brother, on the other hand, had a right to his position by virtue of his conduct and sensitivity to the needs of the people.

Another important aspect distinguishing Disraeli from most other medievalists was the extension of the principles underlying the feudal system beyond its usual rural context. Like Carlyle, he believed that it was the spirit of communality based on hierarchy and reciprocal rights and duties that was at issue. The important point was therefore not where the property was situated or the use to which it was put, nor whether it was inherited or acquired, but what its ownership entailed: 'The merchant or manufacturer may deposit within it his accumulated capital, and he may enjoy the privileges to which its possession entitles him, on condition that he discharges those duties which its possession also imposes.'[53] Consequently, where most medievalists ignored industry and commerce, or expressed their abhorrence of them, Disraeli saw such attitudes as opposed to national interests. The villainous Marney had never seen and never wished to see a factory: 'Our family has always been against manufactories, railroads, everything.'[54] And strangely enough, the brutalised unlettered victims of aristocratic despotism shared the hatred of the machine, believing that it, and not its owners, was responsible for their misery.[55] On the other hand, the educated and broad-minded worker recognised that 'the railways will do as much for mankind as the monasteries did',[56] and his daughter Sybil prophesised that 'with the shuttle and the spindle we may redeem our race if we could only form the minds that move those peaceful weapons'.[57] The first words of Sidonia in the trilogy place industrialism in its historical context. 'The age of ruins is past. Have you seen Manchester?', he asks Coningsby who had just left the storm-shattered forest of ancient trees. The hero then reaches 'the great METROPOLIS OF LABOUR', at which point the chapter ends. The next chapter opens with an eloquent discourse on the significance of the new manufacturing cities that strongly recalls Carlyle in theme and in tone. A great city, Disraeli proclaims, is 'the type of some great idea'. Athens, Rome, Jerusalem, are more than mere places. They stand for whole cultures. The modern world is Manchester, though as yet only the philosopher can discern its 'grandeur ... and immensity of its future' that make it 'as great a human exploit as Athens'. The machine is a 'supernatural slave' that 'neither brings nor bears degradation', and its voice 'roar[s] in jolly chorus, like a strong artisan handling his lusty tools', the Carlylean catchword 'a fair day's wages for a fair day's toil'.[58]

And yet all his enthusiasm for the progress 'to which the annals can afford no parallel' paled before his consternation at the collapse of the moral values and social patterns of pre-industrial times.[59] 'In the hurry-scurry of money-making', what has been ignored was a 'proportionate advance in our moral civilisation'. The outcome was an 'age of infidelity in all things ... [in which] governments were hated, and religion despised ... loyalty was dead and reverence only a galvanised corpse'.[60] As in the *Vindication*, the contemporary crisis was described as a phase of the eternal war between the sons of light and darkness exemplified by Toryism and Whiggism. But in the trilogy, written after the Tories had come to power, Disraeli's historical perspective assumed a new angle: the cyclic decline of the life-giving Tory idea into automatic response, and the clichés of habit. The cancerous growth of egotism had now attacked even Conservatism, so that from the party of the nation it had sunk to that of a power-seeking clique.

The last great Tory was Bolingbroke's disciple Lord Shelbourne. Pitt was well intentioned, but lacked the 'passionate and creative genius' of his predecessors. The French Revolution made him metaphorically lose his head and, abandoning the party's principle of unifying the nation and allaying discontent by judicious reform, 'he appealed to the fears, the prejudices, and the passions of a privileged class [thereby] reviv[ing] the old policy of oligarchy'. The post-war domestic difficulties accentuated the decline, and Lord Liverpool showed himself to be an 'Arch-Mediocrity who presided, rather than ruled, over his Cabinet of Mediocrities'. He was the reverse of the type of Hero, 'peremptory in little questions [while] great ones he left open'. Wellington was chosen as a leader because he had the outward attributes of a Hero, but he was only a man of action, without an ideology and the standards which mark the truly great. 'No one had risen either in Parliament, the universities, or in the press to lead the public mind to the investigation of principles.' An ill-informed party, 'repeating cries which they did not comprehend', chose Robert Peel to lead it, and he was a fitting representative of the 'mere children of routine'.[61] The Tamworth Manifesto was 'an attempt to construct a party without principle' and showed that the 'pseudo-Tories' had sold out to Whiggism. Conservatism had degenerated into 'an unhappy cross-breed'. It 'discards prescription, shrinks from principle, disavows progress; having rejected all respect for antiquity, it offers no redress for the present, and makes no preparation for the future'. In this limbo arose 'that Condition of England Question of which our generation hears so much'.[62]

Like Carlyle, who originated the phrase, Disraeli saw the question as revolving around the paradox of an economy in which 'wealth was increasing to a superabundance' while 'the creators of wealth are steeped in the most abject poverty'.[63] *Sybil* is an analysis in black and white of the dichotomy, summed up along the lines of the Dandies and Drudges in *Sartor Resartus* as the two nations; between whom there is no intercourse and no sympathy ... as if they were ... inhabitants of different planets; who are formed by a different breeding, are fed by different food, are ordered by different manners, and are not governed by the same laws.[64]

The book abounds in descriptions of the worker's daily struggle for mere survival as against the petty quarrels of ignorant aristocratic parasites mouthing their 'mimetic dogmas'.[65] But it also shows how neglect and exploitation have become the dominant ideology of the age.[66] As Disraeli put it elsewhere, liberalism was a cloak to hide the self-indulgence of 'those who would be free from certain constraints and regulations, from a certain dependence and duty which are deemed necessary for the general ... welfare'.[67] Marney justifies on liberal and Malthusian principles the preservation of game on his vast estates, while the inhabitants of the town bearing his name languish in hunger and disease. Seven or eight shillings a week are quite enough for them, he asserts. They have no cares since they can always have recourse to the workhouse, and 'people without cares do not require so much food'.[68] In fact, it is a virtue to reduce the population, and therefore 'I build no cottage, and I destroy all I can'.[69]

The same temper that brought Marney to deny the traditional duties of the landowner to his dependents animated the new class of factory owners who had no tradition of duty to start with. 'Enter with me into a factory in Stockport or Manchester', Disraeli declaimed in one of his speeches, '[and] I will show you human degradation, I will bring you to a hovel where the exhausted slave curses the life which he cannot quit.'[70] On the basis of his own visits and of the correspondence of Fergus O'Connor,[71] he described the industrial and mining counterpart of the Marney estate, Mowbray, where the workers live in 'circumstances that seem to have escaped the notice of the Society for the Abolition of Negro Slaves'.[72] Another example, Woodgate, symbolises the liberal world of the future. 'The most miserable [place] in the most hideous burgh in the ugliest country in the world', it belongs to no one, is governed by no one, without Church, school, municipality, or any other 'meddlesome supervision'.[73] Yet there is in effect an aristocracy of the successful employers who 'intolerant of any tyranny except at Woodgate',[74] enslave their 'hands' and reduce them to 'animals [whose] minds [are] a blank; and their worst actions only the impulse of a gross savage instinct'.[75] Disraeli thus had recourse to the argument already put forward by the Lake poets on the effects of the French Revolution: the antonym of authority is not liberty but tyranny. Liberalism, with its call from freedom, forgot that social co-operation and consideration for others are not innate qualities but must be nurtured through tradition, education and institutions. Released from all these, man falls prey to the Hobbesian struggle in which the most vicious and ruthless emerge as victors. Unlimited freedom leads therefore to the unlimited power of the strong or, as Dostoevsky was to put it, in the final analysis absolute freedom equals absolute slavery. But the opposite, as the romantics equally noted, was no less true, and tyranny leads to anarchy and revolution which involve the destruction of the traditions and institutions that bind society together. The vicious circle is reflected in the participation of the men of Woodgate, led by the most brutal of their despots, side by side with the wretched victims of Mowbray and Marney in an orgy of rioting and arson under the banner of physical-force Chartism. The men of Woodgate sought to impose their egos on others, and their leader admitted that 'as long as there is burning ... I don't care what lessons you teach [the people]'.[76] The victims of Mowbray and Marney protested violently against the egotism of their tyrants. Both, however, proved that, as Disraeli said elsewhere, 'If the Government does not lead the people, the people will drive the government.'[77]

For all this, Disraeli was far from giving up hope. The Tory idea had ceased to guide the age, but, 'even now it is not dead, but sleepeth'. It will yet awake and then the Tory party 'will ... rise from the tomb'.[78] From the throne to the hovel, Sidonia says, all are calling for a guide, a Hero to teach, inspire and lead. True, the spirit of the age runs counter to the idea of the Hero out of despair of finding one. Nevertheless, 'the spirit of the age is the very thing that a great man changes ... prophets, great legislators, great conquerors ... destroy and create'.[79] It was with this mission of revival that Disraeli charged his 'Young Generation', represented by Coningsby, Egremont and Tancred. As a Carlylean Aristocracy of Talent, their duty is to unify the classes and take the lead in the 'reconstructive labours'[80] of reform that would terminate the period of transition and usher in the glorious destiny in store for the country. Thus, Coningsby sees it as especially significant that the three individuals who had greatly influenced his mind were 'a principal landed proprietor, ... one of the most eminent manufacturers, and ... the greatest capitalist [i.e. financier] in the kingdom'.[81]

We are offered a glimpse of the new world when Coningsby first comes to the industrial Midlands. He meets in Manchester a Mr G.O.A. Head who assures him that the 'metropolis of the machine' is not the last word in industrial development, and that he should visit Millbank for a foretaste of things to come. There he finds an industrial village operating according to the latest technological inventions and the personal, communal principles of traditional England, whose owner, in his concern for 'the moral and physical-being of his people', even, like Carlyle's Prudence in *Past and Present*, 'establish[es] singing classes'. A parallel example in *Sybil* is the factory of Tafford, who 'recognized the baronial principle, reviving in a new form, and adapted to the softer manners and more ingenious circumstances of the time'.[82] Each novel ends in a wedding. Coningsby, the heir to landed estates, marries the daughter of Millbank, while Egremont, the new heir of the Marney estate, marries Sybil, who turns out to be the true owner of Mowbray. However, this linking of the two worlds takes the experiments of Millbank and Tafford a step further. Theirs were the reaction of sensitive individuals to the sordidness of the 'cash-nexus' and the parasitism of the landed aristocracy. The younger generation will serve as a model for a society based on a united agricultural-industrial aristocracy and backed by the authority of a strong Crown.[83] To this enterprise Tancred contributes the rediscovered spirituality of the East that will replace the theology of the 'mitred nullities' which always ends in 'concrete expediency' with a creed that will cement the people and a church that will 'share equally among all its prayer, its incense, and its music, its sacred institutions, and the highest enjoyments that the arts can afford'.[84]

The degree to which these doctrines dictated Disraeli's policies after 1846 is debatable. He repeatedly alluded to them, though in the more moderate tone necessitated by his responsibility in the party and the gradual absorption of industrial and commercial forces in its ranks. Yet one must beware of identifying too closely the utterances and actions of a practising politician of his type. For example, one would be hard pressed to relate the 1867 Reform Act to his constitutional theories, but it provided him with an excellent opportunity for repeating his historical thesis. Moreover, his speeches on the issue illustrate a mood of confidence which was to grow as his influence increased. Change, he argued, is a permanent condition of society. The question is whether it should be directed within the framework of the British tradition and constitution or break out of it. 'Whenever [the Tory party] degenerates' change is destructive; 'when the people are led by their natural leaders' change is constructive, as proved by the Act.[85] A later example is his preface to the collected edition of his fiction (1870) where he stated the basis of his ideology: 'The Feudal system may have worn out, but its main principle, that the tenure of property should be fulfilment of duty, is ... the keystone of human progress and without it governments sink into police, and a nation is degraded into a mob.'[86] His harping on his doctrines can equally be shown in his speech on the programme of the Tory party some two years later.[87] The virtue of the English constitution lies in the existence of a united landed and industrial aristocracy of talent leading the rural and urban workers to see their welfare as of mutual interest. He also outlined proposals of meliorative legislation which he expanded in the famous Crystal Palace Speech of the same year.[88] The Hero principle was examined in the following year. Neither Socialists nor Liberals, he claimed, can produce the required leadership to institute reform, the one because its levelling principles preclude the emergence of a leadership, the other because of its principle of uncontrolled individualism free from restraint from above. In both cases 'those who ought to lead feel isolated, and those who wish to obey know not to whom to offer their devotion'. Only the Tories therefore can both unite, lead and guide the people towards a greater future.[89]

One is tempted to see the social legislation which assumed such a prominent position in the activities of the Disraeli government as a direct application of these ideas. Critics have argued that many of the reforms were vote-catching concessions to the working class, were necessitated by official investigations and reports, or were already being worked out by the civil service. It is also true that Disraeli showed little concern for the details of the legislation, although his encouragement and support cannot be questioned. But whether or not we agree with what a recent writer has rejected as the 'neo-opportunist interpretation of Disraeli'[90] is immaterial. What is more relevant is that he developed an ideology which pledged such reforms and exploited their meliorative effects as its confirmation. By bringing the romantic tradition into the service of

Toryism, he was instrumental in bringing the party up to date to suit the needs of the modern world.

III

In the year Disraeli helped to bring about Peel's downfall, Charles Kingsley defined the curse of his generation as total loss of inner faith, the outward expression of which was what he elsewhere called 'mammonite infidelity'.[91] As one who years before had lost and regained his faith, he believed he could guide his generation out of the morass even if 'the sensible folk' dismissed him at first as 'a bigot and a fanatic'.[92] A parallel may be drawn between the early stages in the careers of the two men. Some eight years earlier Disraeli had entered Parliament after a period of vacillation and began the process that was to culminate in his leadership of the Tory party. In that very year Kingsley entered Cambridge and not long after underwent a deep crisis of religious doubt which ended in his abandoning law for theology. In each case the decisive course of development was powerfully affected by the romantic tradition. An ardent reader from youth, Kingsley too had studied the romantics before entering the university and according to his future wife knew the poetry of Southey, Shelley and Coleridge by heart. But the strongest impact was provided by Carlyle's works which she sent him at the lowest point of his undergraduate crisis. Some critics claim that 'to Carlyle ... belongs the credit for saving [him] from the blackness of despair [and] for influencing him towards the life of service'.[93] Such an extreme assertion is difficult to prove conclusively, but there can be no doubt that his ideas helped Kingsley to crystallise his views and played a major part in his decision to follow the example of 'that old Hebrew prophet' who showed 'to prince and beggar' the way of truth.[94]

Following his recovery, Kingsley's letters are full of Carlylean echoes, references and quotations. One or two examples may suffice. The theory that 'we are a part of all we see and hear',[95] and the appreciation of all natural objects as symbols of a spiritual essence offering a glimpse of the ultimate divine purpose, could have come from other romantics. But he acknowledged as from Carlyle the doctrine of the Heroes who appear periodically to 'free man from the bondage of custom and self, the two great elements of the world that lieth in wickedness',[96] and who open his eyes to the moral message of nature. It is just possible that the attack on the 'devil's principle' of considering the labourer as a trader 'who sells you a certain amount of work for a certain sum of money', and the wish to revive 'the patriarchal and feudal spirit',[97] had other origins though the probability is that it came from *Past and Present* which he had recently read. But what is beyond doubt is the source of the observation that contemporary society reflected a world that had broken with the forms and beliefs of the past without replacing the 'old clothes'[98] with new ones, for it was supported by quotations from Carlyle referring to the French Revolution.[99]

However, as Kingsley matured he was not content with merely echoing such ideas. Increasingly, he wrote to his wife, Carlyle brought him to 'a healthy ferment of mind' which issued in deeper speculations and further developments of the Master's principles. In these he found not black pessimism but a 'bright view of life' offering 'clues and threads of light' through the 'infinite Chaos and darkness'.[100] His new insights enabled him to interpret with greater sensitivity the works of the other romantics. This letter was followed by another about *The Excursion*. Wordsworth to him was 'not only a poet, but preacher and prophet of God's new and divine philosophy'.[101] Somewhat earlier he made a comment on Shelley and Byron which about a decade later he was to expand into a full-length essay. The two, he argued, were victims of an age of transition, caught between the breakdown of old codes and beliefs but before their replacement by new ones. In their 'struggle to escape from the "circumstance" of the evil world' they were 'thrust ... down into the abysses of misrule and uncertainty'.[102] Conversely, he read Carlyle through the spectacles of religion, finding new meanings in his works:

> I find that [his] system, or rather chaos, so far from making one unloving, makes me more and more loving, and charitable, at every page. I do not think indeed it would do this, unless *translated* and explained by the great truths of Christianity; but in *their* light, I see *its* light.[103]

This angle allowed him to trace an underlying similarity between Carlyle and Maurice, the other formative influence on his world view. From the start he linked the two in his letters, and in due course their doctrines, for all their differences, fused in his mind into a single philosophy in which religion, society and politics were inextricably combined: 'Maurice is a struggle ... Carlyle is a struggle — all more or less sound, towards true Christianity, and therefore true national prosperity.'[104]

Kingsley's efforts to draw on both in the formation of a point of view of his own were already noticeable in 1842, between his graduation and his curacy. The life of St Elizabeth of Hungary was not originally intended for publication, and concentrated only on one conception which he attributed to Carlyle and Maurice: the source of all religions is equally the search for some ultimate truth. In times of transition all grope for 'a *something* right or wrong which should supply a spiritual want'. The greatness of St Elizabeth and her like is that they provide an answer to such 'controversies'.[105] However, his ministry in the isolated and neglected rural parish of Eversley was devoted to supplying not only the spiritual wants of the impoverished labourers but also their social and physical needs. What he had learned from the theories of his masters he came to apply on the 'field work' of raising the labourers out of 'Barbarism'. By late 1846, he generalised the condition of Eversley to the 'Condition of England Question'. His point of view embraced not only the whole country but demanded action in the combined religious, socio-economic and political spheres for which his experiences, so he maintained, fitted him. The revolutions of 1848 abroad and the threat of upheavals at home were the final stimulus to take the steps he had been readying himself for. The day after the failure of the great Chartist demonstration he and a group of others started their public propaganda campaign, and under the direction of Maurice he drew up his first placard, quoting Carlyle and summing up the central message of his *Chartism*.[106] A month later saw the publication of the Christian Socialist's Journal, *Politics for the People*, to which he contributed regularly under the pseudonym of Parson Lot. The same year he began his first political novel, *Yeast*, shortly to be followed by *Alton Locke*.

In these, and subsequent numerous articles and books written in a similar vein, he freely acknowledged his debt to Carlyle and pressed his readers to take advantage of the 'ennobling knowledge' his writings offered. 'The general effect which his works had on me', says Sandy Mackye in *Alton Locke*, 'was the same as they had, thank God, on thousands of my class and of every other'.[107] Carlyle, for his part, found the book 'very welcome to me', helped to get it published, and regarded its author as a comrade-in-arms in the war 'against the Devil's Dung-heap'.[108] Yet Kingsley's writings were not mere echoes. To the religious quality he attributed to his master's ideas he added further elements from his reading of the earlier romantics, particularly Wordsworth. He also gave prominence to and developed further several strands of Carlyle's thought, especially the radical ones, yet taking due account of the fundamental conservatism of his teachings. For this approach he and his friends found an earlier model in Southey. A 'Champion of Orthodoxy and Conservatism', he proved in his *Colloquies* 'that a coalition and the boldest Progress, is not quite as Utopian as false Prophets of the Press assert it to be'.[109]

In a letter to his wife, Kingsley declared in the fateful year of 1848 that 'the symbolism of nature and the meaning of history must be my studies'.[110] Carlyle, as we have already noted, had opened his eyes to the relations between the two areas of study. He now expressed his intention of pursuing the matter further, and indeed it formed the basis of his future philosophy. His series of articles 'Biblical Politics' (1850-1) and his innaugural lecture as Professor of History at Cambridge (1860) give clear expression to views diffused throughout his *œuvre* and develop those aspects of Carlyle's thought which we have noted bore an affinity to Marxist theory. In contrast to the unchangeable instincts or unconscious biological processes that mark non-human life, man, he posited, is distinguished by his free will which allows him to shape his reality through the constant interchange of his inner world and his outer environment. By divine fiat it is his nature to be both self- and other-creative:

> ... he was meant to be an artificial being; artificial in his manufactures, habits, society, polity-what not? All day long he has a free choice between even physical laws, which mere things have not, and which make the laws of mere things inapplicable to him.[111]

Following the argument and the examples of *Sartor Resartus*, Kingsley took technological inventiveness as the most characteristic quality of the human species and the most prominent illustration of the way its progressive nature unfolds. Moving types, gunpowder or the spinning-jenny are mind working on matter. But 'so strangely interwoven is the physical and spiritual history of man, that material inventions produce continually ... spiritual results'. In short, man's creativity produces machines, thereby changing the phenomenal world which, being part of the human environment, in turn affects his being and develops his mind, leading to yet more advanced inventions.[112]

The motive force that operates this development, Kingsley believed, is morals; for it is they that determine what actions may or may not be taken, and in consequence the kind of world that is created. Yet, since such worlds are always progressing, morals change and are relative to specific societies at specific times. Such a view comes strangely from a parson and perhaps testifies to the depth of the Carlylean influence upon him. More surprising still is that he took the argument to his tutor's conclusion. Morals and religion are interconnected. God is beyond our understanding, but every age interprets him differently, and history is conditioned by the fact that 'Men make the gods in their own likeness; then they copy the likeness they have set up'.[113] Such an assertion logically led to another Carlylean doctrine, that of the 'divine dignity [of] man's labour and man's inventions'. Work is hallowed by the sanction of the God he has created in accordance with his own nature, and therefore it bears the stamp of divinity:

> The humblest artisan, as well as the deepest man of science, may look on his daily labours as a sacred business; a business, for the doing of which rightly, right thoughts and rules are put into his mind direct from the Almighty.[114]

But man not only has a divine element that links him through action to all that is outside him. 'There is in human nature [also] ... a demonic element, defying all law and all induction', that is concerned with satisfying the individual desires irrespective of the outer world. As man reaches the goals he sets for himself, the spiritual systems that fired his activity die down, and his God becomes a fixed prescriptive principle out of step with the dynamics of his nature. As the gap widens, he withdraws into himself and 'every man [becomes] his own God by making [his] spirit the only rule of right and wrong'.[115] Then work loses its spiritual dimension and is no longer the agent of self-fulfilment. All it can serve is the material satisfaction of immediate desires. Echoing *Past and Present*, Kingsley described man as becoming in this stage 'a sort of magnified beaver, or ape, or spider, or very unhappy, quarrelsome, ill-fed beast of prey'.[116]

The Wordsworthian influence on Kingsley's thought is already noticeable in his earliest articles on the social implications of this historical pattern. The poet is quoted to substantiate the argument that the mind of men is formed by nature, whether as it is or as modified by human activity. Society as the entity of men in the aggregate is therefore also determined by nature, and this being the medium by which we perceive God, when we share the admiration of His glorious works we feel with and hence for one another.[117] Moulded by the same environment every individual feels himself a

> member of a body ... which has a life of is own, and a government of its own, a duty of its own, a history of its own, an allegiance to a sovereign, all of which are now his life, his duty, his history, his allegiance.[118]

Such shared sensitivity to 'circumstance', to that which surrounds one, is the source of true pleasure: '... though man [is] the creature of circumstances, he become[s] happy by creating the very circumstances which afterwards ... create him'.[119] The loss of this communality of response to the spirit of God, caused when each man follows his own selfish lusts, spells the disintegration of society. Man becomes a 'tool to buy and sell', and competition becomes the means by which he achieves his private ends. It is 'man eating man, eaten by man, in every variety of degree and method'.[120] So long as he withdraws into himself he is 'a coward'. When he is at one with nature and his fellow men 'he is a hero'.[121]

Though every age knows only its own version of God, Kingsley was confident that the history of many ages can reveal the general laws governing humanity. Moral lessons can be drawn, especially, from 'critical periods'.[122] Thus the French Revolution teaches what happens when instead of a united society we have the tyrannical egotism of a corrupt regime. Unknown to themselves, unrighteous revolutionaries like Robespierre performed a righteous mission as agents of the Almighty. 'Their work succeeded, and remains to this day; they themselves ... were punished for their own wickedness'. However, following a line of thought of Carlyle to be considered in the final chapter, he considered bloody revolution as a lesser form of divine retribution. When the process of degeneration and 'wearing down of the race' is not stopped in time, society reaches a point of no return and must be destroyed root and branch, as with the massacre of the Amalekites or of the American Red Indians. God takes away 'those who might be harmful ... leaving room for others, who are, though no better than those destroyed, more fitted to carry on the great work of increasing and civilising, and raising the human race'.[123]

Such an extreme opinion could be taken as evidence of profound pessimism, for if man shapes the circumstances that in turn shape him, once he starts on the downward cycle there would seem to be little hope of reversing the process. Yet one must bear in mind Kingsley's adoption of Carlyle's doctrine of the Hero. Periodically there appear men of intellectual and moral stature 'the like of whom we have never seen, and cannot explain ... such do, in fact, become leaders of men into quite new and unexpected paths ... and leave their stamp upon whole generations and races'.[124] As initiators of historical turning points they implant in the minds of men 'unseen eternal facts' which bring them 'in harmony with heaven, and earth, and the Maker thereof'.[125] In this way they redirect society in the upward path of melioration and ensure the continuation of human progress. The message of each is the link in the sequences of history.

> Hero spirits
> Pass the lamp from hand to hand,
> Age from Age the world inherits.[126]

Contemporary society, Kingsley believed, was awaiting the advent of such a Hero. Precisely because the century had seen 'more done for science, for civilisation, for agriculture, for manufacture, for the propagation of human life, than any preceeding one for a thousand years and more' it had ignored the nonmaterial and become a 'Dead Church'.[127] The yardstick of both human achievement and human degradation was Political Economy. As a scientific system it reflected the capacity of modern man to comprehend the laws governing economic forces. But having revealed them, it proclaimed that they were immutable. Thereby it denied man's faculty for discovering 'the laws of existing phenomena, in order that he may employ them to create new phenomena', which is the secret of 'his dignity as a rational being [and] ... a progressive animal'.[128] It had truly become 'the dismal science', for it condemned man to live as animals do, only in the present. Moreover, emptying the world of all aspirations and values other than the monetary, it left the individual a single interest — his own immediate personal gain. Work itself had turned into a mere device for money-making, to be avoided whenever possible. Consequently Political Economy 'after ignoring all the higher and holier part of man's nature and destiny, and asserting him to be a mere *"hand"*, a brute, and a machine, has not even the wit to make that machine work decently'.[129] The direct outcome was social exploitation and a growing gap between rich and poor. Sweated labour had become a norm of employment, encouraged even by the state, the representative of the people, on the ground that it was to the benefit of the nation as a whole. The Church itself had given sanction to the God of Mammon, and clergymen 'used the Bible as if it was a mere special constable's handbook — an opium dose for keeping beasts of burden while they were being overloaded — a mere book to keep the poor in order'.[130] England, says Eleanor in *Alton Locke*, was the new Babylon, ruled by 'the plutocrats and bureaucrats, the money-changers and devourers of labour' whose 'merchandise is the bodies and souls of men'.[131]

Poets like Burns, Byron and Shelley illustrated the dilemma of sensitive men who found themselves 'standing between two worlds, amid the ruins of an older order; upon the threshold of a new one'.[132] All three denounced the 'decay and rottenness' of a society whose divisiveness was perpetuated by despotic laws with the benediction of the Church.[133] None, however, could suggest a viable alternative. Burns, having lost faith in degenerate values came to deny all value. He 'ceased to worship, and therefore to be himself worshipful'. Byron, believing in the validity of an ultimate law despaired at being unable to implement it. But it was Shelley, in whom 'God's likeness' shone so clear and bright, who was the most tragic. The contemporary distortions of the ultimate Law so tormented him that he preached the destruction of everything, including law itself, in an orgy of iconoclasm. In so doing he symbolised the feelings of all suffering victims of tyranny and evil, and his blind striking out against all authority became the model for the revolutionaries.[134] The spread of such views, especially among the working classes, explained their 'bloodthirsty threat of revenge' which would be 'utterly ruinous to poor as well as rich, and probably prove the death-blow of the country'.[135]

Two Years Ago presents the issue in the allegorical guise of fiction. Elsley Vavasour, the poet who had 'let sights and sounds, not principles and duties, mould his feelings for him' and become weakened by addiction to opium, falsely suspects his wife of infidelity. He climbs the trackless pass of Snowdonia on his way to escape from his country, his society, his family and himself. Wynd and Naylor pursue him to bring him back and save him from self-destruction. Vavasour's activity is negative; theirs is positive, prompted by the sense of brotherly love, social responsibility, and the desire to defend the sacred values of family.[136] The moral is the same that Kingsley put forward from the first in his *Letters to the Chartists*. The cure for the sickness of the times could not be provided by what Carlyle had described as 'Morrison's pills', the evasion of reality by escape into the fantasy of a cure-all Charter or the drugging of oneself with the panacea of revolution. Rather, it had to be actively attained through the return to those moral and spiritual values in the absence of which all reform is useless:

> God will only reform society on condition of our reforming every man his own self — while the devil is quite ready to help us to mend the laws and the parliament, earth and heaven, without even starting such an impertinent and 'personal' request, as that a man should mend himself.

The first value to be learnt is that of communal responsibility and co-operation. If we refuse to learn it through 'public spirit and brotherly kindness', Kingsley warned, we shall learn it the hard way, through the contagious nature of social evil. By neglecting the health of others, for example, we may ourselves become infected as by cholera.[137]

For Kingsley, the first sign of the possibility of national redemption was the spread of 'great popular ideas as directly divine inspirations'.[138] Such was Owen's idea of Association among the working classes and the growing conception among the landed aristocracy that 'all property is held in trust from God, for the good of the commonwealth'.[139] The co-operative movement was the embodiment of the former. The latter held promise of the rise of a young generation of aristocrats who 'shall settle down in life, and become, as holders of the land, the leaders of agricultural progress, and the guides and guardians of the labouring man'.[140] Both groups could start off processes that would snowball till they engulfed the whole country. The workers should no longer be denied the vote and the right to influence their destinies. But as individuals they are helpless. Only by joining together in co-operatives and trade-unions could they introduce change. Instead of focusing on strikes and protest they should acquire land and establish their own factories and stores to distribute their produce. Money saved by elimination of the middleman would be invested in raising their own standard of living and in establishing more co-operatives. The landed aristocracy should enter long-term contracts with the agricultural workers, establish villages for them and provide them with plots of their own. This would end 'nomadism' and strengthen the loyalty of the rural worker to the landlord and the estate. The outcome would be the restoration of principles that underlay the feudal relationships which had lasted for so many centuries because they proved to be of mutual benefit for all. An additional value would be the reversal of migration from the village to the city which would restore the national status of those that live on the land.[141]

The lessons would not be lost on the urban capitalists. The success of both kinds of enterprise would teach them that the 'cash nexus' is wasteful and inefficient, for 'if you leave [your workers] tempted by want, your property is unsafe; if you leave them uneducated, reckless, improvident, you cannot get your work properly done, and you have to waste time and money in watching instead of trusting them'.[142] They too would therefore come to appreciate the importance of the 'patriarchical bond' and try to follow the example of the countryside by building villages for their workers outside the factory areas, on the model of Carlyle's *Past and Present*. The city would become only a place for work and public utilities, a showcase for the benefits of modern technology without its drawbacks. Industrial feudalism would thus contribute its share to the 'complete interpenetration of city and country, a complete fusion of their different modes of life, and a combination of the advantages of both'.[143] In fact, Kingsley could envision the setting up of entire industrial and agricultural parishes run on a communal basis, in which each inhabitant, 'from the mere paid worker to the capitalist' would receive his 'proportion of the profits, the muscle of the labourer and the skill of the scientific man being credited to them ... as so much money'.[144]

Central authority had also a vital role in ensuring the success of the new society. Again Kingsley followed Carlyle in proposing extensive sanitary legislation carried out by a special ministry, far-reaching laws regulating employer-employee relations and an emigration scheme that would trigger competition for labour among the industrialists. Equally he pressed the educational value of governmental action as representing the nation in its supra-sectional and historical sense:

> All government should be paternal ... it should help and guide all those who are unable to help and guide themselves. It should coerce those who are blind to the interests of their neighbours and the commonwealth ... to raise them to that which they are not ... in short, to restore them to that very ideal from whence they have fallen.[145]

In this way the state would orchestrate the different sections of the people to produce the harmonious composition of a good society. Bringing back the 'compromise between the strictness of military discipline and the *laissez-faire* ideal' it would restore to modern industrial England the values that had made it great for so many centuries. The conception of political life would once more be shaped by the conception of family life, while the spiritual source of all authority would be the God of all.[146] 'I assert', Kingsley wrote in 'My Political Creed', 'that this creed practically unites those extreme popular opinions that I always hold ... with the most loyal conservatism, and that it is at once English, Scriptural, and fit for a staunch High-Churchman'.[147]

IV

Praeterita, Ruskin's unfinished autobiography (1885-9) and the last in the very long list of his works, was written in the lucid intervals of madness. Its charm and wit contrast with the loss of his hold on reality that grew steadily during his final years, and it is fascinating to see how he could still recapture the very feel of his youth and sum up the dominant forces that had made him what he was. 'I was different ... from other children even of my own type', he wrote, for already he had absorbed 'Wordsworth's reverence, Shelley's sensitiveness, Turner's accuracy, all in one', each supplementing, modifying and correcting the other. Now, he continued, 'I find myself in nothing whatsoever *changed*... in the total of me, I am but the same youth, disappointed and rheumatic'.[148]

The choice of the three is significant. His closeness to Wordsworth can be seen in preface to his first great work, *Modern Painters* (1843), where he defined his purpose to 'declare and demonstrate, wherever they exist, the essence and authority of the Beautiful and True'.[149] The words gain further meaning from the lengthy passage from *The Excursion* quoted on the title page of each of the five volumes, part of which runs:

> I now affirm of Nature and of Truth,
> Whom I have served, that their Divinity
> Revolts, offended at the ways of men.
> Philosophers who ...
> ...yet prize
> [the human] soul, and the Transcendent universe,
> No more than as a mirror that reflects
> To proud self-love her own intelligence.

The inclusion of the last two lines takes us back to the 'authority' of the 'Beautiful and True', for Wordsworth's reverence for nature derived from his sense that as a manifestation of God it embodies moral principles that apply equally to mankind. Even after Ruskin abandoned his evangelicism he continued to deduce from nature and the 'constructive accuracy' in perceiving it the laws that govern art and society. However, in so doing he replaced the divine element in Wordsworth's links between God, man and nature by a Shelley-like historical and axiological approach in which the central value is the aesthetic. In consequence he felt obliged, to his regret, increasingly to subordinate his artistic interests to socio-economic criticism. *Fors Clavigera* climaxed a steady progression of works on these issues. More than 'a kind of blackmail levied by his conscience on his artistic activities',[150] it was a direct extension of his concern as an art critic. Yet despite the common foundation on which he and Shelley built their philosophies, namely what the latter called 'poetry in the Universal sense' as the basis of morals and social behaviour, the two diverged thereafter in following the two trends in the romantic tradition. Shelley always remained the radical; Ruskin defined himself as 'socialist of the most stern sort but also a Tory of the sternest sort'.[151]

Any attempt to follow Ruskin's social and political thought must take into account its relation to the ideas of the man he saw as 'a guide to all my work', Thomas Carlyle.[152] At first sight there would seem to be an incompatibility between the outlook of the two. Notwithstanding Carlyle's remarkable capacity for treating words as pigments and his graphic descriptions of men and events, there are virtually no visual depictions of nature in all his works. One does not find in them anything like Ruskin's genius for projecting himself into the spirit of physical phenomena. Moreover, what served as the starting point for his moral views was precisely the conception of the human soul as a battleground between the forces of good and evil that deflected Carlyle from the concern with external nature. From his letters one can even detect a distaste for the plastic arts and what he called in *Sartor Resartus* 'the epidemic, now endemical, of View-hunting'.[153] Nevertheless, one can see in Ruskin the enlargement of the scope of Carlyleanism into new areas of sensitivity. Its first impact on him may serve as an example. In 1842, at the time he was considering a defence of Turner, he read *Heroes and Hero Worship*. The book opened his eyes to new possibilities of treating his subject. He determined to preach the creed that art 'no less than other spheres of life, had its heroes; that the mainspring of their energy was sincerity, and the burden of their utterance truth'.[154] As he developed, the part played by Carlyle increased. He was the 'only ... man in England ... to whom I can look for steady guidance', and he served as a paternal surrogate after the death of Ruskin's father (he called him Papa in his almost daily letters when he was abroad). 'Carlyle is the only living writer who has spoken the absolute and perpetual truth about yourself and your business ... read your Carlyle ... with all your heart', he wrote in his letters to the workmen and labourers of Great Britain.[155] The friendship and indebtedness have been very fully treated by a host of writers, including one complete book comparing the political thought of the two men.[156] It is therefore supererogatory to recapitulate a well-studied theme. We shall restrict ourselves to a brief discussion of three points: Ruskin's philosophy of history, which merits more consideration than it has received; his authoritarian development of the *motif* of state reform which strongly influenced British socialist theory; and the implications of his hatred of industry which distinguished him from the romantics who restricted their denunciations to the capitalist ethos that accompanied it.

The most famous of Ruskin's books is also his lengthiest treatment of a historical theme, *The Stones of Venice* (1851-3). The basic components of his argument were already foreshadowed in his earlier works, but here they were developed and given more concrete and definite form which was to reappear with some variations and greater conciseness throughout his productive life.

The Seven Lamps of Architecture (1849) broadened his connection between art and morals to include building. This involved a further development in his view of the relation between the creator and the creation. The starting-point was that the work was undertaken by teams of craftsmen, guided by a common plan and executed for the use of a community. In *Modern Painters* art was regarded as the expression of an individual's conception of the essence of nature. Now Ruskin turned to the Carlylean doctrine of man as *Homo Faber*, a tool-using animal supplying his needs by changing the world of matter in harmony with the eternal principles that control the universe. Human activity is an 'independent force by which he moulds and governs external things; ... a force of assimilation which converts everything around him into food, or into instruments'. Accordingly, great art was seen as the quintessential expression of human creativity and of national character, the epitome of 'the true life'. The servile copying that marks false art points, on the other hand, to the diminution of the creative element in the individual, the loss of communication with the outer world, and the reduction of man to a self-centred creature who thereby becomes alienated from society.[157]

In *Modern Painters* (volume II, 1846) Ruskin had compared medieval painting with modern painting. The former was characterised by simplicity, innocence, purity and the immediacy of direct perception. The latter turned to artificialities of social life depicted in artificial surroundings which pointed to the distancing from the natural phenomena under whose influence we exist.[158] In *The Seven Lamps* the wider interpretation of art led to a profounder comparison. Of the lamps, only two, power and beauty, were commonly associated with buildings. The rest are the moral virtues at the basis of social life. Sacrifice is the spontaneous uncalculating altruism that prompts the individual to forgo immediate private interests in favour of the future general good. Memory involves the preservation of the best of the past in the present. Life refers to the element of freedom in creative activity and the joy in subjecting material things 'naturally passive and powerless' to the shaping power of human 'vital energy'.[159] However, 'the more the man is an inspired instrument and the less there is of himself',[160] the more he is free. Hence the lamp of obedience stands for the acceptance of guidance and submission to one's superiors. Truth is the result of applying these principles in architecture as a reflection of those in nature and society. Great art, in brief, encompasses both spontaneity and discipline, both the creativity of the individual and his participation as a cell in an organic whole, both the control of the phenomenal world and the subjection to the divine purpose, both the satisfaction of present requirements and the respect for traditional values. It is in the spirit of Carlyle's 'Produce! Produce! in God's name!'. Such were the characteristics of Gothic building and medieval society, reflecting 'the opposite of the prevalent feeling of modern times, which desires to produce the largest results at the least cost'.[161]

In *The Seven Lamps* the argument was illustrated by a comparison of the Greek and Byzantine with the Cis-Alpine Gothic styles. The general theory is continued in *The Stones of Venice* leading to a consideration of the nature of the Gothic through an exhaustive study of buildings and ornamentations in the city and to an analysis of the subsequent 'Fall' from Gothic to Renaissance. But since architecture is 'expressive of some great truths commonly belonging to the whole race and necessary to be understood or felt by them in all their work that they do under the sun',[162] the study developed into a major indictment of modernism by the method of *Past and Present*, that is, presenting it as it were as the photographic negative of medievalism. In fact, the brunt of the attack, particularly in 'The Nature of the Gothic', was against contemporary English society as embodying the spirit of modernism which climaxed the processes begun with the Renaissance.

The first attribute imputed to the Gothic was its 'savageness'. At the close of the so-called Dark Ages, when the Roman 'in the utmost impotence of his luxury and insolence of his guilt' became the model for Europe, the barbarians from the East were held in unmitigated contempt. However, what was admirable was precisely that vital tempestuous vigour born of closeness to nature which the effete 'civilised' West despised. Their architecture was the direct expression of the elemental power of their religious feelings.[163] The contrast with the Romanesque which it supplanted and with modernism represents that between the 'calculating, smiling, self-sustained, self-governed man, and the believing, weeping, wondering, struggling, Heaven-governed man; — between the men who say in their hearts "there is no God", and those who acknowledge a God at every step'.[164] The imperfections of the Gothic style are themselves revealing. They show the preference for aspirations and intentions too high for perfect realisation as against the satisfaction of lesser aims wholly within the grasp. Especially in the ornamentations, workmen were allowed freedom within the overall functional limits, for the masters respected the individual's craftsmanship as the expression of his soul. Yet 'out of fragments full of imperfection' they could raise up 'a stately and unaccusable whole'.[165] The result was the expression in artistic terms of the essence of feudal society: its acceptance of man's place in the universal scale of things, its recognition of his strength and its compassion for his weakness, its hierarchical structure and organic unity. The contrasts with the irreligious vanity of civilised society were inescapable. The very perfections of English architecture pointed to the stress being laid on the end-result rather than on the process of creation. It betrayed an 'ignoble' character that 'causes us to forget the relative dignities of [man's] nature itself, and to prefer the perfectness of the lower nature to the imperfection of the higher'. The argument that there was more freedom in medieval England, 'though the feudal lord's lightest words were worth men's lives', than in contemporary industrial society recalls Carlyle's comment in *Past and Present* on the true freedom of the bondsman Gurth in *Ivanhoe*.[166]

In later works, especially *The Crown of Wild Olives* where Ruskin summarised the historical thesis of *The Stones of Venice*, and in *Sesame and Lilies*, the theory is expressed with greater trenchancy. Man's 'inextinguishable instincts' lead him to act on what is outside him. Employed positively, they are directed to self-enhancing satisfaction through creative interaction, whether with things in art or people in society. Employed negatively, they are directed to egotistic gratification through destructive exploitation of all that is outside the self. Every era has its idea, or 'great national religion', which directs man to the former, but in time these degenerate and 'perish by falsehood in their own main purpose'. New ideas are then needed to bring men back to healthy creativity. The physical and moral attributes of society depend therefore on which expression of man's activity is dominant.[167]

As the years passed, Ruskin's despair at the ascendance among his countrymen of the satanic over the divine aspects of human nature steadily deepened. In *The Stones of Venice* he lashed out against the sending of the multitudes of industrial slaves 'like fuel to feed the factory smoke'.[168] About a score of years later he returned to the image in a terrifying word-painting of the clouds hiding the Heavens:

> The sky is covered with grey cloud; — not rain-cloud but a dry black veil, which no ray of sunshine can pierce ... it looks partly as if it were made of poisonous smoke; ... there are at least two hundred furnace chimneys in a square of two miles on every side of me. But ... it looks more to me as if it were made of dead men's souls.[169]

Nineteenth-century England, he proclaimed in *Fors Clavigera*, was doomed to exhibit in all things 'the elect pattern of perfect Folly, for a warning to the farthest future'.[170]

One cannot but recall Carlyle's pre-Maxian theory of alienation when we read Ruskin's analysis of the predicament of modern man. For this we may go back once more to the seminal chapter on 'The Nature of the Gothic'. The evanescence of the spirituality of religion,[171] and man's focusing on himself as the centre of the universe, he argued, had led to the channelling of creativity from its source in the great forces of nature into the mechanical reproduction of petty objects. What could the workers give of themselves in the making of the point of a pin or the head of a nail? Estranged from their activity and its products they were 'unhumanised'; 'all the energy of their spirits must be given to make cogs and compasses of themselves'.[172] Since man as distinct from the brute is a creator by nature and his work gives meaning to his existence, such labour deprived him of his very purpose in life. Only when he rested or ate, only in what he had in common with the animal, did he feel human. The whole plan of the species was thus inverted and men became estranged from their work, from nature and the products of their work and from themselves.[173] Nor could society as a whole remain unaffected, for alienation from one's self necessarily means alienation from one's fellow-beings. Deprived of happiness in their labour people turned to money as the sole source of happiness. However, those who enjoyed such 'pleasure' were precisely those who do not work. They obtained their enjoyment at the expense of those who did work but were equally doomed to animal existence, and one of physical deprivation to boot. If 'right freedom' means to obey and 'yield reverence' in return for 'liberty from care', the so-called free society which involves neither reverence nor release from poverty is in truth despotism. Man the Maker had split into man the slave and man the slavedriver.[174]

In the final volume of *Modern Painters* (1860) Ruskin

broadened the scope of his diatribe against capitalism to include an onslaught on Political Economy, summed up in the phrase which he proclaimed as the cornerstone of his alternative doctrine: 'Government and co-operation are in all things the Law of Life; Anarchy and competition the Law of Death'.[175] That year he also published the *Cornhill* articles, later collected under the title *Unto This Last*. Together with *Munera Pulveris* (1862-3) they constitute the core of his attack. He dedicated the latter 'to the friend and guide who has urged me to all chief labour, Thomas Carlyle', and acknowledged that his contentions rested on the authority of *Sartor Resartus, Past and Present* and the *Latter Day Pamphlets*.[176] The essence of his argument in both books was that Political Economy gave scientific sanction to all four dimensions of human estrangement, elevating disobedience to the principles of true religion into a religion. It was a form of witchcraft, dissociating behaviour in society from its social consequences. Assuming man to be a mere engine whose motive-power is provided by 'calculable' forces, it revived 'the monkish doctrine of the opposition of body and soul' and ignored the latter together with its emotional fuel.[177] The human being was thereby considered as a mere money-making machine. Seeking to fulfil himself by producing for himself the maximum of riches, he took advantage of the needs of others to exploit them as much as possible, whatever the cost to themselves and to the whole.[178] Since work was valued only for the money it brought, the employers' techniques could include underselling one another and encouraging unemployment, thereby enforcing lower wages and increased working-hours on those employees lucky enough to get work. 'The modern Politico-Economic slave', Ruskin wrote in *Fors Clavigera*, is a new species: not only is he put to compulsory labour as of old but now all too often to compulsory idleness. Carlyle's comparison of man and horse, he claimed elsewhere, was the most telling illustration of the working of the 'dismal science'. Having been stripped of all that distinguishes him from the brute, man indeed had become a beast of burden, and as such was worth far less and treated far worse than the four-legged one.[179] Proper political economy would take into account the 'power of entire human nature, body and soul'.[180] 'There is no wealth but life', Ruskin insisted;[181] it is the vital energy that circulates throughout the body politic like blood in the natural body, quickening its activity and nourishing its cells. The richest country therefore is that which enhances the lives of the greatest number of its citizens, while the richest man is he who 'having perfected the functions of his own life to the utmost has also the widest helpful influence'.[182] On the other hand, what for the Political Economists constituted wealth was in truth 'illth',[183] producing not the flush of health but a fever ending in putrefaction. Not only did it encourage 'monstrous forms of vice and selfishness'[184] but it increased the chance of an 'insane war' between 'wealth and pauperism',[185] of mob violence fed by popular passions.

Such recommendations as were suggested in *The Stones of Venice* were essentially negative: one should not waste energy on producing the superfluous and the uncreative, or demand the achievement of perfection or encourage imitation.[186] In later works Ruskin turned to more positive methods of restoring social and spiritual health. Like Carlyle he always fought shy of the superficiality of panaceas that passed over the moral bases of society. 'No political constitution can ennoble knaves', he argued.[187] Men have in differing degrees their limitations, weaknesses and imperfections, and all forms of government are good only so far as they 'attain this one vital necessity of policy', [188] that they appoint Heroes 'to guide, to lead, or on occasion even to compel and subdue their inferiors, according to their own better knowledge and wiser will'.[189] It is only such as these who can instil in the many a change of heart. The aristocracy must become an Aristocracy of Talent, qualified and ready as 'our quite clear-sighted teacher, Carlyle, had been telling us ... to *govern* the country'. The manufacturers and merchants must never 'consent to any deterioration, adulteration, or unjust exorbitant price', and must be prepared to take on themselves 'distress, poverty or labour' in defence of the trust confided in them as providers of the nation's necessities. All these should constitute the upper classes not only in terms of position but as moral influences on their dependents. 'Invested with a distinctly paternal authority and responsibility', they should teach by example that 'joy without labour' and 'labour without joy' are equally base. As for the worker, he must realise that happiness does not reside in money or status but in the daily attainment of 'more subtle and exemplary skill in his own craft'.[190] The nation will thus become an organic whole, united in purpose like one great army of 'soldiers of the ploughshare'.[191]

Notwithstanding the reservations about the efficacy of constitutions, from *A Joy for Ever* (1857) onwards there appear guidelines for the modes of action of the good state. Basically they are those prefigured by the Lake poets, especially Southey, and developed by Carlyle. As the representative of the entire people throughout the generations the state should operate like 'a farm in which the master was a father and in which the servants were sons'. Just as he allocates to each his work and responsibilities, so should it 'direct the waywardness of national energy'.[192] To check 'the childishness of national fancy', compulsory state education would inculcate true values and virtues and train each child for 'the calling by which he is to live'. Any unemployed person should be sent to the nearest governmental training institute and set to work for which he is fitted 'at a fixed rate of wages'. Objectors would be drafted to the most arduous, degrading or dangerous toil. As with Carlyle's industrial brigades, such state involvement would compel competing private employers to adopt the conditions and level of performance set by government.[193] The establishment of manufacturers and workshops 'entirely under Government regulation' for 'the production and sale of every necessary of life' would thereby create improved standards of 'work done and sold'.[194]

Not content with such a degree of public control of the individual, Ruskin in *Time and Tide* (letter XIII) took the doctrine of the state to its furthest conclusion. Over every 100 families or so an overseer would be elected for life to 'render account to the State of the life of every individual ... so that it may be impossible for any person ... to suffer from unknown want, or live in unrecognised crime'. A detailed report on the principal events in the life of every family would be submitted annually to 'higher officers of State' having 'executive authority' over large districts to 'enforce or mitigate the operation of ... general law'.[195] Though Ruskin took Carlyle's description of Frederic the Great to exemplify his own Hero as King, and his regime to illustrate the good government, he went far beyond anything that his master could have envisaged.[196]

But the mere enunciation of these grandiose principles was not sufficient. As his depression deepened, he sought to initiate operative schemes to reverse the deterioration of society. The best known and most ambitious of these was the St George Guild, to which he devoted so large a part of *Fors Clavigera*. Landlords and masters 'who would like better to be served by men than by iron devils', as well as tenants and workmen 'who can be true to their leaders and to each other', were called upon to set aside ten per cent of their income in order to fund a company for purchasing waste land.[197] On this young families would be settled to lead healthy, fulfilled lives, away from the strains and temptations of the city, each engaged in the work most suited to his natural skills and capacities. The organisation of the guild would be hierarchical. At the apex would be the 'master', Ruskin himself. Below him in descending order would come 'marshals' and 'landlords' called *Comités Ministrantes*, land agents, tenant farmers and hired labourers called *Comités Militantes* and 'independent companions' who give ten per cent of their income to the Guild (*Comités Consilii*). All would be divided by occupation into guilds on the medieval model. Social differentiations would be heightened by distinctive styles of dress for each class, but whatever their status, all would be equally obliged to prove their value to the community. Likewise, all would be trained in 'totally unreasoning obedience to their fathers, mothers and tutors', who in turn must offer the same 'precise and unquestioning submission to the officers set over them'. With time the whole of society would consist of such self-sufficient units.[198] The idea would even be exported and a St Anthony's company founded in Italy on the same lines.[199]

Ruskin was under the impression that his plan was 'following Carlyle's grander exhortation',[200] and in many respects it does appropriate the conception of the manorial system applied to modern circumstances, as set out in *Past and Present*. Indeed he took the theory of the decentralised community to its extreme, just as he did with the theory of the centralised state, thereby bringing into sharper focus one of the main tensions inherent in the reformism of his predecessors. At the same time the scheme reveals the major difference that marked him off from the romantics treated in this book. *Past and Present*, as in the works of Southey and later of Disraeli and Kingsley, was based on the conception of the Middle Ages as an ethical and structural model capable of being adapted to present and future conditions. It could therefore go hand in hand with technological and industrial progress. Carlyle himself even regarded industry as 'the voice of God' in his day. Hence the Captains of Industry were urged to perform the functions of the medieval aristocracy in a neo-feudal system. The metaphor of Ruskin's guild, on the other hand, was of St George pitted against the dragon of industry 'vomiting black venom into the waters of life'.[201]

Like Carlyle, Ruskin saw work in modern society as 'the great reverse of Creation'.[202] However, whereas Carlyle identified the cause not in work as an activity but in the light in which it is regarded, Ruskin attributed it to the mechanical routine and uncreative nature of industrial labour. For him the machine was the antithesis of both nature and humanity: '... the powers of Nature are depressed or perverted together with the Spirit of Man'.[203] Consequently, the feudalism he advocated was a literal return to the conditions of pre-industrial England, with its ideal of the individual creative craftsman. In so doing, he raised the fundamental question of the reduction of the specific quality of man as *Homo Faber* by mass machine-production which transformed the worker into an unthinking robot. He was, more than his predecessors, alive to the modern problem presented so graphically by Chaplin in *Modern Times*, one which actual robotism is seeking to solve in the computer age. His own solution, however, was a reactionary escapism bearing little relevance to modern life. Strangely enough, not only did industrial England carry out many of the reforms which, in the wake of Southey and Carlyle, he had advocated, but as a 'violent Tory of the Old School'[204] he became one of the most powerful influences on British socialism in its most formative period.

Notes

1. See R. McKenzie, A. Silver, *Angels in Marble* (Chicago and London: University of Chicago Press, 1968), especially pp. 18-73. In claiming to have always been the party of national reform, Tory propaganda even advanced the thesis that the party had already championed the Reform Bill prior to the French Revolution, an effort foiled by the machinations of Fox and the Whigs. See e.g. *War and Reform*, Handysheet no. 2, and *The Unreformed Parliament*, Handysheet no. 5, 1880 elections.

2. W.D. Jones, *Lord Derby and Victorian Conservatism* (Oxford: Basil Blackwell, 1956), p. 193.

3. C. Driver, *Tory Radical, the Life of Richard Oastler* (New York: Oxford University Press, 1946), p. 400.

4. J.F. Bulley (ed.), *Speeches on the Conservative Policy of the Last Thirty Years* (London: John Camden Holton, 1870), p. viii.

5. A Tory, 'Lord Beaconsfield — Why we follow him', *The Contemporary Review*, XXXVI (December 1879), p. 681.

6. C.W. Dilke, *Mr. Dilke on Mr. Disraeli's Manifesto* (London: Pit and Son, pamphlet, 1868), p. 2.

7. P.W. Wilson (ed.), *The Greville Diary* (London: William Heinemann, 1927), vol. II, p. 407.

8. *Memorials of Lord Beaconsfield, Reprint from The Standard* (London: Macmillan, 1881), p. 6.

9. B. Disraeli, *Whigs and Whiggism*, W. Hutcheon (ed.) (Port Washington, New York: Kennikat Press, 1971), p. 33.
10. Quoted in W. Maynell, *The Man Disraeli* (London: Hutchinson and Co., 1927), p. 30.
11. R. Blake, *Disraeli* (London: Methuen, 1966), p. 190.
12. R. Blake, 'The Rise of Disraeli' in H.R. Trevor-Roper (ed.), *Essays in British History Presented to Sir Keith Feiling* (London: Macmillan, 1964), pp. 227-8, Cf. R. O'Kell, 'Disraeli's *Coningsby*: Political Manifesto or Psychological Romance'. *Victorian Studies*, XXIII (Autumn 1979), pp. 57-78.
13. B. Disraeli, *The Works of Benjamin Disraeli, Earl of Beaconsfield* (London and New York: M. Walter Dunne, 1904), vol. I, p. 215.
14. Ibid., vol. I, pp. 211, 215.
15. See R. Garnett, *Shelley and Lord Beaconsfield* (London: printed for private circulation, Richard Clay and Sons, 1887).
16. Disraeili, *Works*, vol. X, pp. 290, 284; vol. XI, p. 91.
17. B. Disraeli, *The Revolutionary Epic*, Bk I, XXIX, XXXIX; Bk II, VI, XVI, XLIII.
18. Disraeli, *Works*, vol. XI, pp. 34-5, 98, 61.
19. Disraeli, *Whigs and Whiggism*, pp. 20, 22. Influences on Disraeli's historical conceptions may be traced in earlier writings. An example is Mr Grey's disquisition on the unsteady evolution of mankind towards perfectibility. 'Moral powers', he said, should keep pace with 'our physical ones', and their failure to do so impeded regular progress. Contemporary technological and industrial expansion, whatever its benefits, had outstripped spiritual growth, and consequently, 'we are all studying science [while] none of us are studying ourselves'. But this can only be a passing phase in the onward march of 'an improving race'. Disraeli, *Works*, vol. I, pp. 33-4.
20. Disraeli, *Whigs and Whiggism*, p. 341.
21. Ibid., pp. 124-5.
22. W.F. Monypenny, G.E. Buckle, *The Life of Benjamin Disraeli* (London: John Murray, 1929), vol. I, pp. 311-12.
23. Disraeli, *Whigs and Whiggism*, p. 138.
24. Ibid., p. 140.
25. Disraeli, *Works*, vol. XIV, p. 107.
26. Disraeli, *Whigs and Whiggism*, pp. 328, 349.
27. Ibid., pp. 77, 81, 109, 336, 333.
28. Ibid., p. 338.
29. Ibid., p. 80.
30. Ibid., pp. 91-2.
31. Ibid., p. 230.
32. Ibid., p. 349.
33. Ibid., pp. 226-7.
34. Ibid., p. 340.
35. Ibid., p. 108.
36. Ibid., p. 218.
37. R. Faber, *Beaconsfield and Bolingbroke* (London: Faber and Faber, 1961), pp. 69-70.
38. Disraeli, *Whigs and Whiggism*, p. 221; Monypenny, Buckle, *The Life of Benjamin Disraeli*, vol. 1, p. 462.
39. Hansard, *Parliamentary Debates*, 3rd series, vol. XLIX (1839), pp. 246-52.
40. Monypenny, Buckle, *The Life of Benjamin Disraeli*, vol. II, p. 88.
41. Ibid., vol. I, pp. 564, 527.
42. C.G. Duffy, *Conversations with Carlyle* (London: Sampson, Low, Houston and Co., 1862), p. 13.

43. T. Carlyle, *The Works of Thomas Carlyle in Thirty Volumes*, H.D. Traill (ed.), (London: Chapman and Hall, 1907), vol. XXVII, p. 60.
44. The Marquis of Zetland (ed.), *The Letters of Disraeli to Lady Bradford and Lady Chesterfield* (London: Earnest Benn, 1929), vol. II, p. 9. Disraeli was discussing in this connection his early novel *Alroy*. This is clearly a slip of memory, for the novel preceeded Carlyle's winning of public attention. The admission itself, however, is significant.
45. J.C. Shairp, *Aspects of Poetry* (Oxford: Oxford University Press, 1881), p. 412.
46. D. Blair, *Carlylianism and Christianity: Notes on a Lecture by the Rev. W. Henderson* (Melbourne: W.B. Stephens, 1865), pp. 8, 20.
47. See e.g. Blake, *Disraeli*, pp. 191-2; J. Robertson, *Modern Humanists* (Port Washington, New York: Kennikat Press, 1968), pp. 52-3; D. Masson, *Carlyle Personally and in his Writings* (London: Hodder and Stoughton, 1895), p. 67.
48. J.A. Lovat-Fraser, *Disraeli* (London: Barry Dock News, pamphlet, n.d.), p. 2.
49. Disraeli, *Works*, vol. XV, pp. 190-3; vol. XIV, p. 92.
50. Ibid., vol. XII, pp. 159, 316-19 *passim*.
51. T.E. Kebble (ed.), *Selected Speeches of the Earl of Beaconsfield* (London: Longmans, Green and Co., 1882), vol. I, pp. 50-1.
52. Disraeli, *Works*, vol. XIV, chap. X.
53. Kebble (ed.), *Selected Speeches of the Earl of Beaconsfield*, vol. I, p. 443.
54. Disraeli, *Works*, vol. XIV, p. 176.
55. Ibid., vol. XV, p. 137.
56. Ibid., vol. XIV, p. 117.
57. Ibid. pp. 241-2.
58. Ibid., vol. XII, pp. 203-11 *passim*.
59. Ibid., pp. 94.
60. Ibid., p. 165.
61. Ibid., pp. 93-109 *passim*.
62. Ibid., pp. 132-4.
63. Monypenny, Buckle, *The Life of Benjamin Disraeli*, vol. I, p. 629.
64. Disraeli, *Works*, vol. XIV, p. 93.
65. Ibid., p. 183.
66. Ibid., p. 31.
67. Kebble (ed.), *Selected Speeches of the Earl of Beaconsfield*, vol. I, p. 178.
68. Disraeli, *Works*, vol. XIV, pp. 157, 183, 216.
69. Ibid., p. 283.
70. Kebble (ed.), *Selected Speeches of the Earl of Beaconsfield*, vol. I, p. 139.
71. B. Disraeli, 'General Preface', *The Collected Novels and Tales of the R. Honourable Benjamin Disraeli* (London: Longmans, Green and Co., 1870), vol. I, p. xiii.
72. Disraeli, *Works*, vol. XIV, p. 200.
73. Ibid., pp. 231-2.
74. Ibid., p. 234.
75. Ibid., vol. XV, p. 127.
76. Ibid., vol. XV, p. 154.
77. Bulley (ed.), *Speeches on the Conservative Policy of the Last Thirty Years*, p. 42.
78. Disraeli, *Works*, vol. XIV, p. 395.
79. Ibid., vol. XII, p. 15.
80. Ibid., p. 50.
81. Ibid., p. 341.
82. Ibid., pp. 212-32 *passim*; vol. XIV, p. 214.

83. Ibid., vol. XIV, pp. 262, 159.
84. Ibid., vol. XV, pp. 92-3.
85. Kebble (ed.), *Selected Speeches of the Earl of Beaconsfield*, vol. II, pp. 487-8.
86. Disraeli, 'General Preface', p. ix.
87. Keeble (ed.), *Selected Speeches of the Earl of Beaconsfield*, vol. II, pp. 506-11.
88. Ibid., pp. 531-2.
89. B. Disraeli, *Address as Lord Rector of the University of Glasgow, November 19th, 1873* (London: National Union of Conservative and Constitutional Associations, Central Press, 1873), p. 10.
90. P.R. Ghosh, 'Disraelian Conservatism: A Financial Approach', *The English Historical Review*, XCIX (April 1984), pp. 268-96.
91. F. Kingsley, *Charles Kingsley, His Letters and Memories of His Life* (London: Kegan Paul, Trench & Co., 1884), p. 57.
92. Ibid., p. 58.
93. S.E. Baldwin, *Charles Kingsley* (Ithaca: Cornell University Press, 1934), p. 52.
94. Kingsley, *Charles Kingsley, His Letters and Memories of his Life*, pp. 10, 17.
95. Ibid., p. 28.
96. Ibid., pp. 32-3.
97. Ibid., pp. 41-3.
98. Ibid., p. 49.
99. Ibid., p. 57.
100. Ibid., p. 49.
101. Ibid., p. 50.
102. Ibid., p. 44.
103. Ibid.
104. Ibid. Maurice himself, it should be remembered, owed not a little to the romantics, especially Coleridge and Carlyle. See e.g., C.R. Sanders, *Coleridge and the Broad Church Movement* (Durham: Duke University Press, 1942), pp. 217-39 and H.G. Wood, *Frederick Denison Maurice* (Cambridge University Press, 1950), chap. II.
105. Kingsley, *Charles Kingsley, His Letters and Memories of his Life*, p. 23.
106. Ibid., pp. 63-4.
107. C. Kingsley, *The Works of Charles Kingsley* (Hildesheim: Georg Olms Verlagsbuchhandlung, 1968-9), vol. III, p. 104.
108. Kingsley, *Charles Kingsley, His Letters and Memories of his Life*, pp. 92-3.
109. *The Christian Socialist*, 30th November, 1850.
110. Kingsley, *Charles Kingsley, His Letters and Memories of his Life*, p. 71.
111. C. Kingsley, *The Limits of Exact Science as Applied to History* (Cambridge: Macmillan, 1860), p. 25.
112. Ibid.
113. Ibid., p. 60.
114. *The Christian Socialist*, 8th February, 1851.
115. Kingsley, *The Limits of Exact Science*, p. 34.
116. *The Christian Socialist*, 8th February, 1851.
117. *Politics for the People*, 6th May, 1848, 1st July, 1848.
118. Kingsley, *Works*, vol. XXIII, pp. 297-8.
119. Kingsley, *The Limits of Exact Science*, p. 39.
120. Kingsley, *Works*, vol. I, p. 249; vol. III, pp. xviii, xix.
121. Ibid., vol. XXIII, p. 298.
122. Kingsley, *The Limits of Exact Science*, pp. 8, 35.

123. *The Christian Socialist*, 22nd February, 1851, 22nd March, 1851. See also *Works*, vol. XVI, pp. 6-7.
124. Kingsley, *The Limits of Exact Science*, p. 43.
125. Kingsley, *Works*, vol. XVI, p. 85.
126. Ibid., vol. I, p. 249.
127. Kingsley, *Works*, vol. XVIII, p. 277.
128. Ibid., p. 278.
129. *The Christian Socialist*, 2nd November, 1850.
130. *Politics for the People*, 27th May, 1847.
131. Kingsley, *Works*, vol. III, pp. xxix, 433.
132. Kingsley, *Works*, vol. XX, pp. 37-8, 140, 44-5. Arnold may have had Kingsley's phrase in mind in the well-known passage of the *Grand Chartreuse*, and both are reminiscent of Carlyle's diagnosis in 'Signs of the Times'.
133. *The Christian Socialist*, 26th April, 1851.
134. Kingsley, *Works*, vol. XX, pp. 37-8, 140, 44-5.
135. *Politics for the People*, 13th May, 1848; *The Christian Socialist*, 4th December, 1850.
136. Kingsley, *Works*, vol. VIII, chap. XXI especially pp. 377-9. See H.R. Harrington, 'Charles Kingsley's Fallen Athelete', *Victorian Studies*, XXI (Autumn 1977), pp. 73-86.
137. *Politics for the People*, 13th May, 1848, 27th May, 1848, 17th June, 1848; Kingsley, *Works*, vol. XXIII, p. 304.
138. *The Christian Socialist* 15th November, 1851.
139. C. Kingsley, *The Application of Associative Principles and Methods to Agriculture* (London: James Belzer, pamphlet, 1851).
140. Kingsley, *Works*, vol. II, p. xi.
141. *The Christian Socialist*, 15th November, 22nd November and 29th November 1851; Kingsley, *The Application of Associative Principles and Methods to Agriculture*, pp. 47, 55.
142. Kingsley, *Works*, vol. XXIII, p. 303.
143. Ibid., vol. XVIII, pp. 207, 215-16.
144. C. Kingsley, *Miscellanies* (London: John W. Parker and Sons, 1859), vol. II, p. 196.
145. *The Christian Socialist*, 22nd November, 1851, 15th November, 1851; Kingsley, *Miscellanies*, vol. II, p. 202.
146. Kingsley, *Works*, vol. XVI, p. 263.
147. *The Christian Socialist*, 14th December, 1850.
148. J. Ruskin, *The Works of John Ruskin*, E.T. Cook, A. Wedderburn (eds.) (London: George Allen, 1905), vol. XXXV, pp. 219-20.
149. Ibid., vol. III, p. 4.
150. J. Evans, *John Ruskin* (London: Jonathan Cape, 1954), p. 324; see also the editor's introduction in Ruskin, *Works*, vol. XXVII, p. xix. Contrast the view of N. Shrimpton, '"Rust and Dust": Ruskin's Pivotal Work' in R. Hewison (ed.), *New Approaches to Ruskin* (London: Routledge and Kegal Paul, 1981), especially p. 51.
151. Quoted in P. Quennell, *John Ruskin, the Portrait of a Prophet* (London: Collins, 1949), p. 163.
152. Ruskin, *Works*, vol. III, p. xxiv; vol. XXVI, p. 75.
153. T. Carlyle, *The Works of Thomas Carlyle in Thirty Volumes*, H.D. Traill (ed.) (London: Chapman and Hall, 1907), vol. I, p. 123.
154. Ruskin, *Works*, vol. III, p. xxiv.
155. Ibid., vol. XXVIII, p. 22; vol. XXVI, p. xcvi; vol. XXVII, pp. 179-80, vol. XXIX, p. 539. In his diary Ruskin records how Carlyle even appeared to him in a vivid dream. See J. Evans, J.H. Whitehouse (eds.), *The Diaries of John Ruskin* (Oxford: Clarendon, 1958), vol. II, p. 645.

156. F.W. Roe, *The Social Philosophy of Carlyle and Ruskin* (Port Washington, New York: Kennikat Press, 1969). The recent collection of *The Correspondence of Thomas Carlyle and John Ruskin*, G.A. Cate (ed.) (Stanford: Stanford University Press, 1982) which includes 114 letters hitherto unpublished is a further major contribution to research in this field.
157. Ruskin, *Works*, vol. VIII, pp. 191-2.
158. Ibid., vol. IV, pp. 30-3.
159. Ruskin, *Works*, vol. VIII, p. 190.
160. Evans and Whitehouse (eds.), *The Diaries of John Ruskin*, vol. II, p. 366.
161. Ruskin, *Works*, vol. VIII, p. 30.
162. Ibid., vol. X, p. 214.
163. Ibid., pp. 185-7.
164. Ibid., p. 67.
165. Ibid., p. 190.
166. Ibid., pp. 190, 193, cf. Carlyle, *Works*, vol. X, Bk III, chap. XIII.
167. Ruskin, *Works*, vol. XVII, pp. 137, 444, 447.
168. Ibid., vol. X, p. 193.
169. Ibid., vol. XXVII, p. 133.
170. Ibid., p. 80.
171. Cf. Ruskin's letter to J. Llewelyn Davies, 1st November, 1862: '... the form in which Christianity is at present preached in England is the most fatal cause of human crime and suffering now extant on the earth' C. Davies (ed.), *From a Victorian Post Bag* (London: Peter Davis, 1926), p. 15.
172. Ruskin, *Works*, vol. X, p. 196.
173. Ibid., p. 192. See also vol. XVIII, pp. 426-7.
174. Ibid., vol. X, p. 194.
175. Ibid., vol. VIII, p. 207; vol. XVII, p. 75. For an earlier formulation see vol. XV, p. 26.
176. Ibid., vol. XVII, pp. 145-6, 287.
177. Ibid., pp. 25-30 *passim*.
178. Ibid., pp. 78, 80, 169; vol. XXVII, p. 48.
179. Ibid., vol. XVI, pp. 28-9.
180. Ibid., vol. XVII, p. 149.
181. Ibid., p. 48.
182. Ibid., p. 105.
183. Ibid., pp. 88-9.
184. Ibid., p. 394.
185. Ibid., vol. XVIII, p. 494.
186. Ibid., vol. X, pp. 196-7.
187. Ibid., vol. XVII, p. 328.
188. Ibid., pp. 248, 74.
189. Ibid., p. 79.
190. Ibid., vol. XVIII, pp. 498; vol. XVII, pp. 41, 336, 321.
191. Ibid., vol. XVI, p. 26.
192. Ibid., p. 25.
193. Ibid., p. 27.
194. Ibid., vol. XVII, pp. 21-2.
195. Ibid., vol. XVII, pp. 378-81 *passim*.
196. Ibid., vol. XXVII, p. 47.
197. Ibid., p. 95.
198. Ibid., p. 20.
199. Ibid., pp. 327-8.
200. Ibid., vol. XXX, p. 95. See also vol. XXVII, pp. xiv, xxviii, 22.
201. Ibid., vol. XXVII, p. 293. See P.L. Sawyer, 'Ruskin and St. George: The

Dragon-Killing Myth in "Fors Clarigera"', *Victorian Studies*, XXIII (Autumn 1979), pp. 5-28.
202. Ruskin, *Works*, vol. XXVII, p. 177.
203. Ibid., p. 615.
204. Ibid., vol. XXX, p. 13.

6 THE WORKING MAN AS HERO: HARDIE, BLATCHFORD AND THE ILP

I

In his pamphlet *What made me a Socialist*, F.W. Jowett, a founding member of the Independent Labour Party (ILP) and Commissioner of Works in the first Labour cabinet, described his political development as falling into three stages. At the age of 14 he read Carlyle's *Past and Present* which was his initial step towards the 'Socialist faith'. Later he came across Ruskin's *Unto This Last* and became a full socialist, though as yet ignorant of the term. Finally, he learned the correct label on reading Morris's *Useful Work against Useless Toil*.[1] Morris himself, in an article bearing almost the same title as Jowett's, also claimed descent from Carlyle, 'the glory of England', and Ruskin who 'before my days of practical Socialism was my master towards the ideal aforesaid'.[2] Examples could be multiplied to show how British socialist leaders regarded Carlyle and Ruskin, in Tom Mann's words, as teachers of the 'correct spirit in which the modern crusade against our social villainies is to be conducted'.[3] Indeed, in 1906, of the 51 Labour and Lib-Lab M.P.s, the 45 who answered Stead's questionnaire on 'The Labour Party and the Books that Helped to Make it' concurred that apart from the Bible it was Carlyle and Ruskin who had the greatest formative influence on their views.[4]

From its inception the Labour Party was a coalition of organisations of different ideological tints, and any attempts to go beyond a broad definition of its principles threaten its unity. Moreover, like all systems of ideas employed as weapons in the battle of politics, its doctrines have been subject to fluctuations in priorities and emphases according to circumstances. Nevertheless, some of the doctrines were basic and distinctive. The acknowledgments quoted above trace back to Carlyle and his followers a complex of ideas that marked the party off from its counterparts on the continent. The influence was not restricted to any one group of the British socialists active round about the turn of the century. Morris disseminated Ruskinism from the platforms of various organisations, notably the Social Democratic Federation (SDF). Headlam preached Christian Socialism from within the Fabian Society. But the major stream of British Socialism and the closest to the Carlylean fountainhead was the 'Ethical Socialism'[5] of the ILP. This chapter will examine the romantic heritage of British socialism chiefly as reflected in the speeches and writings of two of the founding members of the Party, Keir Hardie and Robert Blatchford. It will also offer occasional comparisons with the opinions of two other leaders, Ramsay MacDonald and Bruce Glasier, to show that their views were representative of a large body of socialists before the First World War.

Hardie was a practical politician who underwent a long process of soul-searching before he finally found himself, in his own words, as a 'wandering agitator'[6] of socialism and the first ILP leader. He described his intellectual growth as resulting from two related conversions.[7] One was religious. Brought up in a free-thinking home he became a fervent Christian, and though later he no longer attended Church regularly, a strong religious tinge always coloured his thought. The other was political. Brought up to believe in self-seeking individualism he adopted the principle of altruism as the true basis of social life. This was largely due to the early influence of two fellow Scots, Burns and Carlyle. The reading of *Sartor Resartus* at the age of 16, he wrote, was 'a real turning point, and I went through the book three times in succession until the spirit of it somehow entered into me. Since then ... I still remained a worshipper at his [Carlyle's] shrine'.[8] To the end of his life he could 'pity the man ... who can read Carlyle without finding light'.[9]

The convergence of these religious and social attitudes accounts for the close kinship between Hardie's opinions and Christian Socialism during the early phase of his political career as a trade union leader and Liberal activist. Broadly recalling the monied Dandies and day Drudges of *Sartor Resartus*, he argued that 'there must always be some "born to rule" just as the great majority of us are "born to obey" '.[10] This demanded of the former the sense of responsibility and obligation which had become so eroded that a gap had grown between the 'walking money bags' and the workers who were 'compelled to drudge'. The employers who cannot 'occupy the position of commander[s] will perish in the future "struggle for existence" between "Mind v. Money" '.[11] But the moral elevation of the workers was no less essential for national salvation, and 'the first step towards the coming emancipation [was] that the liquor traffic be put down'.[12] A practical step towards the good society was to follow the prescription of *Past and Present*, the book which he said gave him his first insights into politics and economics. Enlightened employers would advance the good employees through profit-sharing schemes, providing thereby a stimulus for other workers and ensuring the close collaboration of leaders and led. The value to both would serve as a general model to all, till 'Capital and Labour shall meet together' and consign to oblivion 'all feelings of discord that ever existed between those twin brothers whose best interests are united'.[13]

When Hardie became a convinced socialist is in dispute.[14] It came upon him not as a revelation but as the result of the gradual realisation that good-will alone was not sufficient. What was required was the intervention of the state by legislation and nationalisation, and this could only come about through the efforts of a dedicated and independent Labour party. The process had already started by the end of 1886, when he persuaded the Cummock Debating and Literary Society to support Henry George's scheme for legislation 'on the lines of Socialism until the People are in possession of the land'. But the decisive step came with the ruthless suppression of the miners' strikes of 1887. The reluctance of the Liberals to put up working-class candidates for Parliament and the hesitations of the Lib-Labs to support such labour reforms as the reduction of working hours of boy-miners strengthened his conviction that 'if there was to be a labour party in the House of Commons at all, it would require to be a party pledged to the interests of labour alone, and not tacked on to the tail end of any political party'.[15] In the parliamentary elections of 1888 he unsuccessfully stood as a Liberal candidate for Mid-Lanark against the expressed will of the local party and in opposition to their official nominee. Though he pledged loyalty to the general party line he reserved the right of independent action in support of such legislation as setting up Arbitration Courts, fixing minimum wages and maximum working hours, and compulsory cultivation of all unexploited arable land. Such government action and the breaches of the principle of the freedom of contract were justified by appeal to the authority of Carlyle.[16] What was in his mind can be judged when one remembers that he had been engaged for nearly a year in planning the Scottish Labour Party which was formally launched only a month after the election. Furthermore, the scope of his proposals for the collective melioration of the conditions of labour can be understood in the light of his later declaration that the campaign brought home to him that what was needed was not only a party to look after the interests of workers, but a party to represent the ideology of socialism.[17] As yet, however, he still thought of an independent party as a lever for bringing pressure to bear on the policies of the major parties. In his December 1889 invitation to the Tory Randolph Churchill to address the Ayrshire Miners' Association he wrote: 'As working men we are prepared to give support to any candidate for parliamentary honours who will, when returned, support measures for ... the general social elevation of the masses.'[18] In the same year he was sent as a delegate to the Paris Convention which established the Second Socialist International. This, as well as the correspondence he held with Engels, led to the final crystallisation of his thought. Henceforth he looked for a radical change of the economic structure of society to be achieved by a self-reliant party seeking to organise the working classes to become the leading political power of the land. The leading role he played in the founding of the ILP was the first step towards the realisation of this ideal.

As chairman of the Bradford Conference at which the new party was set up, Hardie crossed swords for the first time with Robert Blatchford, the leader of the 'Clarionettes' who formed a distinct group within the Socialist-Labour movement. A brilliant largely self-taught journalist and author, Blatchford arrived at his socialism by a very different route. Unlike Hardie, whose views were forged on the anvil of political activity and experience, his were the outcome of the intellectual education he imposed on himself and the connections he drew between his reading and the grim facts he observed in the slums of the big industrial cities. 'Largely,' he wrote, 'we are made by what we *read when we are young.*'[19] He himself had been 'roused' in childhood by Dickens, and in maturity by other authors — more particularly 'Grand old Carlyle, Giant, hero, genius, master of us all. Greater than we of his own day can see; the most forcible, the most imaginative, the most virile, the most poetical prose writer the world has ever known'.[20] As 'a kind of recruiting sergeant'[21] whose particular duty was 'to make Socialists' he urged his readers, taking himself as a model, to start their study of socialism with the works of Carlyle which would be 'a revelation and education to [them]'.[22]

Blatchford's first encounter with the writings of 'the master' occurred during his service in the forces, where he rose to the rank of sergeant and gained the army's second-class certificate of education. 'I have read some ... of Carlyle's [books] over and over again', he confided to his future biographer Laurence Thompson, 'I have read *Heroes and Hero Worship* through about six or seven times, slowly and carefully. I have studied *Sartor Resartus* and some others.'[23] After his demobilisation he worked for some years as a clerk, but continued his self-education spurred on by the ambition of a writing career. This he began as a desultory journalist, and by 1885 he became a regular staff member of a London newspaper. His transfer shortly afterwards to the Manchester *Sunday Chronicle* owned by the same proprietor proved a decisive step in his development. Shocked by the appalling poverty and housing conditions in the slums of the great industrial city and searching for a remedy, he came across the famous pamphlet by Hyndman and Morris, *A Summary of the Principles of Socialism* (1884). As he stated in his autobiography, it showed him the way in which a cruel chaotic society could be made to conform to those values that he had absorbed through his reading and experienced in the army: '... human brotherhood and co-operation ... collective action ... [and] a large, deeper, nobler *ésprit de corps*'.[24]

Stimulated by his discovery, he took part in establishing the Manchester Fabian Society, formed a close relationship with the local SDF, and toyed for a while with the idea of contesting the coming elections as Independent Labour candidate for East Bradford. He found, however, that he could be more useful to the cause by following his natural bent. According to Thompson, Carlyle's comparison in *Heroes and Hero-Worship* of the Church and the press as means of directing the people towards right living strongly affected his decision as well as his style of writing. In a letter to a friend Blatchford wrote: 'I can see what no other man in England can see, and that is the way to convert the people to Socialism. But ... it means the sacrifice of my life.'[25] The first of his sacrifices was his resignation from the *Chronicle*, following on the owner's demand that he cease using the paper as a platform for his socialist sermons. He thereupon took the lead in starting *The Clarion* with a view to hastening the coming of the new order and preparing his readers for the inevitable change. In line with this objective he came to support the SDF demand for an independent Labour course as against the Fabian 'permeation policy' of working through other parties. The outcome was the founding in May

1892 of the Manchester ILP in the office of *The Clarion*. Blatchford drafted its constitution, the fourth clause of which stipulated that socialists must abstain from voting where no socialist or Labour representative stood for election. This was to be the grounds of the first clash between him and Hardie at the Bradford Conference.

What came to the fore was not merely disagreement over tactics but their fundamentally different temperaments and conceptions of what constituted a socialist party. For Hardie, the first stage on the road to socialism was the improvement of the educational and economic conditions of the working classes to render them capable of constituting the vanguard of the nation in the march towards a better society. The party therefore was an organisation whose primary function was to fight for their political representation and to utilise such power to raise their standard of living and cultural status. In a way, it was analogous to a trade union, 'a federation for political purposes on the same lines as the Miners' Federation is for trade purposes'. This required a 'broad tolerant catholicity' of views, a considerable degree of flexibility, the capacity to compromise and the readiness to co-operate with any individual or party if the cause could benefit thereby.[26] Blatchford's major premise, on the other hand, was the pre-eminence of principle and the preservation of ideological purity. What the workers lacked, he argued, was not power but the compass by which its direction could be charted:

> If the people, having so much power now, make no use of it, why are we to assume that all they need is a little more power to make them healthy, and wealthy, and wise? ... practical politics are hopeless and ... practical politicians — not *quite* so wise as they imagine.

Compromise and expediency were therefore anathema to him. Rather, the party should be an educational organisation consisting of 'a small army of devoted and heroic volunteers' whose duty is 'to fan the divine embers of love into a flame ... [and] make clear to all men the truth, justice, and wisdom of socialism'.[27]

The differences of opinion between Hardie and Blatchford were not confined, however, to party strategy or issues that turned on matters of theory. They were liable to flare up whenever some major concrete policy had to be decided. A critical example, which led to the ILP boycott of *The Clarion* and all the publications associated with it, was their policies on the Boer war, which also serves to show that they were far from being single-minded in their views. Hardie, the practical politician, took his stand on socialist principles, denouncing the war as one of 'financiers seeking to secure higher dividends through reducing the wages of white workers and enslaving the black workers'.[28] Blatchford, the ideologist, was moved by emotional nationalism and personal attraction to army life to direct his vituperation against the 'cant' of the anti-imperialist 'peace-mongers' among the radicals and socialists:

> I am a Socialist ... but I am also an Englishman ... I am also an old soldier and I love Tommy Atkins ... I cannot go with those Socialists whose sympathies are with the enemy. My whole heart is with the British troops.[29]

Such incompatible approaches, theoretical and practical, led to considerable personal rancour. Hardie, while expressing appreciation of his opponent's service to socialism through his books, considered that for his own peace of mind he would well be advised to leave politics to others.[30] In a less charitable mood he accused him of appealing only to the 'narrow, selfish, egotistic, hen-brained type of reformer, whose mission in life is to keep the average man humble'.[31] Blatchford for his part tried for some 20 years to incite the rank and file against Hardie and the ILP leadership. 'I cannot honestly give any public support to [him], nor write about him in an appreciable way', he wrote in *The Clarion*.[32] In private letters he was more forthright: '... he has been vain, greedy, crooked, and bumptious. I think he has been a failure and has done a great deal of harm. I think he has nearly ruined the ILP which would have done well but for him'.[33]

And yet, seen in the lengthening perspective of time, the differences, so acute when viewed in detail and at close quarters, pale before the general ideas they held in common. What takes shape is precisely the Carlylean element that inspired them and which each tinged in his own way.

II

Any consideration of the mainstream of British socialism at the turn of the century must take account of the impact of diverse, earlier and contemporary forces such as Owenism and Marxism in addition to the influence of Carlyle, whether direct or mediated through the first generation of his disciples. We may indeed begin by noting where the doctrines of the nascent Labour movement departed from Carlyleanism. The first difference relates to their egalitarianism. On the face of it, this was the logical conclusion of the antipathy for the 'parasitical Dandies' and industrial exploiters and the sympathy for the toiling victims of capitalism, emotions so widely felt and so powerfully expressed by the romantics we have discussed. In fact, Shelley had adopted such a position, and his impact was still considerable. *Queen Mab* was declared to be 'the Chartists' Bible', other poems were repeatedly printed in the working-class press, and Bernard Shaw described himself in youth as plunging 'head over heals' into his works and reading 'every word he published'. Nor was the ILP unaffected by Shelley's theories. For example, an article entitled 'Shelley as a political thinker' that appeared in the party's *Labour Leader* described the poet as anticipating the ideas of the Fabian Society and enunciating 'some of those great truths that are only now beginning to find a home in the hearts and minds of men'.[34] Nevertheless, within the tradition under consideration, the main influence was rather that of Carlyle, Ruskin and to a lesser extent Kingsley, a group that sought greater distributive justice as a means for preserving the paternalism of the hierarchical order of society. Carlyle described the call for freedom and equality as a mere negative reaction, the despairing cry of a nation under the heel of uncaring and selfish governors; Kingsley still looked to the aristocracy as the natural rulers of the people; and Ruskin proclaimed: 'Liberty and equality — I detest the one and deny of possibility of the other'.[35]

Another departure of the ILP from Carlyleanism touches on the nationalisation of the means of production and distribution. This again would seem to be a normal development of the conception of the state as a supra-class entity and the major agent of reform that has been noted in the theories propounded by the romantics, especially since the British Socialists unlike their continental counterparts envisaged its strengthening rather than withering away with the coming of the new order. However, their commitment to egalitarianism led them to demand nationalisation of a scope wholly incompatable with the Southey-Carlyle-Ruskin tradition. Though the effect of late-nineteenth-century theorists such as

Marx and Henry George must not be discounted, it should be remembered that such ideas had their roots in the doctrines of earlier radicals like Hodgskin, Bray and the Owenites.

Finally, one might point to a third difference relating to the part played by the working class in instituting the new order. Francis Johnson, Hardie's friend and colleague, claimed that his efforts in building up a party to represent the workers were inspired by Carlyle's prediction in *Past and Present* that 'this they call organisation of Labour is the problem of the whole future'.[36] Yet, whatever the weight to be attached to such testimony, there can be little doubt that Carlyle's use of the Saint-Simonian phrase 'organisation of labour' could in no way imply the setting up of a workers' party. For Southey the attempt to organise the workers politically was a threat to society. Carlyle regarded the Chartist Movement as indicating a severe crisis characteristic of a period of transition. Kingsley, it is true, advocated the extension of the franchise to the workers, and Ruskin joined in his call on them to play a part in the building of the new society. But both accepted the Master's conception of the just order as brought about by a leader or by superiors in the social hierarchy.

Notwithstanding such discrepancies, there was some common ground between the Socialists' idea of their party as fulfilling an essentially ethical function and the doctrines of Carlyle and his school. This lay in the shared view that society is based on moral principles from which the interrelations between its members and the nature of its institutions derive. 'Every ... problem of life', Hardie wrote, 'is at bottom a question of morals';[37] while Blatchford suggested that man's activities spring from instinct and from sentiments that have their origins in basic moral attitudes, whereas reason merely serves 'to support their action'. Efforts to eradicate social ills by tinkering with the 'machinery of society' were consequently no more than the treatment of external symptoms.[38] The policy of the Socialist Party therefore was to achieve its goals through the moral persuasion of the nation, or in Ramsay MacDonald's words, 'the bombardment' of a 'morally inefficient state of society' by 'new crusading ideals'.[39] The very vocabulary they used was that of religion. Just as Carlyle's Hero served as a channel for the *lux mundi*, so the 'new theology' would replace the egotism which had filled the vacuum left by the waning of true belief. For Hardie it answered the need to 'bring dead and decaying and putrifying creeds out of the dustholes'.[40] Blatchford, drawing on the imagery of *Past and Present*, declared the 'New Religion' as engaged in a holy war against the gospel of the 'dead sea apes', the industrial 'buccaneers' and 'scalp-hunters'.[41] A.M. Thompson summed it all up in his declaration that socialism was 'a religion or a moral system rather than a party programme'.[47]

This did not preclude differences on the relationship between the new religion and the old. Hardie, as an avowed Christian, regarded socialism as the 'embodiment of Christianity in our industrial system'[43] and believed that if the Church would reassume her rightful place as the 'repository of the national conscience'[44] she could guide the forces working the change. Blatchford, as an avowed agnostic,[45] preached 'the most uncompromising standard of holiness ... without any admixture of "spiritual Christianity" '[46] and saw no role for the Church to play in bringing about the new order, though he joined Hardie in claiming that the 'New Religion' represented the unperverted basis of Christianity.[47] Nevertheless, both agreed that the established Church had connived at the evils of society and encouraged the ousting of brotherly love by egotism. 'It had bowed the knees to Baal', Hardie charged. Drawing on 'Signs of the Times' and *Sartor Resartus* he denounced it as having become an empty husk: '... between a ritual ... or Carlyle's steam-motored automation, I prefer the latter. There can be neither insensitivity nor hypocrisy about the iron parson worked by steam.'[48] Blatchford maintained that socialism began where the teachings of the contemporary church ended. The latter started with the love of God but stopped short before it came to the neighbour. The former started with the neighbour and was reaching for the stars.[49] Drawing on the *Latter Day Pamphlets* he denounced the statues to Hudson and Mammon set up by the Anglicans moved by the spirit of gentility, the Romanists inspired by pomp and ritual, and Calvinists preaching fire and brimstone. As against all these the only true faith for the age, he proclaimed, was that propagated by Carlyle and his followers.[50]

In spite of the frequent appeal to the authority of Carlyle and the repeated references to his writings, one must beware of regarding him as the 'onlie begetter'. It should not be forgotten that towards the end of the century religion had a strong hold on the main body of miners and industrial workers from among whom Labour recruited its members. As pious Nonconformists brought up on the Bible, it was only natural to appeal to them by presenting socialism as a moral gospel. Nor did such a style originate with the founders of the ILP. Even before Hardie and Blatchford became socialists the term 'new religion' was used by Hyndman and Harris in the pamphlet which helped Blatchford to crystallise his political views. However, such issues as egalitarianism, nationalisation, the worker as Hero and the 'new theology' should not be examined in isolation as self-sufficient doctrines. Rather, they cohere as elements in a wider world-view which leads us back to the stream of thought which is the subject of this book.

The foundation on which Hardie and Blatchford rested their arguments was a theory of man which the former attributed to the gospel of work of Carlyle, to whom the latter added Kingsley.[51] Hardie's approach was coloured with mysticism. We are urged on by an eternal craving to realise the potential within us, thereby fulfilling the supreme fiat of self-fulfilment. This unappeased hunger, 'away down somewhere at the well-spring of life, beyond what the intellect can grasp or the tongue fashion into words', is the reason for our restless ambition, ever reaching for what is beyond our grasp. Art, literature and the intellectual pursuits are one aspect of our striving, but we cannot rest content with them. We must always seek to shape and control the material world, impressing on it the imprint of our own image. Every generation seeks more and better means of satisfying its hunger, and the appetite grows with the eating.[52] The same urge is the source of religious feeling. Echoing *Heroes and Hero-Worship*, he argued that all the religions of the world are no more than different forms of the same 'ideal', the attainment of peace in the human heart by directing man's energy in the right channels[53] towards the principle of perfection which we call 'the Divine Life'.[54]

Blatchford presented a similar belief, though clothed in a secular dress. For him too all religions are attempts to plot the future direction of humanity on its course, which in truth is not towards some undefinable spiritual goal to which we apply the term 'Divine' but towards the 'perfect human ideal', the fullest exploitation of the resources within us by which we may attain 'mental and moral perfection'. Man's final destination, however, is no less mysterious. We are navigators of a ship moving towards a distant unmapped territory and 'cannot steer for the promised land, for it is out of sight'. We can only gauge our direction by the wake, noting and correcting any zig-zagging from the straight line. The track is the record of human culture, of all that has led to our understanding of the world and of our transforming of inert matter into an extension of ourselves. Rare geniuses such as Plato and Shakespeare create the touchstones by which to measure the purity of our spiritual systems. The rest of mankind express their creativity through physical labour, but the hands being 'tools of the brain', this too is a 'fine form of moral and mental discipline and training'. In fact, 'contact with nature and the facts of life is ... more effectual culture than can be got from books or lectures'.[55]

Both men arrived, then, at the conclusion that work is the 'expression of ourselves'[56] and that the freedom to employ one's energies in following one's bent begets the true nobility. Man's creations, springing from his essential creativity, not only modify the way he lives but develop his powers and affect his being. He creates himself by creating his world. Since every generation builds upon the creative achievements of its predecessor, transmitting them with its own to those following as a cumulative legacy from the past to the future, the general advancement of the race along the 'upward path which leads from degradation to we know not what' is assured.[57] Nevertheless, the movement is not in a straight line but constitutes a series of progressions and retrogressions mounting à la Carlyle in a rising spiral, or to use Bruce Glasier's simile, like a deciduous tree which loses its leaves and remains dormant through the winter to renew its growth and foliage in the spring.[58] Like Teufelsdröckh, the god-begotten devils' dung, man has a dual nature, 'the beast-like and the god-like',[59] and the 'spirit of Altruism' wages an eternal combat against 'the isolated Ego'.[60] This, Hardie and Blatchford believed, is true of the individual as well as of the group and forms the basis of all social relationships. Hardie asserted that when the spirit of altruism is in the ascendant social affections are strong and the community represents 'a huge family organisation', assuring constant and harmonious development.[61] Blatchford said that the god-like aspect of man teaches him that 'it is better to become something than to have something', and the resulting activity links the worker to his co-workers and to what he fashions, 'to nature and especially to his fellow man.'[62] However, both agreed that rapid material progress brings with it the domination of the satanic element in man. The hoarding of material wealth is a Frankenstein monster that destroys its creator, Hardie maintained.[63] For, as Jesus taught in the Sermon on the Mount, 'the more [a man] accumulates the more are his thoughts diverted from life itself to the things of life until the things become more important than the life'. Then the craving in our hearts degenerates into possessiveness, greed puts an end to human creativity, and the energy that should be expended in co-operative effort is directed by the individual to snatching whatever he can at the expense of his neighbours.[64] This, Hardie concluded, is what Carlyle meant by the 'cash-nexus'. Blatchford likewise thought that material success leads to the yielding to physical satisfactions which he called 'sensuality' and to its concomitants, 'vanity, narrowness, greed'. These direct human energy from creativity to acquisitiveness, for 'Devil worship' gives neither peace nor joy to those who follow it but ever demands more and more.[65] Such spiritual disease brings each member of society to withdraw into himself and seek his gratifications whatever the cost to others; religion, in Blatchford's special sense of the word, withers, for 'competitive individualism is too rank a weed to allow religion to thrive in the same field'.[66]

The theory of alternative patterns of social relationships as expressing the domination by one or the other of the aspects of man's dual nature, the godlike-altruistic-co-operative or the breastlike-egotistic-competitive, taken in conjunction with their moral or 'religious' dimensions, clearly derived from romanticism as developed by Carlyle and his school. But even an ILP leader like MacDonald, who did not trace his legacy from any of the figures hitherto discussed, was not immune from its effects. Historical epochs, he argued using the terminology familiar from Saint-Simon and the Carlyleans, can be considered as either organic or mechanical. The slow process of natural growth that marks organic communities is periodically disrupted by rapid economic development, in which the social organisation is captured by the strong and exploited by them. In due course the masses revolt, politics 'rises to heroic proportions ... inspired by religious fervour ... or philosophical conviction', and a new epoch of organic growth is re-established. 'This double thread of exploitation and revolt against exploitation runs right through history.[67]

Together with Hardie and Blatchford, MacDonald held that periods of selfish individualism and the class antagonism which it breeds, if unchecked, threaten society with extinction. The thesis that social harmony is not, as the Marxists held, a final state to be striven for but a persistent pattern of social life, despite periodic temporary interruptions, was buttressed by an appeal to the argument of the survival of the fittest. Hardie claimed that Darwin had proved social survival to be conditioned by the ability to live in 'sympathetic association and not individualistic competition', and this provides a key to the understanding of the rise and fall of civilisations. When the strong communal element characteristic of early Greek society was undermined by excessive individualistic wealth it degenerated and became a satellite of Rome. Rome in turn thrived so long as land was held in common. But the influx of wealth from the empire led to the emergence of a rich privileged class which took over the communally held property. The resulting social polarisation led to the decline and fall of the Roman Empire, and a comparable pattern is observable in medieval Europe.[68] A similar interpretation of Darwinism caused Blatchford to rank it along with Carlyleanism as a pillar of the 'New Religion',[69] while MacDonald took it as proof that the English 'moral' socialism was scientifically sound, whereas the 'scientific' socialism of Marx and Engels was at fault.[70]

At this point the socialists were caught in a logical predicament arising from the typically romantic synthesis of idealism and materialism that premised their theory of social periodicity. On the one hand, the spiritual element in man activates his natural propensity to progress by directing him to fulfil himself through extending his intellectual horizons and shaping his environment to suit his growing needs. On the other, man is created by his environment, and his increasing involvement in the material world bolsters the importance of his physical surroundings, stifling his spiritual being. This leads to selfishness and the exploitation of human beings as tools for the creation of wealth which further strengthens the element of 'sensuality'. Consequently, just when it is at its weakest the need is at its strongest for the spiritual element to reshape the social and physical environments and release society from the clutching embrace of the inferior side of man's nature.[71]

One attempt to rescue the thesis from the threat of self-negation was to suggest a technique resembling that of Baron Munchausen who pulled himself out of the quicksand by his hair. Bruce Glasier, for example, argued that

> we cannot, it is true, alter our character without altering our social environment but we are each of us ourselves our own chief environment, and if we cannot alter our own environment we shall make a poor job of altering the environment of society.[72]

A more satisfying solution was that of the poet-prophet-seer, developed by the romantics from the earlier debates on the distinction between genius and talent, and most fully expounded in *Heroes and Hero-Worship*. Hardie put his finger on the problem as well as on the way out when he argued that 'in every set of circumstances individuals are to be found greater than their surroundings, else would progress come to a full halt; but a community is, and always must be, what its circumstances and surroundings make it'.[73] An individual of this kind is a 'heaven-sent genius' whose spirit has 'soared into and explored the limitless expanse which lies outside the ken of common vision'. By virtue of this gift he blazes a trail which later followers beat into a broad highway leading to new frontiers of social experience.[74] The greatest of all Heroes was Jesus, but all the prophets of old were like him 'neither more nor less than Labour agitators'. Among the moderns Hardie singled out Shelley and Burns, though he regarded Southey's *Wat Tyler* as the greatest individual poem.[75] Shelley typified the Hero far in advance of his age. From being a lonely voice out in the wilderness he finally received universal recognition, and his statue was set up in the very college in Oxford that had expelled him.[76] Burns represented reform through railery: *castigat ridendo mores*. He heaped contempt and ridicule upon the evils of his day until, by getting the people to laugh with him, he 'laughed these out of being'.[77]

In many respects Blatchford's approach resembled that of his rival. He too believed that 'triumph over evil environment' is possible only by drawing on the power of 'poets and seers' to awaken the potential dormant in man.[78] Carlyle and his followers were the chief models he chose as those who 'taught the truth that will spread'.[79] He divided them into three generations. Carlyle was the main source and a personal proof of the social truth that spiritual self-development makes for an active Aristocracy of Talent replacing the passive aristocarcy of inherited power and wealth.[80] As Jesus was a son of a carpenter, he was the son of a mason, yet they brought a new gospel to the world.[81] The second generation included Ruskin and those disciples who amended the essential doctrine to conform to the democratic ideal, Morris and Walt Whitman.[82] Blatchford himself, he half insinuated, belonged to the third generation of those who called upon the people to follow the example of Carlyle's Hero by abstracting themselves from their material surroundings to confront their inner selves, thereby refreshing and strengthening their spiritual powers.[83]

However, there was a crucial difference in the attitudes of Hardie and Blatchford which points to the difficulty of applying Carlyleanism to socialism. Just as the acceptance of the doctrine of the Hero was a natural consequence of espousing the 'gospel of work', so the principle of hierarchy followed from the theory of the Hero. Hardie's attempt to reconcile egalitarianism and hierarchical authority rested on the assumption that full socialism would arrive only as the end-result of a long evolutionary progress: for a long time to come democracy will mean 'finding the fit person, and loyally and generously trusting him' in the performance of the allotted task.[84] Blatchford seized on this view to justify an attack on the leader of the party who, he claimed, having swallowed Carlyle's doctrine whole, illustrated in his own person the flaw in it. In demanding a superior being both to guide and to rule, Carlyle had failed to note that the qualities required for each function are not the same 'and are seldom found to be united in one soul'. The ruler or leader wields his authority to impel others to accept his decisions. The guide points out a direction and recommends others to follow it. The choice must be theirs; he can only explain and persuade. But morality cannot be enforced; it must be nurtured till the people learn to distinguish between good and evil. Therefore, until they have learned the right way they need guides and not rulers. In fact, the greater the inability to recognise the truth, the greater the need for a guide and the more likely it becomes that they will choose the wrong leader. Significantly, neither Carlyle nor Ruskin could devise a means for overcoming this difficulty. Hence 'we must have *guides*, but we must resist rulers'. 'Real democracy' in a party as in a state demands that 'all the genius of the nation shall be placed before The People in council' and measures of importance will be decided by referendum. Able men of action to make good the will of the people should be appointed or dismissed by a similar process. 'In a nation where a free, educated, and independent People really studied and took part in national and international affairs' Blatchford believed that even this 'machinery' would become increasingly unnecessary. Leaving aside speculation about how society could be run, one is still puzzled to know by what steps such perfection could be reached. Clearly, 'The People in council' cannot be on the model of the Greek polis for reasons of scale. Moreover, the central question is still left unanswered: who chooses 'the genius of the nation' if 'the public is incapable of choosing well'?[85] In the final analysis, Blatchford's own acceding to the doctrine of the Hero undermined his criticism of Hardie. Once the two had accepted it, the bogy of hierarchical principles popped up like a Jack-in-the-box, and averting their gaze from it failed to make it disappear.

The same ambivalence lay behind their adoption of the typically Carlylean interpretation of history, both as the record of the achievements of great figures and the 'essence of innumerable biographies'. It is to 'the dreamer, the possessor of imagination' that the world is indebted for what progress it has made, Hardie wrote;[86] and Blatchford, pitting his evolutionary doctrine against the static religion of the church, saw the history of civilisation as 'successions of brave "Heretics" and "infidels", who have denied false dogmas or brought new truths to light'.[87] Such individuals, they both held, were the initiators of mass social movements which snowballed to overwhelm the evils of their society. The ideas they set in motion reached ever-widening sections of the people just as a great scientific discovery initiates a series of further discoveries till the very life of the nation is transformed.[88] Indeed, MacDonald described civilisation as progressing as it were along a double axis, 'Romantic history [which] is the story of heroes [and] scientific history [which] is the story of peoples'. There is a reciprocal influence between 'the colossal historical figure' and the 'masses and organisations'. The Hero epitomises the existing 'life of his time' and at the same time leads the people in a new movement to change it.[89] Contemporary socialism, they all agreed, was the latest manifestation of the eternal struggle of mankind for freedom, waged 'since long ere yet history carried any record of man's doings'. It spread again the gospel of those few who, in an age dominated by selfishness, strive to save society by re-establishing contact with the ultimate scheme of the universe. Far from being 'a thing recently invented by a few discontented, shiftless fellows', or as Glasier put it with obvious reference, by 'a few refugees and philosophers', it was 'a power that began with the beginning of the world'.[90]

III

The corollary of such ideas was the validation of abandoned traditions which, modified to suit new realities, promised a better future. The socialist is not a mere iconoclast but one who seeks 'to resuscitate a phase of British life which produced great and good wealth in the past', for 'the trend of progress ... is towards a similar condition of things to that which formerly obtained, but adapted, of course, to meet modern conditions'.[91] The possession of a sense of historical perspective was the proud claim of several ILP leaders. Hardie, for example, described himself as 'a student of history',[92] while MacDonald urged his fellow socialists to 'read history in the historical spirit'.[93] Both believed that a recurrent pattern runs through history; the good society dies, and rises again from the ashes like Carlyle's Phoenix. The archetypal paradigm was the ancient community of Israel. It too knew periods of rapid economic growth which brought about the polarisation of society into rich and poor, and which evoked the denunciation of the prophets. But on the whole it was characterised by the 'adjustments of social and individual right and ... moral restraints imposed upon economic processes' as laid down in the Mosaic code. Although it finally went down 'before a capitalist civilisation', its ideals remained in the minds of men and inspired them to strive for a return of the ancient spirit.[94] For the two socialists the Reformation was a result of the growing concentration of wealth in the hands of the few, and it brought to an end the latest appearance of the good order in British history. Hardie's imaginative and largely imaginary picture of the late medieval period is interesting more as a rough blueprint for the kind of society he envisioned than as a piece of history. Every private interest was held in subordination to the common weal, while civic institutions protected the liberty of each individual. The land belonged to the nation but was given in tenure to the Church and the barons on the condition that they assumed responsibility for the welfare of the people, their health and education. In town the authorities bought on behalf of the inhabitants the basic necessities, saw to their just distribution, fixed prices and prevented profiteering. In times of economic distress, food was shared out to everyone according to his need. The communal spirit also found aesthetic expression in the architecture of the cathedrals and public buildings, and both secular and ecclesiastic bodies provided music and public plays for the edification and pleasure of the whole.[95] MacDonald, citing More's *Utopia*, concentrated on the decline of this system as a factor in bringing about the Reformation. Accompanying the growing prosperity of the wool merchants and the expansion of foreign trade, the spirit of commercialism took firm hold of England. The appetite of the abbots grew and they enclosed the common lands for the grazing of sheep, depriving the peasants of their livelihood and opening thereby 'a new epoch in the history of ... poverty ... The ownership of the soil no longer carries with it the heavy social obligations to maintain men on it.' This process was clinched when the nobles forcibly seized the accumulated wealth of the Church, justifying their unscrupulousness by a doctrine that 'lent the sanction of religion to the selfish creed of each for himself'.[96]

Unlike these two self-styled explorers of the past Blatchford modestly acknowledged that he was 'not versed in history'.[97] Nevertheless, he devoted what became the most popular piece of socialist writing in Britain to the thesis that the old order was in essence the best model for the new. The very title *Merrie England* and its spelling are loaded, recalling as they do the happy spirit of an earlier pre-industrial age. It suggests a contrast between an old way of life rooted in the soil where small communities were bound together in close fellowship, and the way of life of a people in the anonymity of sprawling industrial urban centres that were spreading their tentacles over the countryside.[98] The implication was that it was the Industrial Revolution and the new wealth it brought about that fuelled the desire for personal gain and created, to use the title of another of his books, a *Dismal England*. The historical perspective differs somewhat from that of Hardie and MacDonald, yet they were all of the opinion that the accelerating tempo of industrial and commercial expansion which gave the death-blow to traditional England was a direct consequence of acquisitiveness, resulting in an ever-widening gap between technological know-how and moral values. Quoting Carlyle, both Hardie and Blatchford described England as falling under the curse of 'long-eared Midas', starving in the midst of plenty. Man who had 'solved the riddle of production' found himself in 'commercial and industrial vassalage' till 'every improvement in civilisation ... [became] a burden and a curse', and the workshop of the world was turning into 'the most horrible and the most miserable country the world has ever known'.[99]

The similarity in their analysis of the consequences of the Industrial Revolution is largely attributable to their dependence on opinions widely held since the end of the eighteenth century. Carlyle, as we have seen, had taken up the romantic dread of the encroachment of industrialism, systematised it, and had given it a philosophic expression closely recalling Marx's theory of alienation.

Ruskin and Morris adopted his main arguments, stressing their aesthetic implications but turning them into a one-sided rejection of industrial civilisation. The following generation of socialists relied equally on Carlyle and on his disciples. Blatchford advised his readers that in order to understand and to demolish the industrial system they should 'get the works of Thomas Carlyle'. Hardie urged them to add to the list the writings of Ruskin and Morris, whose 'denunciation of machinery and ... glorification of the beauties of nature' showed how far commercialism was 'killing art as well as life, since the one is but the expression of the other'.[100]

Both took the loss of 'communion with the silent, yet all powerful forces of nature'[101] as the starting point for their criticism. When the better faculties are uppermost, they argued, man strives to realise his full identity through creative co-operation with the world outside him, people as well as things. He is 'as much a piece of Nature as the birds of the air or the lilies of the field'.[102] When the lower faculties are dominant and he falls under the sway of possessiveness, all that is outside him becomes raw material to be exploited and manipulated for selfish gratification. He thereby estranges himself from nature and withdraws into himself. In the first situation the economic basis of social existence is chiefly tied to the land while 'the manufacturing portion of [the] nation's industry is subsidiary'. In the second, society uproots itself from its natural surroundings and creates an aritifial environment in the form of industrial cities. The result is cumulative. Those who first take the step benefit at least from the early influences of nature. Their descendants, born and reared in the city and 'shut off from the purifying and ennobling influence of nature', are stunted from birth.[103]

A different aspect of the same phenomenon is the estrangement from the process and the product of work. The craftsman, like the artist, is 'continually called upon to put part of himself into the work of his hands'. The industrial worker by contrast 'sees in his toil a dull mechanical task'. Hardie concluded that 'work without art is brutality'.[104] Blatchford, comparing the sculptor or the surgeon with the collier, pointed out that the former is engaged in work of his own choice, enriches himself by it, and may acquire the further satisfaction of fame. The latter, on the other hand, has no say in his work and sees in it mere drudgery 'never to be made to yield pleasure, or praise, or profit'.[105] In short, what he makes means nothing personal to him. His sole concern is with the number of shillings he is given for his pains.[106] Moreover, over-efficient production will sooner or later lead him to the degradation of unemployment.[107] Little wonder therefore that 'we live in jerry-built houses, wear shoddy clothes, and eat adulterated food'.[108]

This psychological analysis was reinforced by the argument that to toil without love is to weaken or destroy one's humanity. The worker whose indifference betrays his creative faculties 'is robbing himself ... of his manhood'.[109] The sole concern left him is the satisfaction of physical needs and he is reduced to 'living the life of [the] beast'.[110] Worse still, where work is valued solely by the money it brings in, man sees himself and his fellow beings as mere machines for producing wealth. The individual, the family, society, are affected by the blight. They are equally sacrificed at the shrine of the God Mammon.[111] Nor are the victims only from the working classes. The same sordid desires, destructive of all free life, reduce the wealthy too to the level of beasts. They are no less slaves of the market forces, living in constant fear of the penalties imposed by the iron laws of supply and demand.[112] Indeed, Glasier wrote, the poverty of the rich is perhaps the greatest of all for, money having become an 'emblem of their own degradation and their fellow's slavery', the more they possess the more barren their lives.[113] The direct consequence of such dehumanisation, they all agreed, was the disintegration of the organic society. Selfish divisiveness accentuated social tension, replacing the community sense of co-operation between individuals, groups and interests by the competitive sense that pitted individual against individual, group against group and interest against interest. The new ideology of class warfare was a symptom of the disease which is sought to cure homeopathically, by arousing social hostility. It was 'glorified animalism dangerously akin to bestiality'.[114]

Much of Hardie's polemic against class struggle was aimed at Marxism, whether as expressed in Marx's teachings or in the policies of his British followers (SDF). It permeated his writings throughout his career but was crystallised in his 'An Indictment of Class War', published in two instalments in the *Labour Leader* of September 1904. This in turn provided the inspiration for Glasier's 'Socialism and Socialist Dogma, the Class War Hypothesis', published likewise in two instalments in the same paper some two months later. The interest of these articles lies less in the lack of understanding of Marxism they reveal than in their view of continental socialism as a foreign doctrine. Over a decade earlier Hardie had recognised that British socialism belonged to a separate tradition originating in essence in the 'great message of deliverance' brought by Carlyle and his disciples who rescued the movement from 'foundering on the rocks of materialism' and elevated the 'spiritual side of man's being'.[115] 'The class war dogma', the ILP leaders insisted, was an excrescence on socialism similar to the hairsplitting biblical hermeneutics of the medieval scholastics. Modern schoolmen had done great disservice to the cause by latching on to slogans and catchwords, but of all those that they 'thrust upon the socialist movement, surely ... the class war is the most unscientific and un-socialist'. Such jargon could become current only in a brand of socialism which inverted the relations between the moral and the material dimensions of social life, positing that moral values are derivatives of economic factors and thus denying man's unique position in the living world and the special factors explaining his evolution. Because it failed to understand the roots of capitalism it assumed that the predicament of modern society lay in its polarisation into rich employers and poor employees, whereas in truth the gap between the classes derived from a deep-lying moral obliquity. The sought-for overthrow of the wealthy would consequently achieve little save the changing of roles within the same framework. After all, both rich and poor were infected by a single malady. The same attitude that leads the rich employer to engage cheap sweated labour, or the landlord to charge exorbitant rent, motivates the workers themselves whenever the opportunity arises. When, for example, a master worker exploits his apprentice, or the employee in a co-operative store is overworked and underpaid, the exploitation is not of an employee by his employer but of one worker by another. And the subjugation of women in the home is further evidence of 'man's universal inhumanity to man [which] respects no class or person, race or creed, youth or age, sex or virtue'. The poor in their degree are therefore 'as much landlords and capitalists as are the rich. The rich are only the more fortunate, the poor the more unfortunate exploiters.' The kind of socialist that advocated the class war inflamed the savage element in mankind to foment further hatred. British socialism on the other hand sought to allay this fever by reviving the embers of fellowship. It was not a movement built on the exclusion of classes and sections of the people but a movement of the whole nation which 'transcends the self interest of all classes and sections'.[116] 'When I used the expression "communal consciousness" ... as the antithesis to "class consciousness"', MacDonald recalled, 'he [Hardie] wrote me saying that that was exactly what he felt.'[117]

Blatchford's views up to the beginning of the twentieth century were fundamentally in accord with those of the ILP leadership. He too argued that 'the average workman is just as much an individualist and a profit-seeker at heart as the average employer. Why not? They are both bred under the same system.' He was also at one with them in stressing the necessity for a nation-wide campaign to rise above personal selfishness and sectional interest. If anything, he was more trenchant in the expression of his ideas. While rejecting class hostility, Hardie was forced to acknowledge that society had split into two opposed divisions. Blatchford denied even this. Only 'angry and unreasoning Socialists', he maintained, could pigeonhole the members of society in a clearly defined class structure consisting of the rich and the poor. In reality, 'from the crown to the crossing [sweeper] there is no distinct line of division between class and class'. Every profession, trade or employment, even the fraternity of beggars, has its aristocracy and its plebeians, and in every group the higher exploits the lower. One cannot speak therefore of one struggle between two great groups but of a thousand struggles among a thousand groups, at every point of the social continuum.[118]

By the turn of the century these opinions underwent a steady change. Following the socialist defeat in the parliamentary elections of 1895, Leonard Hall of *The Clarion* suggested a change of tactics. Instead of relying on such abstractions as 'universal brotherhood', the socialist movement should appeal to the self-interest of the man in the street. Not till 1899 did any indication appear that Blatchford himself was thinking along the same lines. In that year he admitted that he still adhered to the kind of socialism advocated by Morris, but 'the crowd ... are incapable of rising to such an ideal, and I have come to think that Socialism must move slowly, taking the crowd with it'.[119] By 1902 his book *Britain for the British* showed the line he thought socialism must take, as 'the first stage on the road to what I call real socialism'.[120] In it he came round to the idea that society had indeed split into two classes, the wealthy minority and the indigent majority. The only way in which the many could recover their lost rights was to follow their interests and gain control of the state by sheer numbers. An article published in the same year explained the purpose of the book: 'I want a nation of men and women, not of masters and servants, and I believe that one of the best ways of helping towards that end is by appealing to the class consciousness of the masses.' Nevertheless, he stressed that his ultimate objective was no different from that of those socialists who repudiated the struggle between the classes. The difference was only one of tactics. Class consciousness was no more than a means of drawing the masses to support a movement whose ultimate aim was to change the value system at the basis of society so that it could rise above class consciousness by virtue of reaching higher moral standards.[121]

This faithfulness to a principle explains why he never abandoned his belief that revolution was the most evil aspect of 'foreign' socialism. Nearly 40 years later he opened his last book with the declaration, 'I hate revolution and violence', claiming that his mission had always been to avert them.[122] The metaphor that both be and Hardie used was the same: revolution was a childhood disease which mature socialism had outgrown.[123] The brotherhood of man, they argued, could not be achieved by bloodletting; hatred and violence breed hatred and violence, and the victor is the one in whom hatred and violence are the strongest. Revolution therefore 'would put the worst kind of man into power', so that 'the people would ... slip down into worse evils than those against which they had fought'.[124] Glasier saw it as a regressive force, a recurring tragedy of history which it was the function of socialism to end,[125] and Hardie concurred that 'socialism offers the one chance left of saving our civilisation from being destroyed by wealth and poverty'.[126] Moreover, the Marxist view, that there was no alternative for revolution since the capitalists could not be expected to give up their ill-gotten gains without a struggle, rested on an assumption that was false in Britain at least. There the people had the vote, and all that was required of them to change the system was a change of heart to be achieved by education and persuasion.[127]

Such a conviction was rooted in a conception of the state as 'the expression of the will of the people',[128] not the representative of a class but 'an organ of society', upon which devolved the duty of instituting and carrying out the reforms that would bring about the new moral order.[129] As such the state could not be opposed to the will of its members, or as Hardie and MacDonald put it in a joint article, to think of man *versus* the state is as impossible as to think of a square circle.[130] Glasier even argued that 'we can only conceive of man being fully human *in* the State', for it is only by and through it that he can develop himself.[131] Holding such a position, the ILP was at daggers drawn with the anarchistic streams of the socialist movement. In 1894 the National Administrative Council of the party met to express their total repudiation of anarchist principles and methods as injurious to the cause of the worker and calculated to check the progress of true socialism.[132]

It is hard to pin down any specific theorist or movement as the main source of such attitudes, for similar views were widely held from the earliest years of the Victorian reign. Some eight years before the Reform Act of 1867 J.S. Mill had already attacked the demand for massive state interference in the social and economic life of the nation which followed on the extension of the franchise as a new threat to freedom. The introductory chapter of *On Liberty* opens with a discussion that strongly recalls de Toqueville's analysis of State control as 'caressive tyranny'. On the face of it, Mill argued, once the 'magistrates of the State' become the people's 'tenants and delegates, revocable at their pleasure', many will come to think that there is little necessity for limiting their authority further on the grounds that the nation does not need to be 'protected against its own will'. On the contrary, the greater the activity of the state the greater the control by its citizens of their own destiny, for the power of the state is 'the nation's power, concentrated, and in a form convenient for exercise.[133] Mill was thankful that such a belief, though prevalent on the continent, was not widely held at home. However, by the eighties and early nineties it seemed that his confidence was premature. Radical theorists like Henry George, the vigorous propaganda of the Land Nationalisation Society and of the Land Restoration League, and the state socialism of the Fabians were in effect logical continuations of the trend set by the social legislation of the Disraeli and the Gladstone Ministries. Blatchford's assertion that socialism was already in the making since 'nearly all law is more or less socialistic', implying as it does 'the right of the state to control individuals for the benefit of the nation',[134] sounds less extravagant when one remembers that the Liberal John Morley could state in 1881 that socialism was advancing through the increasing state regulation of life and work in the interest of the general welfare.[135]

Actually, the call for the intervention of an overriding national authority preceded even the Victorian era. Previous chapters have shown that the conception of the state as a supra-sectional agency of reform was already present in the germ in the doctrines of Wordsworth, and was developed by Southey in the period of the Anglo-French wars. This was taken over by Carlyle and reached a degree of virtual totalitarianism in the writings of Ruskin. A comparison of their views of the nature and scope of state activity with those of the ILP would suggest at first sight that the influence, if any, was negligible. For the romantics the state represented the nation as an entity transcending particular times and conditions, entrusted with the mission of moulding contemporary society to conform to ultimate principles. For the socialists it expressed the will of the people, and its activities were directed from below. Both, it is true, believed in the advent of the great spiritual leader to guide society into new directions. But for the ILP leaders the 'Hero', 'prophet' or 'poet' inspired the people to direct the state, not the governors to direct the people.

For all that, an examination of the proposals for state action put forward by Hardie and Blatchford reveals that romantic political doctrines in the form developed by Carlyle and Ruskin exerted important influence on both. One of the clearest examples appears in a series of articles entitled 'The Unemployed' in which Hardie, who was dubbed 'the member for the unemployed', formulated the theoretical bases of his thoughts on reform. Imitating the rhetorical devices of *Chartism* (Chapter 10) he argued that unemployment was not only a problem for its individual victims but a problem for society as a whole. Governors whose only answer to the plea of the unemployed for help, to the proof that there was ample land available for exploitation, that there was ample capital available to exploit it, and that there was ample manpower available to work it, was the single word 'impossible!', would not escape the nemesis of revolutionary violence.[136] If the authorities were not content to await such inevitable doom they had two choices before them. One was on the lines of Carlyle's version of Swift's 'Modest Proposal', the whole of which was quoted almost verbatim from *Sartor Resartus*, that the unemployed be shot as game, pickled and fed to the paupers. The other was for the state to accept its responsibility as the representative of the nation not only to deal with immediate contingencies but to lay down a framework for the future. He always insisted that 'generations of population come and go, but the state remains'; therefore, while the individual thinks only of today, it must 'organise industry' in the interest of tomorrow. The basic model it should follow was that of the work brigades, quoted at length from the *Latter Day Pamphlets*. The direct participation of the state in the national economy as a large-scale employer capable not only of absorbing the slack of unemployment but also of giving security to the 'nomads of the labour market', would serve as a lever for the reorganisation of the entire society. It would compel the captains of industry to improve working conditions or fail under the pressure of competition with the state, and at the same time to educate all to the value of work and of fair and just relations.[137] From this starting point he drew on schemes adopted from various sources, most important of which was that of the co-operative estates outlined in Reverend Herbert Mills' *Poverty and the State* (1886).

Blatchford's temperament led him to engage far less in proposals for state action. Moreover, whereas for Hardie the problem of reform was an immediate concern, for him it was something to be taken up only after the coming to power of a socialist government. Nevertheless, *Merrie England* provides a scheme for solving the unemployment problem that shows the strong mark of Ruskin's *Fors Clavigera*, supplemented from various sources, including Mills with whose ideas Blatchford felt 'very strong sympathy'.[138] Again the cure lay in the state becoming a large-scale employer. The unemployed would be registered according to their specific qualifications. Unskilled labourers would engage in constructing roads and other public improvements, builders in improving housing estates, and agricultural labourers would work on state farms. The latter would provide the groundwork for the setting up of communal townships to which the state would direct all manner of artisans, tradesmen and professionals necessary to maintain them as self-sufficient bodies. After paying rent and other expenses to the state, the remaining profits would belong to the community. The standard and quality of life would become such as to attract more and more people to similar experiments. By degrees, the great impersonal cities would shrink, the new communities would bring back the spirit of merrie England, and, to quote Blake, Jerusalem would be rebuilt in England's green and pleasant land.[139]

Both Hardie and Blatchford held, then, that the state, in solving such problems as unemployment, would create the conditions which would encourage the liberation of the god-like aspects of human nature. Such a conception led them, as it had the romantics, to view reform as a self-generating evolutionary process initiated by the activation of the moral element in society. 'Reforms', Hardie wrote, 'will come in any case; it is the rebellious spirit of self-sacrifice in the people which is going to renovate the life of the nations'.[140] This optimism explains in a large measure why they did not find it necessary to draw up a detailed blueprint of the envisaged new order but contented themselves in the main with large generalisations which left many questions hanging in the air. It also throws light on the importance they attached to the issue of distributive justice. The workers under socialism, as public employees of municipal or state authorities, would be serving the common weal and none would be parasites living at the expense of others. All would enjoy 'a living wage for an eight-hour day', and profits would accrue to the benefit of all. This, the socialists made clear, did not deny the right of private ownership. On the contrary, it would 'render it possible for all honest and industrious people to enjoy the fruits of their labour', provided it did not take the form of land or capital. The individual will be just as free as he is now to 'hoard his savings ... [and] spend them in any way his taste might dictate', on condition that he would not invest it in the expectation of adding to his money by the work of others. Blatchford even favoured a degree of private enterprise. Land could be rented from the state to the highest bidder for agriculture, mining, building and other purposes, though how this was possible without private employment of labour was left unanswered.[141] Nor would the nationalisation of land and capital entail changes in the technical division of labour. In Hardie's words, the managers, engineers and the rest would carry on as before, 'just as well and profitably employed by society as they are now by the private capitalists'.[142] Or as Blatchford put it, 'the *Captain* of a ship is necessary. The owner of the ship is not. There must be captains as well as sailors, and managers as well as workmen. But there is no need for the usurer and the thief.'[143]

In sum, the sociological and moral bases of the ILP doctrines gave birth to a conception of an economic transformation that was extremely limited in scope. Hardie and other party leaders, as well as Blatchford, actually took pride in the fact that it was modelled on national and municipal services such as the post-office and the waterworks which had already proved themselves, and on the extension of the principles on which they were based.[144] This, they claimed, made British socialism an eminently practical movement as against the continental socialist movements which have 'a tendency to be philosophic, abstract, and dogmatic'. It offered, Glasier implied, socialism for the wise, for 'dogmas are always doubtful, and only the unthinking ever accept them implicitly'.[145]

IV

'Marx's theory may be right or wrong, but not one Socialist in a hundred, or in a thousand, maybe, in these islands has ever grasped [it] ... the validity of Marx's theory no more forms the basis of Socialism than does the theory of undulating ether form the basis of the desire for light'.[146] Written in 1909, the pronouncement may have been somewhat exaggerated, but not much. In part, the explanation why so few people were familiar with Marx's ideas and why these had so little influence on the course of British socialism lies in their late publication in English. If one discounts the pot-pourri of passages from *Das Kapital* serialised in *Today* (1885-9), the work was first published in Britain in 1887. By 1880 Hyndman had read it in French and founded the Democratic Federation (SDF from 1884) to propagate its message. Before the century ended the Fabians too proclaimed Marx as one of their sources. However, by the time *Das Kapital* became generally available, the ideas of the mainstream socialist leaders were already largely crystallised and their political activity already marked. Blatchford expressed a widespread attitude when he stated, about ten years after the first English edition appeared, that Marx was probably an excellent man and a scientific socialist, 'but I am not answerable to [his] opinions, nor [he] for mine. I never read one of [his] books and doubtless never shall'.[147] Two years later he repeated his admission of total ignorance of Marx and his intention of never reading him, adding 'I am ... and always have been ... a communist of the William Morris type'.[148] His comments on the dictatorship of the proletariat in his autobiography written towards the end of his long life confirm that he kept his word. The Marxists, he believed, sought to replace 'all the trained ability of the professions and the commercial and industrial and scientific afterguard' by manual workers, that is to say, 'the efficient are to make way for the non-efficient'.[149]

Such irony, based on hearsay rather than knowledge, hints at another reason for the limited influence of Marx on the British socialists. Some of the most widely circulated apophthegms, maxims and principles associated with Marx's philosophy were in stark contrast to the British socialist's doctrines and sounded alien to their ears. Glasier, for example, accused him of diverting 'socialist teaching from its true line, — i.e., the righteousness of socialism and the theory of commonwealth';[150] and Hardie attacked Hyndman for his 'cold, soulless materialism' and foreign theory of class war which proved that he 'never understood the working class, nor could ... get into touch with their point of view'.[151]

And yet, a third reason for the slightness of Marx's impact on the main body of the British socialists was precisely that whatever was not felt as alien and mistaken had much in common with the doctrines they had inherited from the later thinkers of the romantic tradition. There were certain key issues that they were familiar with from Carlyle and Ruskin and did not see as new and worldshaking; others that they regarded as merely confirming and clarifying opinions that they had arrived at themselves. MacDonald's comments are representative. Marx, he conceded, had 'opened a new volume of the history of the Socialist movement' by organising the proletariat into a political movement with a clear programme and defined objectives.[152] His philosophy contained cardinal errors and was out of date and misleading, but it enabled him to inspire the workers and 'start them on their march'. Now that he had achieved for Europe what English socialists had been doing under more favourable conditions, it was time that he be revised along the lines that British socialism had long laid down independently: '... as the authority of [continental] autocracy decreased, the policy of the International Socialist movement must tend towards ours. In France, in Belgium, in Germany, that tendency is already well marked'.[153]

Hardie concurred with such views, adding that what Adam Smith had done for the bourgeois, Marx had done for the workers. He also agreed that the doctrine of class struggle was mistaken and that European socialism must change in conformity with 'the constitutional evolution of the socialist idea' in England.[154] Paradoxically, however, though among the leaders of the ILP he was the closest to Carlyle, he also stood out as the one who saw himself close to Marx; but it was a Marx that he retailored to fit the views of the party. According to his interpretation, Marx's main contribution to socialist theory was that he uncovered the causes of social discontent and showed that it must persist so long as the state did not supplant the individual as the owner of land and capital.¹⁵⁵ This would arrive only as a result of a revolution, but those Marxists who attacked the ILP misunderstood his use of the term. What he had in mind was not the revolution of violence but a revolution of the spirit, such as took place 'two thousand years ago, when John the Baptist called upon men to repent for the Kingdom of God was at hand'.¹⁵⁶ Marx understood too that to achieve this end all workers, socialists and non-socialists alike, must become members of a single great Labour Party that would attract by degrees the support of the entire people. Hence, whoever appeals to the workers alone, and of them only to those who proclaim themselves socialists, reduces Marx's 'great historical formula to a set of quite meaningless phrases'. It was therefore safe to assert that 'the founders of the ILP, and even more so, of the Labour party were ... in the direct line of apostolic succession from Marx and the other master minds of socialist theory and policy', and that if Marx were alive he would surely join the ILP.¹⁵⁷

The general tenor of the Party's attitude can perhaps best be gauged by the special issue of its *Labour Leader* on the eve of the 1899 New Year. It distributed a large-scale portrait of Karl Marx accompanied by Hardie's editorial message, recommending with mock seriousness the exact specifications for mounting the picture, framing it and hanging it next to that of William Morris. In a more serious vein he proceeded to explain the reason for distributing the picture. As a true disciple of Carlyle, he wrote, he believed that 'a people who fail to show reverence to their mighty dead are a small-souled people who can never be anything but a race of pettifogging shopkeepers'. Every movement, therefore, must have its heroes to worship, and it was only right that the followers of the great English thinker should pay due tribute to the great German thinker.¹⁵⁸

In a sense, this editorial illustrates the contribution of the ILP leaders and of Blatchford to the theory and practice of the British Labour movement. On the day Hardie died, John Burns described him in his diary as 'narrow fanatical doctrinaire ... devoted to his ideal and quest'. His tragedy, he wrote, was that he failed. But he must be judged 'less by his achievement than by his aims', which were to elevate the workers both morally and materially.¹⁵⁹ In retrospect this estimation could be seen as truer if the word 'not' were inserted before the list of failings. Hardie and the non-Marxist majority of the Labour movement were eminently successful when judged by their practical achievements and not by their theoretical aims. If they were fanatics it was in their single-minded devotion to the cause of reform; they were certainly not doctrinaire on the continental model but flexible to a degree, incorporating important elements of English thought and looking back to the native tradition as well as forward to a new order. In so doing they helped to fashion a party whose policies and tactics were acceptable to large segments of the nation and who could appeal to all walks of life. Glasier put his finger on the unique quality of the ILP socialism:

> It has been the means, I think, of restoring the English tradition into our ... agitation — a tradition which was lost by the usurpation of the Marxists and Communards. For myself, I feel as one set free now that I am able to speak and work for socialism without feeling that I belong to a different cast of beings from that of the ordinary Liberal or Tory.[160]

The success of the Labour party may be measured by the fact that within a few years of Burns's comments, it came to power and thereafter formed the main alternative to the Conservatives. The price was the watering down of its final vision of a moral renaissance and a new structure of society. British socialism indeed joined Conservatism as just another party. Perhaps, however, that was also because a major stream of British conservatism, drawing from the same springs, had long adopted many of the attitudes and policies that elsewhere had been the prerogative of the left. Nothing could be more telling than a letter sent by Blatchford to a socialist friend long after he abandoned socialism for conservatism:

> We have not drifted apart. I was always a Tory Democrat and you a French Democrat ... from the first ... we loved the humour and colour of the old English tradition ... The England of my affection and devotion is not a country nor a people: it is a tradition, the finest tradition the world has ever produced.[161]

Notes

1. F.W. Jowett, *What Made me a Socialist* (London: ILP pamphlet, 1925), pp. 12-13.
2. Quoted by L.W. Eshleman, *A Victorian Rebel* (New York: Charles Scribner's Sons, 1940), p. 157; *How I Became a Socialist* (London: The Twentieth Century Press, pamphlet, n.d.), pp. 19-20.

3. T. Mann, *A Socialist's View of Religion and the Churches* (London: Clarion pamphlet no. 10, 1896), pp. 12-13.
4. W.H. Stead, 'The Labour Party and the Books that Helped to Make it', *Review of Reviews*, XXXIII (January 1906), pp. 570-87.
5. See S. Pierson, *British Socialists, the Journey from Fantasy to Politics* (Cambridge, Mass. and London: Harvard University Press, 1979), especially Chapters 1, 4.
6. *The Pioneer* (Merthyr Tydfil), 6th December, 1913.
7. *The Aberdare Leader*, 21st April, 1906.
8. Stead, 'The Labour Party and the Books that Helped to Make it', p. 570.
9. *Labour Leader* 14th December, 1895.
10. *The Ardrossan and Salcoats Herald*, 22nd July, 1882.
11. Ibid., 27th March, 1885.
12. *Labour Leader*, 24th October, 1903.
13. *The Ardrossan and Salcoats Herald*, 19th January, 1883; *Rules of the Ayrshire Miner's Association*, 22nd March, 1881 (Scottish Record Office, Edinburgh, Fs 7/3).
14. I. McLean, *Keir Hardie* (London: Alan Lake, 1975) dated his socialism with the formation of the ILP in 1893; K.O. Morgan, *Keir Hardie, Radical and Socialist* (London: Weidenfeld & Nicolson, 1975) held that he became a socialist by the beginning of 1890; and F. Reid, *Keir Hardie, The Making of a Socialist* (London: Croom Helm, 1978) dates his socialism at mid-1887.
15. *The Ardrossan and Salcoats Herald*, 16th September, 1887.
16. Obviously unaware that Carlyle was quoting from Owen he proclaimed: '"Freedom"', says Carlyle, 'is a divine thing, but when it means freedom to starve it is not quite so divine.' J. Keir Hardie, *To the Electors of the Middle Division of Lanarkshire* (Glasgow: W.M. Robertson, leaflet, n.. (1888)).
17. *Labour Leader*, 6th January, 1905.
18. Hardie to Lord Randolph Churchill, 6th December, 1889, *National Library of Scotland*, De. 176, Box 1. Some weeks later Hardie tried to come to an arrangement with the Liberals on regulation of mutual support for each other's candidates.
19. *The Clarion*, 12th January, 1901.
20. Ibid., 23rd July, 1892.
21. Blatchford to John Burns, 11th June, 1894, BM MS. adds. 46287, ff. 200.
22. *The Clarion*, 21st May, 1892.
23. L. Thompson, *Robert Blatchford: Portrait of an Englishman* (London: Victor Gallancz, 1951), p. 43.
24. R. Blatchford, *My Eighty Years* (London, Toronto, Melbourne & Sydney: Labour Library, 1931), p. 37.
25. Thompson, *Robert Blatchford: Portrait of an Englishman*, pp. 30, 49, 124. About a dozen years later Blatchford estimated that 'socialism has meant a loss of 20,000 pounds to me, or more', letter to John Burns BM MS. adds. 46287, ff. 214.
26. *Labour Leader*, 18th July, 1906; J. Keir Hardie, *My Confession of Faith in the Labour Alliance* (London: ILP pamphlet, 1909), p. 12, and see J. Keir Hardie, 'Introductory Letter' in H. Russell Smart, *The ILP, its Programme and Policy* (Manchester: Labour Press, pamphlet, 1893).
27. R. Blatchford, *Practical Politics, an Object Lesson* (London: Clarion leaflet no. 1, n.d.); R. Blatchford, *Altrusism* (London: Clarion pamphlet no. 22, 1898), p. 16.
28. J. Keir Hardie, Letter to *The Trust* (New York), 10th July, 1901.
29. R. Blatchford, *The Clarion*, 21st October, 1899.
30. Hardie, *My Confession of Faith in the Labour Alliance*, p. 21.
31. J. Keir Hardie, *Labour Leader*, 12th January, 1895.

32. R. Blatchford, *The Clarion*, 10th January, 1902.
33. Thompson, *Robert Blatchford: Portrait of an Englishman*, p. 139.
34. *Labour Leader*, 10th June, 1889.
35. J. Ruskin, *The Works of John Ruskin*, E.T. Cook, A. Wedderburn (eds.), (London: George Allen, 1905), vol. XVII, p. 431.
36. F. Johnson, *Keir Hardie's Socialism* (London: ILP pamphlet, 1922), pp. 3-4.
37. J. Keir Hardie, *From Serfdom to Socialism*, R.E. Dawse (ed.) (Hassocks, Sussex: Harvester, 1974), p. 35.
38. R. Blatchford, *The New Religion*, (*Clarion* pamphlet no. 20, 1895), p. 6.
39. J. Ramsay MacDonald, *Socialism and Society* (New York: Kraus, 1970, reprint of 6th edn, ILP, 1908), pp. 165, 126.
40. R.J. Campbell, J. Keir Hardie, J. Bruce Clasier, *The New Theology* (London: ILP pamphlet, n.d. (1907)), p. 6.
41. Blatchford, *The New Religion*, pp. 4, 5.
42. *The Clarion*, 19th December 1922.
43. *Labour Leader*, February 1894.
44. Ibid., March 1893.
45. R. Blatchford, *Real Socialism: What Socialism is and What Socialism is Not* (London: *Clarion* pamphlet no. 23, 1898), p. 7.
46. *The Clarion*, 30th December, 1893.
47. R. Blatchford, *Not Guilty, A Defence of the Under Dog* (New York: Albert & Charles Boni, 1913), p. 158.
48. J. Keir Hardie, *Labour Leader*, 13th April, 1901.
49. R. Blatchford, *God and My Neighbour* (Chicago: Charles H. Keir, 1907).
50. Blatchford, *The New Religion* p. 6.
51. *Labour Leader*, 30th March, 1906; *The Clarion*, 19th February, 1904.
52. *Labour Leader*, 30th March, 1906, 17th October, 1903.
53. J. Keir Hardie, 'Address in Browning Hall', *Labour and Religion* (London: W.A. Hammond, pamphlet, 1910), p. 53.
54. Hardie, *From Serfdom to Socialism*, pp. 87-8.
55. Blatchford, *The New Religion*, p. 6; *The Clarion*, 19th February, 1904.
56. *Labour Leader*, 29th April, 1910.
57. *The Clarion*, 15th April, 1893; Blatchford, *Altruism*, p. 8.
58. *Labour Leader*, 21st September, 1906.
59. *The Clarion*, 15th April, 1893.
60. Hardie, *From Serfdom to Socialism*, p. 34.
61. Ibid., pp. 87-8.
62. R. Blatchford, *The Clarion*, 26th February, 1904.
63. *Labour Leader*, 12th January, 1895.
64. J. Keir Hardie, *Can A Man be a Christian on a Pound a Week?* (London: ILP pamphlet, 3rd edn, 1905), p. 10; *Pioneer*, 25th October, 1913; *Labour Leader*, December 1893.
65. *The Clarion*, 12th February, 1904.
66. R. Blatchford, *Socialism: a Reply to the Encyclical of the Pope* (London and Manchester: *Clarion* pamphlet no. 1, 1893), p. 15.
67. J. Ramsay MacDonald, *The Socialist Movement* (London: Thornton Butterworth, 1911), pp. 25,17; MacDonald, *Socialism and Society*, p. xii.
68. Hardie, *From Serfdom to Socialism*, pp. 94, 17-21.
69. Blatchford, *The New Religion*, p. 3.
70. MacDonald, *Socialism and Society*, pp. 109-10.
71. See e.g. *Labour Leader*, December, 1893; R. Blatchford, *Three open Letters to the Bishop of Manchester on Socialism* (London: *Clarion* pamphlet no. 3, 1894), p. 7. The argument was more fully developed in *Not Guilty, a Defence of the Under Dog* which Blatchford considered to be a new philosophy of socialism.

In it he emphasised the deterministic factors of heredity and environment on behaviour. However, while removing the moral responsibility for crime and evil from the 'under dog' he placed it squarely on those who not only have created the environment that conditioned vice, but thereupon have condemned those whom it infected. The existing laws and institutions, he argued, constitute an immortal trap set by the few for selfish reasons to keep the masses in a condition which renders vice inevitable.

72. *Labour Leader*, 22nd February, 1907.
73. J. Keir Hardie, *Can A Man be a Christian on a Pound a Week?* (London: ILP pamphlet, 1906), p. 11.
74. *Labour Leader*, 24th January, 1903.
75. Ibid., 7th February, 1903; J. Keir Hardie, 'Christ and the Modern Movement' in C.G. Ammon (ed.), *Christ and Labour* (London: Janda and Sons, 1912), pp. 77-91; *Labour Leader*, 29th March, 1907.
76. *Labour Leader*, 18th April, 1896; 5th April, 1899.
77. Ibid., 17th October, 1907; 22nd January, 1909.
78. *The Clarion*, 12th January, 1901.
79. Ibid., 21st May, 1892.
80. Ibid., 26th December, 1891.
81. Ibid., 20th February, 1892.
82. Ibid., 21st May, 1892.
83. Ibid., 26th October, 1901.
84. *Labour Leader*, 10th April, 1897.
85. *The Clarion*, 16th June, 23rd June, 30th June, 5th November, 1894.
86. J. Keir Hardie, *Labour Leader*, 17th October, 1903.
87. R. Blatchford, *God and My Neighbour* (Chicago: Charles H. Keir, 1907), p.4.
88. *The Pioneer*, 25th October, 1913; *Labour Leader*, 24th September, 1898.
89. MacDonald, *The Socialist Movement*, pp. 15, 17.
90. Hardie, *From Serfdom to Socialism*, p. 71; J. Keir Hardie, *The Red Dragon and the Red Flag*, speech at the Drill Hall, Merthyr Tydfil, October 16th, 1911 (London: Labour *Pioneer* pamphlet no. 1, 1912), p. 12; Glasier to Carpenter, 17th June, 1903, quoted in Pierson, *British Socialists*, p. 60. Cf. MacDonald, *Socialism and Society*, pp. 41, 164.
91. Hardie, *From Serfdom to Socialism*, p. 21; J. Keir Hardie, *The Common Good* (Manchester: National Labour Press, n.d. (1910)), p. 8.
92. J. Keir Hardie, *The Pioneer*, 25th October, 1913.
93. MacDonald, *The Socialist Movement*, p. 22.
94. Ibid., pp. 20-2.
95. Hardie, *From Serfdom to Socialism*, pp. 18-21, 48; Hardie, *The Red Dragon and the Red Flag*, p. 11; *Labour Leader*, 1st May, 1913.
96. MacDonald, *The Socialist Movement*, pp. 39-40.
97. *The Clarion*, 23rd June, 1894.
98. R. Blatchford, *Merrie England* (London: Clarion, 1894), p. 51.
99. Blatchford, *Merrie England*, pp. 16, 21; Hardie, *From Serfdom to Socialism*, pp. 6, 53, 80-3; *Labour Leader*, 17th October, 1903; *Labour Leader*, 1st November, 1896.
100. *The Clarion*, 21st May, 1892; *Labour Leader*, 29th June, 1895.
101. *Labour Leader*, January 1893.
102. Blatchford, *The New Religion*, p. 3.
103. J. Keir Hardie, *The Unemployment Problem* (London: ILP pamphlet, 1904), p. 4; Hardie, *Labour and Christianity*, p. 50; *Labour Leader*, 6th May,
104. J. Keir Hardie, *Labour Leader*, January 1893.
105. Blatchford, *Merrie England*, p. 39.
106. Hardie, *From Serfdom to Socialism*, p. 53.

107. *Labour Leader*, 30th March, 1906.
108. Ibid., 1st January, 1898.
109. Ibid.
110. *The Clarion*, 12th December, 1891.
111. *Labour Leader*, 13th February, 1894.
112. J. Keir Hardie, *After Twenty Years — The ILP, all about it* (London: ILP pamphlet, 1913), p. 7; *The Clarion*, 16th April, 1892.
113. J. Bruce Glasier, *Labour: Its Politics and Ideals* (London: ILP pamphlet, 1903), p. 14.
114. *Labour Leader*, 17th August, 1901; Blatchford, *Altruism*, pp. 5-6.
115. *Labour Leader*, January 1893.
116. Ibid., 2nd and 9th September, 11th and 18th November, 1904.
117. J. Ramsay MacDonald, 'Introduction' in W. Steward, *J. Keir Hardie* (London: ILP, 1925), p. xxii. Cf. MacDonald, *Socialism and Society*, p. 144.
118. *The Clarion*, 16th April, 1892.
119. Ibid., 10th June, 1899.
120. Ibid.
121. Ibid., 3rd January, 1902.
122. R. Blatchford, *What's All This?* (London: Labour Book Service, 1940), p. 1.
123. Hardie, *My Confession of Faith in the Labour Alliance*, p. 11; J. Keir Hardie, 'The Labour Movement', *The Nineteenth Century and After*, vol. 60 (December, 1906), p. 878; Blatchford, *Real Socialism: What Socialism is and What Socialism is Not*, p. 4.
124. Blatchford, *Real Socialism: What Socialism is and What Socialism is Not*, pp. 4-5.
125. Glasier quoted in Lawrence Thompson, *The Enthusiasts* (London: Victor Gallancz, 1971), p. 190.
126. Hardie, *From Serfdom to Socialism*, p. 28.
127. Blatchford, *Real Socialism: What Socialism is and What Socialism is Not*, pp. 4-5; *Labour Leader*, 9th September, 1904.
128. Hardie, *From Serfdom to Socialism*, p. 7.
129. J. Ramsay MacDonald, *Socialism and Government* (London: Socialist Library, 1909), vol. II, p. 12.
130. J. Keir Hardie and J. Ramsay MacDonald, 'The ILP Programme', *The Nineteenth Century*, 454 (January 1899), p.32.
131. *Labour Leader*, 8th January, 1909.
132. *Minute Book of ILP National Administrative Council*, London School of Economics MS., coll. ms. 464 m. 890, vol. 1, f. 1/1, 2nd-3rd February meeting.
133. J.S. Mill, *Utilitarianism, On Liberty and Essays on Bentham*, M. Warnock (ed.), (London: Collins, 1962), pp. 127-8.
134. Blatchford, *Merrie England*, p. 105.
135. J. Morley, *The Life of Richard Cobden* (London: Longmans, 1881), vol. 1, p. 303.
136. *Labour Leader*, 26th January, 1895.
137. Ibid., 19th January, 1895; Hardie, *The Unemployment Problem*, pp. 14-15.
138. *The Clarion*, 11th June, 1892.
139. Blatchford, *Merrie England*, pp. 105-8.
140. *Labour Leader*, 21st August, 1906.
141. R. Blatchford, *The Living Wage and the Law of Supply and Demand* (London and Manchester: *Clarion* pamphlet no. 2, 1893), p. 4; Blatchford, *Socialism, a Reply to the Enyclical of the Pope*, pp. 5, 12; R. Blatchford, *Land Nationalisation* (London: *Clarion* pamphlet no. 26, 1898), p. 2. Cf. Hardie, *After Twenty Years — The ILP, all about it*, p. 8.

142. Hardie, *From Serfdom to Socialism*, pp. 12-14.
143. Blatchford, *Socialism, a Reply to the Encyclical of the Pope*, p. 13.
144. E.g. Hardie, *Can A Man be a Christian on a Pound a Week?*, p. 14; R. Blatchford, *What is this Socialism* (London: *Clarion* pamphlet no. 45, 1908), p. 10.
145. *Labour Leader*, 22nd February, 1907.
146. Ibid., 29th January, 1909.
147. R. Blatchford, 'Socialism and Republicanism', *The Clarion*, 8th July, 1897.
148. *The Clarion*, 10th June, 1899.
149. Blatchford, *My Eighty Years*, p. 219.
150. Glasier's diary for 15th September, 1908, quoted in Thompson, *The Enthusiasts*, p. 90.
151. *Labour Leader*, 17th August, 1901, 26th November, 1909. MacDonald, *Socialism and Society*, p. 122.
153. MacDonald, *The Socialist Movement*, pp. 208-11; *Labour Leader*, 5th April, 1907.
154. J. Keir Hardie, *Karl Marx: the Man and the Message* (Manchester: National Leader Press, pamphlet, n.d.), p. 14; *Labour Leader*, 13th June, 1896, 5th August, 1899.
155. *Labour Leader*, 27th June, 1903.
156. Hardie, *Karl Marx: the Man and the Message*, p. 15.
157. *Labour Leader*, 26th August, 1904; Hardie, *My Confession of Faith in the Labour Alliance*, p. 14.
158. *Labour Leader*, 24th December, 1898.
159. J. Burns Diary, *British Library MS*, add. MS. 46, 337 ff. 161-2.
160. Quoted in Thompson, *The Enthusiasts*, p. 132.
161. Quoted in Thompson, *Robert Blatchford, a Portrait of an Englishman*, pp. 230-1.

7 THE ROMANTIC TRADITION IN BRITISH IMPERIALIST IDEOLOGY

I

The first time in his life that he became a pessimist, Bruce Glasier wrote, was when he learned that a friend of his, 'a man who has read and delighted in Ruskin and Carlyle', had become a jingo and a sympathiser of Rhodes and Chamberlain.[1] The pessimism is explicable in the light of the inseparable connection that had developed in the latter part of the century between domestic issues and imperial policies. It is illuminating, for it also shows up the double inheritance bequeathed by Carlyle and his school to British political thought. For the ILP socialists, imperialism signified all that they rebelled against at home. To quote Hardie, it was a conspiracy 'to destroy all self governing people ... in the interests of a rich and privileged class, whose greed of gold blinds them to every interest of humanity, black, white or yellow'.[2] As followers of Carlyle and Ruskin they read into their doctrines social values that were diametrically opposed to all that imperialist power politics stood for. Carlyle himself, however, has been described by a modern critic with considerable justice as 'the Grand Old Man of the New Imperialism',[3] and in such matters too Ruskin's unswerving faith in his master did not fail.

Perhaps the clearest illustration of their 'jingoism', as well as of the link between domestic and external affairs, was provided back in 1865-6 by the Governor Eyre controversy. This was sparked by the brutal suppression of local disturbances in Morant Bay, Jamaica, in the course of which some 1,000 houses were burnt down and 450 Negroes killed or executed, including a preacher and member of the legislature. Coming as it did in the wake of the heated debates over the American Civil War, it aroused similar reactions at home, but this time evoked by activities in a colony for which England was directly responsible. Again J.S. Mill put himself at the head of radicals, liberals and men of 'advanced opinions' in demanding that Governor Eyre be brought to book for crushing, by atrocities and 'what were called court-martials', a legitimate protest against oppression. There was, he argued, much more at

235

stake than justice to the Negroes. 'The question was whether ... Great Britain itself were to be under the government of law or of military licence.'[4] Against the humanitarians were the members of the Conservative establishment who had earlier proclaimed sympathy with the slave-owning 'Gentlemen of the South'. This time their ranks were reinforced by Carlyle, Ruskin and other distinguished men of letters, including Kingsley, Froude and Dickens. It was essential to 'protest against the spirit in which a servant of the State, who has saved to us one of the Islands of the Empire is ... hunted down', wrote Tennyson with the memory of the Indian Mutiny fresh in his mind.[5] But the issue for the Carlyleans was a yet higher one. Governor Eyre was a Hero, an instrument of divine retribution against those who had transgressed the moral law of the universe according to which inferior peoples who failed to develop civilised values should be guided by the 'corporation of the best' whose judgement it was not lawful to question. Interestingly enough, in the Bulgarian atrocity case, some years later, Carlyle saw the Turkish overlords as transgressing the same moral law by the savagery with which they put down the revolt against the Ottoman empire. This double standard suggests that his reasons were emotional rather than ideological and were motivated by a sense of closer kinship with the more Europeanised Bulgarians than with the Muslim barbarians.

That the conflicting opinions on imperial questions could not be reduced to a simple liberal-reactionary dichotomy may be further illustrated by Glasier's admiration for Kidd. He stressed the close affinity between his opinions and those of Kidd, noting such Carlylean trends in his thought as the moral basis of society, the conflict for mastery between the altruistic and egotistic elements in human nature, and the cyclic pattern of historical evolution.[6] Yet, in his acknowledgement of the service Kidd was doing by advancing 'scientific proof' of principles which were those of British socialism, he failed, as he did with Carlyle and Ruskin, to mention that the man whose doctrines he described as 'the philosophy of Fellowship' was one of the important imperialist ideologies. What he and other ILP socialists did not appreciate was that the very values that prompted their revolt against Victorianism, and many of the basic assumptions on which their political theories rested, underlay an important current of imperialist ideology.

The romantic tradition in British political thought has so far been considered in relation to its contribution to the emergence of peculiarly British varieties of conservatism and socialism. This chapter will consider the way in which it contributed to the emergence of a peculiarly British variety of imperialist ideology that became current during the nineteenth and early-twentieth centuries. However, to provide a better perspective and a clearer understanding of its special attributes, it may be worth considering some other varieties that were current in the period.

There is a natural temptation to justify or explain physical superiority over others by qualities less tangible. This is true of territorial conquest at least from classical times. The Romans, for example, regarded the nations incorporated into their empire as primitive barbarians, and felt it as a civilising mission and to their own greater glory to bring them under the domination of the natural masters of the world. Expansion thus implied an assertion of the values, spiritual, material and social, held by the empire-builders. However, ideologies of imperialism not only provided a mirror of what they were but also a vision of what they could be, given the new opportunities bestowed by empire of realising their potential and giving fuller effect to their ideals. Such dreams of the future often enough involved criticism of conditions at home and dissatisfaction with prevalent codes and norms. The criticism took on added importance at periods when the clash between the 'is' and the 'ought to be' was felt to be sharpening. In times of rapid social change and acute self-questioning when conflicting world-views strove for mastery, it could lead to the division into separate and even opposing ideologies, each reflecting an aspect of the domestic conflict, and all pointing to the search for new certainties.

A prominent example would be the contrast between Dilke and Froude. Both associated empire with conditions at home, believing that by exporting her virtues and benefits England was promoting not only her own good but that of humanity at large, thereby fulfilling a moral mission to the world. However, the former identified the country's glory with the pre-industrial order, while the latter identified it with the rapid growth of a new industrial one. The two concurred that 'the power of English laws and English principles of government is not merely an English question — its continuance is essential to the freedom of mankind'.[7] But whereas the one believed such laws and principles to be contingent on a return to the true path England had followed for centuries, the other associated them with the experimental innovations of private initiative and the spirit of dynamic change that marked the new society. Consequently, what the one regarded as evidence of impending decline was advanced by the other as evidence of progress.

In the course of his extensive travels Dilke became aware that the race of 'Anglo-Saxons' exhibited valuable traits lacking, or to be found only in a limited degree, in others. Their respect for law and honesty enabled them to work together in mutual trust, while their energy, technological expertise and initiative contributed to their outstanding efficiency. The very discarding of old forms and codes in the mother country was proof of their energetic nature and adaptability to the challenge of new conditions. These virtues, inherited from the parent stock, led the English colonists to compete with the other races of the world, and enabled them to emerge as the acknowledged victors. 'The discovery of gold-fields on any coast or in any sea-girt country in the world', for example, 'must now be followed by the speedy rise there of an English government. Were gold ... found in Japan, Japan would be English in five years.' Dilke's visit to the United States so impressed on him the enormous industrial and commercial potential of its great urban centres, that he prophesied that the world would be ruled by the English race from three cities: San Francisco, New York and London.[8] Such expansion necessarily meant the spread of British civilisation and the disappearance of all lower cultures, for wherever the Anglo-Saxons went they brought the advantages of their way of life. Those races that could not assimilate the new conditions would not survive: 'The vigour of the English race' involved 'the defeat of the cheaper by the dearer people ... the Saxon is the only extirpating race on earth.' The race is to the swift, the battle to the strong, and 'the gradual extinction of inferior races is not only a law of nature, but a blessing to mankind'.[9]

For Froude, on the other hand, colonisation was a kind of salvaging operation, a means of rescuing the virtues that had won England her empire and were now swamped by the new culture. True authority rests on the existence of a natural leader to guide and protect the led: one who is responsible for their welfare and relies on their unswerving loyalty. Should he be found wanting, 'Nature shakes him off and puts a better in his place', for the pattern, promising both the material progress and spiritual liberty of mankind, derives from God himself. The fittest lead the way, while 'there is no freedom except in obedience to the laws of the Maker'.[10] The history of England was an exemplary illustration of the principle in practice. From the time of the clan chief surrounded by his retainers, individuals and groups were related to one another by traditionally defined rights and codes of behaviour. At the local level they found expression in the bonds between tenant and landlord, while the nation as a whole was essentially the manor writ large. In such a network of organic relationships the Englishman had been 'proud of maintaining the traditions and habits of his family'.[11] The landlord showed paternal concern for his dependents, while they were animated by obedience and respect. As in the army, 'each man is free, because he has relinquished his freedom in the service of his country'.[12] To such traditions England owed its prosperity and empire. England, like Rome in its day, was the fittest to lead the world, since the same principles of authority that obtained at home held for relations between peoples. Freedom 'is only attainable by weak nations when they are subject to the rule of others who are at once powerful and just'.[13]

However, Froude maintained that rapid success had gone to the head of the English. The 'disintegrative theory' of *laissez-faire* was being advanced to justify the greed that led to the mass production of cheap and nasty goods by cheap labour. The whole nation was affected, for 'if the beginning and the end of each man's business is to better his own condition, the attractive forces that bind together the constituents of society become repellant forces'. The anonymity and impersonality of the great industrial centres had snapped the link between individuals, leaving only the 'breathless race of competition' and an alienated society in which 'the upper half of the world knows nothing of the under, nor the under of the upper'. Social misery was increasing as responsible authority diminished, and the code of values upheld by the landowner and the village clergyman was being replaced by money which 'breeds dishonesty as carrion breeds worms'. In the polluted atmosphere of innumerable chimneys, 'vomiting their smoke into new black heavens' the Englishmen were becoming powerless pygmies.[14] It was only a matter of time before Britain served to point a moral in the world's future history similar to that of the fall of Rome.[15] It was now the turn of the colonies to help save the mother country by drawing off her excess population. 'Let broad bridges be established into other Englands' and the immigrants will live 'a life which is not a life in the foul alleys of London and Glasgow'. At the same time, a less crowded England would reduce the industrial and commercial city to its rightful proportion in the land and enable it to be supported by a large agricultural hinterland.[16] Moreover, with the reduction of available manpower industrialists would compete for labour by reviving the manorial system of mutual and communal responsibilities adapted to modern times. The English would thus return to the natural balance of forces and social patterns that had made Britain great, while renewed moral superiority would 'show the world that [she] is still equal to her great place'.[17]

Dilke and Froude represented the extremes of a broad range of thought. As has been indicated in the introduction and elaborated in the succeeding chapters, no less common were the ambivalent attitudes towards the conflicting world-views symbolised by the twin myths of 'merrie England' and the 'brave new world'. The same thrust and counter-thrust that marked Morris's utopian narratives and the Garden City Movement found expression in imperialist visions that yoked together what John Davidson called 'the splendid Past' and 'the splendid Future'.[18] Much of this composite view was propagated through adventure stories, novels and romances that provided excitement, interest in the exotic and a surrogate for the pioneering outdoor spirit. Without demanding active participation and a consequent disruption of the equal current of day-to-day routine, they effected the release of powerful tensions by fantasy. One feature was the glorification of the British soldier and army life which epitomised many of the qualities that typified the 'good old days': loyalty from below and commitment from above, the hierarchical structure of the military in which every individual found his right place (often based on social rather than professional qualifications), the sense of *esprit de corps*, innate chivalry and acceptance of self-sacrifice for the good of the whole. To these old-fashioned virtues, writers like Henty added the almost feudal loyalty of a retainer to his lord in the form of the relationship of the native soldier or servant to his white master. But such an idealisation was not restricted to army life. The depiction of white superiority was equally presented through the empire-builder's control of the machine, technology and the production of riches. A common ending of such tales was the return home of the hero, covered with glory and blessed with fabulous wealth. The often non-too-savoury eighteenth-century Nabob of fact had thus become a dashing hero of fiction.

Among the major romantics considered earlier there was at least one, Shelley, who was opposed to the expansion of British power abroad. Nevertheless, the principles which he shared with the rest did allow the reconciliation of the 'discordant elements', not through the operations of fantasy but by being incorporated as mutually supportive components of a total philosophic structure. The conception of spiral historical progression, the attack on the abuses of the present by demanding a return to the patterns of the past but on a higher level rising to a better future, the epistemological theory of creativity in which man both made his reality and was formed by it, and the axiological interpretation of society with its two-way traffic between moral values and the material world, all could be, and indeed were, harnessed to the idea of empire. From such springs issued a current of imperialist thought that, like the waggon that bore the Ark of the Lord, turned neither to the right nor to the left, neither to capitalism nor to socialism. In opposition to the former it sought to create a communal society inspired by shared ideals and interests, where no individual would be exploited by another. As distinct from the latter it did not believe in class warfare but aimed at drawing on all national forces, while preserving a hierarchical organisation of society. The typical imagery of these thinkers derived from the structure of the family or the army, but their concern embraced the entire international scene, or the human race. Their justification of Great Britain as the supreme imperial power was that it was the most advanced, technologically and bureaucratically. However, a condition of such world leadership was that the English prove themselves worthy of their mission of enlightenment by turning to the moral ethics of religion and the sense of common purpose. Accordingly, they demanded social reforms which basically implied a nostalgic return to pre-industrial England. The hopes of a thrust towards a 'brave new world' could therefore best be realised by refashioning a new 'merrie England'.

II

Again one may take Wordsworth as a paradigm. Books VIII and IX of *The Excursion* discuss at length, though in general terms, 'the brighter' and 'the darker' sides of industrialism and the place of national expansion as a solution to the problems raised by 'an inventive Age'.[19] The epistemological base of the thesis has already been dealt with, together with Wordsworth's view of the dangers inherent in the upsetting of the delicate equilibrium between man, nature and society consequent on the rapid social and economic changes that marked the period. *The Excursion* takes up the argument of *The Prelude*, stressing not only the disrupted relationship between man and nature but the inversion of the essential qualities of each. Whereas man had imparted 'almost a soul ... to brute matter',[20] he himself had been reduced to becoming 'a tool/Or implement, a passive thing employed/As a brute mean'.[21] The price of 'intellectual mastery exercised/O'er the blind elements'[22] was the turning of man into a 'senseless member of a vast machine'.[23] The Wanderer sums up the paradox in his personification of technology. Man, the creator of the machine, was being destroyed by his own 'new and unforeseen creations' which rose

> From the labours of a peaceful Land
> Wielding her potent enginery to frame
> And produce, with appetite as keen
> As that of war, which rests not night and day,
> Industrious to destroy![24]

However, Wordsworth maintained that technological progress could also serve as the very agent by which man's control of his inventions could be re-established and his humanity restored. This would be achieved by way of the revolution that had taken place in the means of communication which was at once affected by and promoted further the revolution in technology. It had brought the ends of the land and the ends of the earth together. The 'lone pedestrian with a scanty freight' following the 'foot-path faintly marked' had given way to 'stately roads',[25] and the 'sails of traffic' gliding with 'ceaseless intercourse'[26] had linked England with the world just as 'the element of air affords/An easy passage to the industrious bees/Fraught with their burdens'.[27] The conquest of time and space resulting from the rapidity of industrial growth and its universal import invite the thronged hive of England

> ... to cast off
> Her swarms, and in succession send them forth
> Bound to establish new communities
> On every shore.[28]

The benefits would extend to all mankind, till 'earth's universal frame shall feel the effect',[29] and even the smallest habitable rock shall 'hear the songs/Of humanised society'.[30]

These words expounded a view that was to become increasingly popular as the nineteenth century progressed, namely, that the Industrial Revolution had given birth to a new 'culture, unexclusively bestowed'[31] on England, and that its diffusion justified overseas expansion. It is noteworthy that Wordsworth had changed the adverb from 'universally' to 'unexclusively', implying that it was the duty of England to export its material benefits and not keep them to itself. At the same time he maintained that imperialism could restore

> The old domestic morals of the land,
> Her simple manners, and the stable worth
> ... the character of peace,
> Sobriety, and order, and chaste love,
> And honest dealing ...
> That made the very thought of country-life
> A thought of refuge, for a mind detained
> Reluctantly amid the bustling crowd.[32]

Emigration would put an end to the growth of the huge industrial cities under the permanent pall of smoke which swallowed up the countryside, 'hiding the face of earth for leagues'.[33] Instead of the increase of population becoming a curse it would bring a blessing both to the uncivilised world and to the mother country. No less important, the wealth deriving from the empire and the sense of national mission would reverse the process of moral and social transformation that was undermining the whole fabric of the country. Commercial relations based on selfish profit-and-loss calculations that had brought about the alienation of the masses and their degradation to 'a savage horde among the civilised'[34] would be replaced by a stable and ordered hierarchy in which, as in the family, 'duties rising out of good possessed'[35] would tie all in bonds of interreliance and mutual generosity. The needs of all the people, 'like a prayer/That from the humblest floor ascends to heaven'[36] would 'reach the State's parental ear',[37] and she, owning 'a mother's heart',[38] would see to it that none of those 'born to serve her and obey'[39] would be left to 'run/Into a wild disorder; or be forced/To drudge through a weary life'.[40] Instead of the 'discipline of slavery'[41] the country would be united by a 'discipline of virtue'[42] encouraged by moral guidance, national education and 'timely culture'. 'Genuine piety' would thus 'descend/Like an inheritance from age to age'.[43] Unlike the countries of the continent, where revolutions had cast away long-reverenced titles, overturning laws and dividing up territories, England would remain 'entire and indivisible'.[44]

Imperialism, then, was for Wordsworth a step towards realising his vision. It would enlist the forces of industrialism to fortify the fundamental patterns and values that marked pre-industrial 'merrie England', relating the past to the future and the permanent to the transient in seamless continuity. The structure of human relationships would thus be brought into harmony with the powers that operate the universe, where all that exists has its place in the eternal hierarchy which assigns

> To every class its station and its office
> Through all the mighty commonwealth of things;
> Up from the creeping plant to sovereign Man.[45]

The machine could be made to serve as a missionary to propagate spiritual truths that would unite the people of the mother country, and in due course of all lands, into one organic whole. Man, 'strengthened, yet not dazzled by the might/Of ... dominion over nature gained'[46] would learn, 'though late, that all true glory rests,/ All praise, all safety, and all happiness,/Upon the moral law'.[47]

The similarities between this imperialist doctrine and that of Southey, especially in his seminal 'Inquiry into the Poor Laws', are too obvious to warrant elaboration. It is difficult to ascertain with confidence which of the two close friends and neighbours influenced the other more. By the time the 'Inquiry' was written (1812), Southey had come to acknowledge the enormous importance of industry and its value in promoting British power and expansion. Employing the identical metaphor of *The Excursion* he wrote 'let the reader cast a thought over the map, and see what elbow-room there is for England ... It is time that [she] should become the hive of nations, and cast her swarms'.[48] Likewise he saw imperialism, with its opportunities for economic growth, the outlet it provided for commercial and industrial energies, and the sense of national mission it encouraged, as a key factor in the moral and social regeneration of the mother country. However, his contribution to the political ideas of the major romantics is illustrated by his taking a step further two issues that Wordsworth barely touched on. Wordsworth regarded imperialism as a means of conserving the essential spirit of pre-industrial England and preventing its erosion by the evil aspects of the new economy with its weakening of the nation's moral fibre. Such an approach underlay his letter of 1818 to Lord Lonsdale, where he gave it as his firm opinion that 'the feudal power yet surviving in England is eminently serviceable' in counteracting the destructive tendencies of the day.[49] Southey, in line with his cyclic view of history, held that imperialism could play a central part not in conserving but in resurrecting the old order by facilitating the adaptation of the new economy to earlier patterns such as the manorial system. On the model taken from 'wise antiquity', England should 'enlarge herself and send forth her blessings to the remotest parts of the globe', and in so doing promote both at home and abroad, the 'happiness and domestic morals' which proceed from the ancient 'laws and institutions with which Providence has favoured us above all others'.[50] The second issue relates to the function of the State in the imperial venture. Wordsworth, as we have just seen, envisioned the State as a tender mother answering the cry for help of her young. Her duty was to ensure that the wealth accruing from expansion overseas be used for the good of the entire people. Southey entrusted the State with a more active and authoritarian role. For him it embodied the permanent values and traditions of the nation, and as such was the power which, transcending all particular and transient interests, imposes its will on the generations. Accordingly, it devolved on it to initiate and preside over the extension of England's God-given virtues for the good of its people and of humanity at large. Government, as the temporal representative of this permanent entity, was therefore 'required ... to encourage emigration by founding settlements, and facilitating the means of transport'.[51]

It was, however, Carlyle who epitomised this combined Promethean and Epimethean view of national expansion. As with so many of the other social and political ideas examined in this book, he drew on what was 'in the air' at the time, and more avowedly on Southey, systematising, elaborating and developing, to form a doctrine that was to make a powerful impact on the British idea of empire. His biographer, Froude, and his disciple, Ruskin, have already been mentioned in this connection. Among others one could name his friend Forester and his followers,

Kingsley and Disraeli. Even as late as the First World War we find critics describing Kipling as 'Carlyle re-vitalised'.[52] Growing out of a wide, all-embracing, world-view and as a part of a theory of social order, his opinions propelled him steadily away from earlier and contemporary imperialists, whose interests lay chiefly in the economic, demographic and organisational aspects of empire. What is surprising is that in the voluminous works on Carlyle and on imperialism, this side of his thought has barely received recognition beyond an occasional brief comment or, at best, a page or two.

At the heart of his doctrine of empire lies his vision of England as the new Prospero, who 'can send his Fire-demons panting across all oceans ... from end to end of Kingdoms; and make Iron his missionary, preaching its evangel to the brute primeval powers, which listen and obey'.[53] The image of a divinely appointed magician transforming demons into missionaries in order to bring nature under control gains its force from his conception of man as the initiating impulse of change, the foreman in the 'universal workshop', whose sacred mission is to shape the world of matter and his place in it. The English as world pioneers of the Industrial Revolution were the race chosen to spread a new gospel, for industry was 'the voice of God'.[54] The justification of national expansion as the means of bringing light to the benighted in itself differed little from the doctrines of Wordsworth and Southey, but Carlyle added a further dimension. The backward races had not been creative, thereby contravening the nature of man and the laws of God. This was tantamount to being self-centred and worshippers of that aspect of man which he called the 'Devil'.[55] Since all men are brothers, it was the religious duty of the English to emancipate them from egotism and direct them to self-fulfilment.

However, technology had its satanic dimension too, for 'not the external and physical alone is now managed by machinery, but the internal and spiritual also'.[56] In the wake of the Industrial Revolution the old had been thrust aside, and the new without the spirit of the old had become unbalanced. All the weight of society had shifted to the mechanical side, and the product was elevated above the activity of production. In other words, materialism had exchanged the spirit of creativity and co-operation for the pursuit of wealth. The craftsman was forced into becoming an industrial automaton and the gospel of Mammon had replaced the Heroical, devotional and moral ideals of the rulers. God himself had become an 'absentee God',[57] and England had lost 'the wisdom, the heroic worth of our forefathers'.[58]

In *Past and Present* Carlyle pointed to the fulfilment of the prophecy in *Sartor Resartus*, that the breakdown of the social structures and values of pre-industrial England must lead to the economic collapse of the new mechanistic society. The 'hungry forties' showed that the concentration of wealth in the hands of the few had caused an imbalance between supply and demand. The increase in population had not resulted in a proportionate increase in demand, for improved technology meant fewer hands, and increased production which could not be absorbed. To maintain their profits the industrialists reduced production and dismissed more and more workers, who thereupon competed for a dwindling number of available jobs by lowering their wage demands. This caused a further decline in demand, further reduction of production, and so on in a downward spiral of cause and effect. The self-defeating scramble for profit was thus plunging the country into a vicious circle of misery, and incurring the threat of revolution. 'What is the use of your spun shirts', he accused the industrialists, 'they hang there by the million unsaleable; and here by the million are diligent bare backs, that can get no hold on them.'[59] The country's very existence hinged therefore upon the achievement of two goals. The first, and more immediate, was to end unemployment. The second, long-range one, was the re-creation of the good society, similar to that which had been destroyed in the wake of industrialism. In the early thirties Carlyle conceived of colonial expansion as the chief means for the realisation of the first objective. From the end of the same decade he increasingly saw it also as a means for transforming the structure of English society.

In *Sartor Resartus* the blame was placed on the rulers for the social misery that must lead to class warfare. In times of unemployment it was the duty of leaders to promote mobility among the workers and to show the way by emigrating overseas. This, however, they were unwilling to do, since they themselves were free from economic hardship.[60] The idea of emigration as a remedy for unemployment was not new. At the end of the eighteenth century it was raised to deal with those out of work in the highlands of Scotland, while in the 1820s Sir W. Horton was active in a scheme to send paupers to the Colonies. In later works, however, Carlyle developed it in the light of the increasing social distress in England

and the ongoing debate concerning the relations between the white settlers and the natives in the empire. This reached a climax following the Kaffir wars, the recommendations of the parliamentary committee headed by Buxton (1835), the propaganda of the Society for the Protection of the Aborigines founded in 1837, the final abolition of slavery (1838) and, in the year Carlyle wrote *Past and Present* (1843), the assassination of Arthur Wakefield and other whites by the Maoris.

In *Chartism* (1839) he saw the emergence of the Chartist movement as a sign that the class struggle he feared had begun. Once more he demanded emigration as a major solution to a major problem. This time he did not restrict emigration to the unemployed but demanded, like Wakefield and the colonial reformers, 'an emigrant host, larger than Xerxes' was' consisting of 'trained men educated to pen and practice'.[61]

In *Past and Present*, written in the darkest hours of the 'hungry forties', he was no longer content to echo the proposals of others. Rather, he made emigration the moving force for comprehensive social reform. At the core of his scheme lay the theory that mass emigration would induce the employers to offer their employees security of tenure, or as he called it — 'permanent contracts instead of temporary', as well as better working conditions, and this would lead to the formation of mutual interrelations which are a feature of the good society. He appealed to all those who for whatever reason disapproved of the social system to emigrate. Such free emigration would be in inverse ratio to conditions in England. The worse the situation the greater the rate of emigration until, after all the unemployed were absorbed, the balance would be tipped and a shortage of labour would result. This in turn would enable workers to choose their place and conditions of work. The employers, on finding themselves competing for manpower, would not only offer better terms of employment but try to ensure the permanency of the workers in their posts by long-term contracts.[62]

All this turned on the possibility of intensified mass emigration based on freedom of choice. However, many of those who would wish to emigrate would lack the means to do so. Carlyle therefore demanded massive State intervention in the form of a special emigration department with adequate funds to provide transport to various parts of the empire and an ample budget to aid the settlement of the colonists. The scheme for the formation of industrial brigades, put forward in the *Latter Day Pamphlets* under the impression of the 1848 upheavals and the feeling that 'the hour of crisis has verily come', was a device for accelerating this paradoxical process of putting an end to labour 'nomadism' by promoting labour mobility.[63] It too was involved with imperial expansion. The extent of Britain's overseas possessions would guarantee the ability of government to offer work under fair conditions for all those who would enroll: the brigades would move flexibly, according to economic needs and opportunities in the mother country and 'the forty colonies'.[64]

Since this was an afterthought to the scheme put forward in *Past and Present*, one must look for the rationale of that earlier work. There Carlyle emphasised that his plan would be to the benefit not only of the workers but also of the industrialists. A 'Permanent Contract' would give the worker a sense of security and strengthen his loyalty both to his employer and to his place of employment. This would result in increased production. At the same time, the national and cultural links between the colonials and the mother country would ensure the reliability of the economic partnership between them. The colonies would therefore expand the British markets, increase the demand for industrial products and prevent the recurrence of economic crises. Similar arguments apply to the increase of wages and the improvement of workers' welfare. True, these would raise the cost of production. But this cost would fall as a result of increased productivity, while higher wages would increase home consumption. Furthermore, the rise in wages would be relative to the increase of production, and hence would stimulate the workers to further efforts. Likewise, improving sanitary conditions in factories, promoting superior workmen, and even giving the workers a share in the ownership, would prove to be 'an excellent investment' for the employers. Additional reforms, such as the building of hospitals to serve the community of workers, the improvement of housing and environmental conditions, and the encouragement of leisure occupations for the workers and their families, would strengthen the bonds already created, extending them to become the basis of communal life. The last reform would be to retire elderly workers on pension. In this way the personal connection between employer and employee would be maintained even after the worker's retirement from active service.[65]

All in all, emigration would lead to the infusion in society of the religious concept of production as a collective mission to fulfill the divine injunction of 'Produce! Produce! In God's name'. It would transform the organs of society into self-contained harmonious communities, based on principles deriving equally from the pre-industrial community system and the capitalist one which had overthrown it. In this way Carlyle sought to preserve and combine the best of two worlds. On the one hand, he could revert to the world of merrie England. Society would again fall into hierarchical organic communities, within which there obtained semi-feudal relationships and mutual responsibilities. On the other hand he looked forward to a dramatic expansion of production, with its blessings of increased consumption and higher standards of living, leading to internal social harmony based on widespread well-being and co-operation in creative exploitation of all natural resources.

All this led Carlyle to reflect increasingly on two problems of empire currently aired in public debate, namely, the problem of the relationship between Britian's ability to expand and her moral right to do so, and the problem of the lot of the primitive races in the colonies. His views on these issues were already developed by 1837, but the crisis in the West Indies in the late forties led to their greater clarification and crystallisation. The freeing of the slaves had brought about a desperate shortage of labour, while the Sugar Duties Act declared that by 1851 the differential duties on sugar would be abolished. The banks in Jamaica, British Guinea, Trinidad and Mauritius collapsed, and with them the whole system of credits. Many plantations lapsed back into jungle and the population was rapidly reduced to poverty and unemployment.

In essence the views advanced by Carlyle in reaction to these events were a generalisation of his social doctrines. As we have seen, he saw society not as the aggregate of its members but as the complex network of beliefs and relations by which the aggregate co-operates in matters of mutual interest. In other words: in itself society is an abstraction. Such a view does not accord with the nationalistic mystique which asserts territorial rights of a nation, as though it were a concrete entity. Rights of societies or nations are meaningful only as the sum total of the rights of their members; and these are proportionate to their relative contribution to the fulfilment of mankind's mission to create. The control of property, including land (or in the broadest sense — territories), is one of these rights. Therefore, the aggregate of creative people in one contiguous area living by the same norms have combined rights over territories inhabited by an aggregate of people who are less creative. Since Britain was the 'workshop of the world', the British were justified in exploiting territories in all the backward and underdeveloped parts of the world. Furthermore, authority should reside in men of strong moral standards who could propagate their values and direct their subordinates. This principle has so far been considered here only as it applies within a single society. Yet, mankind being one, it would apply no less to individuals and groups of different societies. Accordingly, it was the right and duty of members of advanced societies to control and direct members of backward societies for their own benefit and the benefit of humanity at large. Such backward people have remained so because of their inability to create, owing ultimately to their egotism. For the same reason they would be likely to resent the altruism of those enlightened people who stand in relation to them as 'viceregents of the Maker'.[66] They would rather be left alone to be guided only by self-interest and indolence. Carlyle therefore set the seal of his approval on any action by an enlightened nation to 'civilise' primitive peoples, and thereby elevate them to their full potential as human beings. Such missionary work might involve slavery for a time.

In the *Lectures on the History of Literature* (1838) this principle was enthusiastically applied in defence of the conquest of the Barbarians by the Romans.[67] In *Chartism* an analogy is drawn between ancient Rome and modern Britian. It was the Englishman's mission to conquer 'half the world' and bring the message of productivity and true social order to the benighted peoples.[68] Crabb Robinson was disgusted by Carlyle's 'outrageous declamation in favour of slavery ... he declared the tyranny of the Anglo-Americans to be a natural and just Aristocracy'.[69] Robinson noted that these views were dictated by an instinctive aversion to the Blacks. True, Carlyle claimed in several places that any white man has 'a miraculous head on his shoulders' and 'is worth ... from fifty to a hundred horses', whereas the Negro's value, like that of a beast of burden, is to be measured only in terms of money. He also based his justification of imperialism on the claim that the English stood in relation to the backward peoples as Aristocrats, creative producers and leaders of men. Yet it was on the ground that the English in his day lacked these qualities and were impeding progress that he propounded his reforms. However, it should be remembered that the term 'nigger' in his day was not restricted to blacks but was commonly applied to any of the native races of the empire (as, for example, Indians or Maoris), and that the 'niggers' were naturally lazy was a commonly held cliché.⁷⁰ Carlyle's attacks on the lazy niggers must be seen, therefore, less as a racist attack and more as praise of the English, the masters of the machine. That he also attacked them for abandoning the ways of their fathers shows how difficult he found it to combine the Utopian myth of a 'brave new world' and the nostalgic myth of 'merrie England'.

III

'Imperialism in the air!', Beatrice Webb noted in her diary in 1897, 'all classes drunk with sightseeing and hysterical loyalty'.⁷¹ The theory developed in the first half of the century by such men as Wordsworth, Southey and Carlyle derived in a large measure from their sense of crisis and transition. During the second half of the century there was a general feeling that things were settling down and an equilibrium was establishing itself. However, as the century closed a renewed sense of anxiety increasingly prevailed. A telling phrase to describe the atmosphere was the title of James Bryce's article 'The Age of Discontent' in which he summed up the general mood in the metaphor of a group of mountaineers who had been following a clearly defined upward track but now had lost their way. Some were afraid to climb further and thought they should go back. Others held that they should risk continuing in the hope of reaching the peak. All shared the conviction that they could not stay where they were.⁷² Coming at a time of global imperialist competition and an intensification of interest in empire, the ideas diffused by the romantics swelled to a national chorus. Their spread may be illustrated by three diverse and influential writers. The first is Rudyard Kipling, a man of letters described as 'the Cecil Rhodes of Literature' and as 'the unofficial Poet Laureate of the British Empire'.⁷³ The second was a professional colonial administrator — Alfred Milner. The third was a civil servant who wrote widely on historical and political issues — Benjamin Kidd.

The starting point for Kipling's idea of empire is what T.S. Eliot called 'a deliberate reversal of the values of industrial society'.⁷⁴ This is already abundantly clear in 'The Conversion of Aurelian McGoggin' (1887) which the pseudo-narrator calls 'a Tract'. It begins by criticising the abstractions of philosophers like Spencer and Comte who reflect the anti-social self-sufficiency of the city dweller, 'shut in by the fog' and cut off from close contact from nature and his fellow-men.[75] The natural man, like the Indian, should be intimately related to his environment and 'keep his own caste, race and breed'.[76] His individuality should be defined not only by his separate identity but also by his functional position in the group hierarchy, and measured by his readiness to contribute to the good of the whole. The same principles apply to relationships between entire groups. Each assumes its place in a scale ranging from God to the lowest caste, and each should play its part for the welfare of the human race.[77] In later writings this concept was summarised in the notion of the Law. Every social group has its specific localised laws, 'and every single one of them is right' (*In the Neolithic Age*). All, however, are particular exemplifications, determined by space and time, of a universal pattern. This view, familiar from the romantic writers, finds its clearest form in *The Law of the Jungle*. 'As old and as true as the sky', it is the eternal and uncontrovertible condition of life, so that '[he] that shall keep it may prosper, but [he]/That shall break it must die'. Like the creeper that girdles the tree-trunk, it grows and changes direction with society, running at different times 'forward and back', but always rising higher and higher as it and the tree develop. The central principle is mutual dependence co-existing with individual independence in a paternalistic hierarchy which determines the rights and duties of every part of the whole: 'For the strength of the Pack is the wolf,/and the strength of the wolf is the Pack'. While the essential is the Law, the contingential is determined by the leader in the spirit of the Law: '... in all that the Law leaveth open,/the word of the Head Wolf is Law'. All, however, are equally subject to discipline and obedience, for 'the head and the hoof of the Law/and the haunch and the hump is — Obey!' Within this framework there are the sacred duties of protecting the weak and helpless, and respect for the individuality of all. Thus, the leader is not only he who must be obeyed, but a servant of the society whose interests he directs and a representative of the true faith that binds society together.

Like Carlyle's credo of work, Kipling's notion of Law and the society based on it encompasses the notion of continual activity. The fulfilment of the Law as the basis of the good society leads to growth and production. Society is like a garden, whose beauty is the outcome of the work of the gardeners and of 'the tools and potting sheds which are the heart of all'. As in the garden of Eden, though 'Adam was a gardener', he never forgot that 'half a proper gardener's work is done upon his knees' (*The Glory of the Garden*). Though the image is rural, it applies also to industry and machinery. Like Tennyson, who described himself in his poem *Mechanophilus* as a lover of the machine, Kipling was one of the few contemporary men of letters who openly admired the machine and its master, the mechanic. 'The men to reverence ... and to erect statues to', he wrote, 'are those Prometheuses and Ixions ... who chase the inchoate idea to fixity up and down the King's highway with their ... right shoulders to the wheel.'[78] The machine indeed came to serve him as a symbol for all that typifies the good society: 'Law, Order, Duty an' Restraint, Obedience, Discipline' (*M'Andrew's Hymn*). Britain's technological superiority was the fruit of these qualities, imbedded in the tradition that for a thousand years 'our fathers in a wondrous age' had built up (*The Heritage*). It devolved upon the English to spread the benefits and to lead in carrying the 'White man's burden', bringing light to 'lesser breeds without the Law' (*Recessional*), and bridges, railways and telegraphs to establish the link between England and the lesser developed areas of the world, so that they too may become in time 'a garden'.

However, precisely at their moment of greatness, the English abandoned the Law and thereby debased the function of the machine. In the *Secret of the Machines* the machine warned its masters: '... but remember, please, the Law by which we live ... though our smoke may hide the Heavens from your eyes ... we are nothing more than the children of your brain!' Society had become subservient to technology, and complacently watched 'the old life shrivel like a scroll' (*The Reformers*). Materialism, the snapping of the organic links that held society together, the degradation of the workers into mere 'wage slaves' (*The Wage Slaves*) on the one hand, and the spirit of parasitism on the other, all these were symbolised by the industrial city. Its 'beastly fog' hid 'the horror' and 'heathendom' of a society 'whose Gods are luxury and chance' (*In Partibus*), while the free spirit of its dweller was tamed like a horse 'put into a stable/To run to order ... and earn all he's able'.[79] The rule of Law had degenerated into the law of the masses, an amorphous collection of individuals, each seeking his own immediate private interests and 'gross delights'.[80] Religion, with its concern for that which is beyond the self, likewise weakened and lapsed with the growing egotism of those who considered themselves 'above, beyond, outside', 'the bondslaves of our day'. 'We sinned and our rulers went from righteousness', Kipling wrote in *A Song of the English*. If the Lord is to forgive our transgressions, we must return to 'the Faith our Fathers sealed us', and follow His injunction: 'Keep ye the Law — be swift in all obedience.'

In spite of all his diatribes Kipling did not advocate any specific reforms. The only cure was that of the spirit, 'to lose yourself, in some issue not personal to yourself — in another man's trouble, or, preferably, another man's joy'.[81] Imperialism was a chief means to effect such a cure. It not only brought the benefits of technology and the Law to the undeveloped races; it also meant the liberation of the self in serving the needs of others. Self-sacrifice, hardship, even death in the sevice of humanity, fulfilled both 'the Vision' and 'the Need'. The idealists, 'dreaming greatly, in the manstifled towns', by promoting the good of the natives of the empire, purified themselves and their land of the curse of self-centredness and isolation, thereby allowing the return to the healthy modes of the traditional, pre-industrial society. The sickness of the industrial society would thus be relieved as Britain assumed its rightful place as the workshop of the world. The English, muses the Indian in *Kitchener's School*, have become powerful because of their magic, but 'the magic whereby they work their magic ... may be that they show all people their magic and/Ask no price in return'.

Like Kipling and Carlyle, Milner asserted the belief that by virtue of its achievement as pioneer of technology and industry, and because of the scope of its experience in administration, the British race 'stands for something distinctive and priceless in the onward march of humanity'. It was to the advantage of both England and the natives in the empire that England should be 'energetic in promoting the material progress of these backward countries'.[82] Again like Carlyle and Kipling he held that society was based on a set of values which must always be updated and which ensures that the nation be 'a great family ... striving after all that makes for productive power and social harmony'.[83] Like them too he linked social and spiritual reform in the mother country with her imperial mission. The two, he asserted, were 'inseparable ideals, absolutely interdependent and complementary to one another'.[84] However, differences between him and the other two imperialists are no less marked. First and foremost, he advocated the consolidation rather than the extension of empire: '... the era of expansion is over; the era of organisation is only just beginning'.[85] Milner, of course, was writing of a phase of imperialism which was later than that which concerned the other two. But a new element had entered his considerations: the rivalry among the nations of the West for economic and territorial supremacy, both as nations and as empires. 'The competition between nations, each seeking its maximum development', he maintained, 'is the Divine order of the world, the law of life and progress.'[86] The race is to the strong, and to be strong England must reform itself. Like Carlyle and Kipling, Milner saw the problems that beset England as stemming from the breakdown of an inherited tradition under the strains of the new technology which had proved both a blessing and a curse. 'The immense economic superiority of large-scale production', he wrote,

> created a problem, as formidable as it is really novel ... the question is how to combine the economic advantage of large-scale production with that of keenness and feeling of personal responsibility in the individual worker, that pride and pleasure in his work, which belonged of old days to the independent craftsman.[87]

What he wrote of his mentor, Arnold Toynbee, after the latter's death, applies to himself to a great degree. Toynbee had an instinctive 'reverence for the past', the power of 'vividly realising the conditions of the past', and 'sympathising with the thought and aims of bygone generations ... The industrial revolution had shattered the old social system ... Society left to itself would not right itself.'[88] He therefore proposed numerous reforms that had as their final objective the return to the traditional organic society, based on the model of the aristocratic paternalistic patterns of essentially rural England.

To counteract the 'evil effects of aggregation in large cities' he proposed to restore the lost balance between town and country, so that 'rural occupations and interests, and the rural spirit, may once more count for something in our national life'. This could be realised by encouraging a return to the countryside, promoting emigration to the colonies and improving the ecology of the towns through parks, sanitary reforms and the abolition of slums. He also advocated giving 'greater influence' to the landed aristocracy and the agrarian interests in parliament.[89] To restore the conception that 'the state, like the human body is indivisible', 'not a mere multitude of competing individuals, but a genuine household', he demanded that education develop the idea of service in the empire. To induce discipline, a co-operative spirit, and the ability to give and receive commands, he proposed the formation of a militia, following on the fostering of the scout movement in the schools. To pay for these reforms he supported high tariff walls for England and the empire but excluding all other nations. After the First World War he suggested further means of consolidating the economic and organic structure of society through joint industrial councils of employers and employees, the formation of a complete 'parliament of industry', and various other measures. Once more, the direction was to progress to the future through revival of the spirit of traditional England.[90]

Unlike the two writers discussed hitherto, Kidd was fully aware of the double pull in his thought, as is evident from his self-description as 'radical to a degree beyond anything which current radicalism conceives but at the same time conservative to a degree beyond anything conceived by present conservatism'.[91] In common with Milner he held that the society which combined the qualities of organic cohesion, effective scales of leadership and altruistic responsibility would take the lead in the evolutionary struggle between the nations as expressed in technological superiority and territorial conquest. However, such qualities, he maintained, run counter to the 'intellect, uncontrolled by ethical forces ... [which] must always be individualistic, disintegrating, destructive'.[92] As with Carlyle, the Satanic egotism is opposed by the principle of self-transcendence through religion. Therefore, the basis of all the above-mentioned virtues is religious faith. In his words, 'the organic growth endowed with a definite principle of life, and unfolding itself in obedience to law, is the social system ... founded on a form of religious belief'.[93]

Hitherto it had been the English that had proved themselves foremost in turning the world 'into a vast workshop where all the powers of nature [are held] submissively in bondage to supply [their] wants'. This was the justification for empire. The native races are like children; they must be rigorously, and if necessary ruthlessly, disciplined, and the resources of their territories exploited for the benefit of mankind. He quoted with approval the words of a 'leading colonialist' who demanded that 'the natives must go; or they must work laboriously to develop the land as we are prepared to'.[94]

Kidd admitted, however, that the qualities and faith which had made England great had weakened. His criticism of contemporary failings in English society was not dissimilar to those offered by Kipling and Milner. Nevertheless, history proceeds cyclicly in an ever-rising spiral pattern. The success of the British had led to the disintegration of the structures and codes of behaviour that had produced it. But all the negative aspects of contemporary society were signs of a 'transition period preliminary to and preparatory to a more important stage upon which we are already entering'.[95] He could already point to the 'deepening and strengthening of the altruistic feelings ... and the consequent ever-growing sense of [mutual] responsibility' in English society. Returning the compliments paid him by the socialists he saw in the fervour of 'the religion of socialism'[96] a portent of a better society to come. No less significant was the transformation of the relations between the state and the people, as government assumed its true position of representing the concern of the community as a whole and not of priviledged sections within it. The movement towards regulating, controlling and restricting the rights of wealth and capital, he predicted, must continue 'even to the extent of the state itself assuming these rights in cases where it is clearly proved that their retention in private hands must unduly interfere with the rights and opportunities of the body of the people'.[97] A new England was forming which would revive the noble qualities of the past and raise them to an even higher level. It would harness them to the production of further scientific and technological revolutions, thereby elevating yet further the material standards of mankind.

> Although we are as yet far from fully anticipating how principles of the past may ... be applicable to the future ... continuity with the past will clearly be visible as the past transition stage upon which we appear to be entering develops.[98]

The First World War, however, produced in him a deep sense of disillusionment. The leaders had betrayed their mission, both of reviving the best of traditional England and of developing new technological skills that could serve mankind as a whole. Society was divided, and inventiveness was directed solely to means of destruction. The best of the past had not fused with the best that the future should bring. Kidd's final words were:

Oh, you blind leaders who seek to convert the world by laboured disputations! Step out of the way or the world must fling you aside. Give us the young! Give us the young and we will create a new mind and a new earth, in a single generation![99]

The attack, bordering on a total repudiation of contemporary politics, marks the turning of the theory back on itself. What has been called here the romantic tradition in British political thought always included a strong condemnation of the socio-political values and practices of the day. However, its double focus on the past and on the future offered grounds for fundamental optimism. By restoring the virtues of time past without forfeiting the anticipated benefits of time to come it offered solutions to a present in crisis. The transitional quality of that present, dark though it might be, was in itself essential, for it presaged the dawning of a new day. The romantic tradition could thus provide grounds for a vision of stability in a troubled age. But was it a vision or a dream? Can the myth of the past ever become the reality of the present? Can the pot of gold at the foot of the rainbow of utopia ever be seized? Paradoxically, the hope of stability could only be held at a period felt as one of instability and rapid transition. When the integration of the three tenses at the basis of the tradition was no longer regarded as possible, when the horizons of the past and of the future receded further and further and neither the values and forms of the splendid past nor the anticipation of a splended future were felt to be realisable, then the present appeared to provide stability, but of gray, unending ordinariness, without direction or meaning. This may explain Carlyle's bleak pessimism after the watershed of 1850 and his yearning for a new kind of leader, the 'Hero as a drill sergeant', who would knock sense into the faceless blockheads of the British people. It was this feeling of being caught up in the statis of a society without memory or expectation that gave rise to his growing misanthropy and to the style of his later writings so reminiscent of Hieronymus Bosch or Breughel, in which he depicted his own distorted fantasies of the victory of evil and stupidity, of the *Ship of Fools* and the *Day of Doom*. Such a sense of social paralysis, compounded with the disillusion caused by the Labour Party's position on the issue of the House of Lords Reform and the failure of Grayson's candidacy in Colne Valley, may have led Blatchford too to renounce his life-long hopes. 'If the people are selfish and foolish our religion [of socialism] is too good for them', he wrote in 1910. 'I no longer believe in the British people. They are a degenerate race, and their star is setting.'[100]

Their disappointment should not distract us from the influence of the romantic tradition. In the course of the nineteenth century it left an indelible mark on British conservatism and on British socialism, in effect, on those who flanked the mainstream of liberalism. If anything, its importance grew during the twentieth century, as the Liberal party was squeezed out between the Conservative and Labour parties, and as the left wing of the former and the right wing of the latter overlapped to form a tacit consensus on basic issues later known as the Baskellite consensus. And yet, the romantic tradition of political thought expressed for many the deep longing for the certainties of the past and the equally deep need for the creation of something new, the desire for tradition and experiment, for permanence and change together. The bitterness of such figures as Carlyle, Blatchford and Kidd shows that the backward-looking nostalgia for the known cannot be easily yoked to a forward-looking eagerness for the unknown, and that a 'merrie England' at one with a 'brave new world' is a dream that the present cannot make real. The open-eyed sanity of mediocrity had defeated them.

Notes

1. L. Thompson, *The Enthusiasts* (London: Victor Gollancz, 1971), p. 117.
2. *Labour Leader*, 14th October, 1899.
3. R. Faber, *The Vision and the Need* (London: Faber, 1966), p. 115.
4. J.S. Mill, *Autobiography* (New York: Columbia University Press, 1944), pp. 207-8.
5. H. Tennyson (ed.), *Alfred Lord Tennyson, A Memoir* (London: Macmillan, 1899), p. 450.
6. *The Clarion*, 19th January, 1901.
7. C.W. Dilke, *Greater Britain: A Record of Travel in English-Speaking Countries during 1866 and 1867* (London: Macmillan, 1868), vol. II, p. 407.
8. Ibid., vol. I, pp. 273-5.
9. Ibid., pp. 127-50, 308, 405-6. Some 20 years later Dilke published his second major book, *Problems of Greater Britain* (London: Macmillan, 1890). In this more detailed and substantiated work he admitted to important defects in his previous book, notably his earlier dismissal of Russia which he now saw as threatening British supremacy, and his recommendation of colonial settlement in Africa. However, central principles did not change. The English still combined 'the best qualities of the foremost races of the old world'. Nor did he abandon the doctrine of the battle for the survival of the fittest and the belief that 'as to the ultimate result of [the race's] high deeds there can be no doubt'. Nevertheless, his confidence was now tinged with a note of anxiety. Greater efforts were called for

Romantic Tradition in British Imperialist Ideology 261

to ensure that the law of nature would not be thwarted by complacency, for a coalition of rivals was forming which might well draw the British empire into a war that would deal her 'a blow from which she would not recover' (vol. 1, pp. 1-3, 6).

10. J.A. Froude, *Short Studies on Great Subjects* (London: Longmans, Green and Co., 1907), vol. IV, p. 304; vol. III, p. 115, 118.
11. Ibid., vol. III, pp. 23-4.
12. Ibid., vol. IV, p. 337.
13. Ibid., vol. III, p. 122; J.A. Froude, *The English in the West Indies, or the Bow of Ulysses* (London: Longmans, Green and Co., 1888), pp. 182, 361.
14. Froude, *Short Studies on Great Subjects*, vol. III, pp. 21-2, 24, 135, 149-87, 212-22, 138, 151, 208, 218-19.
15. J.A. Froude, *Oceana, or England and her Colonies*, (London: Longmans, Green and Co., 1886), pp. 4-7.
16. Froude, *Short Studies on Great Subjects*, vol. III, p. 31, vol. IV, pp. 292-321, 13-14. Froude, *Oceana*, pp. 15-16.
17. Froude, *Short Studies on Great Subjects* vol. III, p. 222; *The English in the West Indies*, p. 359.
18. J. Davidson, *St. George's Day* (New York: John Lane, 1895), p. 8.
19. W. Wordsworth, *The Excursion*, Bk VIII, l. 87.
20. Ibid., ll. 203-4.
21. Ibid., Bk IX, ll. 115-17.
22. Ibid., Bk VIII ll. 201-2.
23. Ibid., Bk IX, ll. 158-9.
24. Ibid., Bk VIII, ll. 91-5.
25. Ibid., l. 109.
26. Ibid., ll. 112-13.
27. Ibid., Bk IX, ll. 369-71.
28. Ibid., ll. 377-80.
29. Ibid., l. 386.
30. Ibid., ll. 388-9.
31. Ibid., l. 392.
32. Ibid., Bk VIII, ll. 236-45.
33. Ibid., l. 121; see also Bk IX, ll. 363-8.
34. Ibid., Bk IX, l. 309.
35. Ibid., l. 355.
36. Ibid., ll. 325-6.
37. Ibid., l. 327.
38. Ibid., l. 328.
39. Ibid., l. 298.
40. Ibid., ll. 305-7.
41. Ibid., l. 351.
42. Ibid., l. 353.
43. Ibid., ll. 361-2.
44. Ibid., l. 345.
45. Ibid., Bk IV, ll. 341-3.
46. Ibid., Bk VIII ll. 210-11.
47. Ibid., ll. 214-16.
48. R. Southey, 'Inquiry into the Poor Laws', *Quarterly Review*, VIII (December 1812), p. 355. See also R. Southey, *Sir Thomas More: or, Colloquies on the Progress and Prospects of Society* (London: John Murray, 1829), vol. II, p. 263.
49. *The Early Letters of William and Dorothy Wordsworth*, E. De Selincourt (ed.) (Oxford: Oxford University Press, 1935), vol. II, p. 380.
50. Southey, 'Inquiry into the Poor Laws', pp. 355-6.
51. Ibid.

52. T. Hopkins, *Rudyard Kipling: A Literary Appreciation* (New York: Frederick A. Stokes, 1966), pp. 214-15.
53. T. Carlyle, *The Works of Thomas Carlyle in Thirty Volumes*, H.D. Traill (ed.) (London: Chapman and Hall, 1907), vol XXIX, p. 181.
54. Ibid. vol. XXVII, p. 60.
55. Ibid., vol. I, p. 177.
56. Ibid., p. 130.
57. Ibid., p. 30.
58. Ibid., vol. XXVII, p. 81.
59. Ibid., vol. I, p. 185; vol. X, p. 22.
60. Ibid., vol. I, pp. 183-4.
61. Ibid., vol. XXIX, p. 203.
62. Ibid., vol. X, pp. 265, 277-80.
63. Ibid., vol. XX, p. 32.
64. Ibid., p. 28.
65. Ibid., vol. X, pp. 254-336 *passim.*
66. Ibid., vol. XXIX, pp. 373-4.
67. *Lectures on the History of Literature Delivered by Thomas Carlyle, April to July 1838*, J.R. Greene (ed.) (London, Ellis and Elvcy, 1892), p. 43.
68. Carlyle, *Works*, vol. XXIX, p. 205.
69. H. Crabb Robinson, *On Books and their Writers*, E.J. Horley (ed.) (London: J.M. Dent and Sons, 1938), vol. II, pp. 541-2.
70. Carlyle, *Works*, vol. I, pp. 200-1; vol. X, p. 263; vol. XXIX, p. 350; see V.G. Kiernan, *The Lords of Human Kind* (Boston: Little, Brown, 1969), pp. 32-70, 232, 233. Cf. R. Horsman, 'Racial Anglo-Saxonism before 1850', *The Journal of History of Ideas*, XXXVII (July-September 1976), pp. 387-410, especially pp. 399-401.
71. B. Webb, *Our Partnership* (London: Longmans, 1948), entry for 25th June, 1897.
72. J. Bryce, 'The Age of Discontent', *The Contemporary Review*, XXXVII (January 1891), pp. 14-19.
73. F.L. Knowles, *A Kipling Primer* (Boston: Brown and Co., 1899), p. 60; see also *A Kipling Notebook*, 5 (June 1899), p. 79. For a comparison of Kipling and Carlyle, see A. Rutherford, 'Carlyle and Kipling', *Kipling Journal*, xxxiii (June 1966), pp. 10-19, (September 1966), pp. 11-19, (December 1966), pp. 11-16.
74. T.S. Eliot, *On Poetry and Poets* (London: Faber and Faber, n.d.), p. 249.
75. R. Kipling, *Plain Tales from the Hills* (London: Macmillan, Sussex edn, 1937-9) pp. 153-4.
76. Ibid., p. 235.
77. Ibid., pp. 153-4. Verse quoted in text hereafter may be found in the *Verse, Songs from Books* and *Miscellaneous* volumes of the same edition, and is cited within brackets without volume and page number.
78. R. Kipling, Letter to F. Young, cited in F. Young, *The Complete Motorist* (London: Hethusen and Co., 1904), p. 283.
79. Lines in a letter to Edmund Gosse, 24th May, 1980, BM MS Ashley, 3493.
80. See, e.g., R. Kipling, 'The Ritual of Government', *A Book of Words* (London: Macmillan, Sussex edn. 1937-9), pp. 59-61.
81. R. Kipling, 'Values in Life', *A Book of Words*, p. 19.
82. A. Milner, *The Nation and the Empire* (London: Constable and Co., 1913), p. 496.
83. A. Milner, *Questions of the Hour* (London: Thomas Nelson and Sons, 2nd edn, 1925), p. 173.
84. Milner, *The Nation and the Empire*, p. 139. See also pp. xxxiii, 24, 163, 293.

85. Ibid., p. 466.
86. Milner, *Questions of the Hour*, pp. 83-4.
87. A. Milner, 'Reminiscence', A. Toynbee, *Lectures on the Industrial Revolution of the Eighteenth Century* (London: Longmans, Green and Co., 1913), pp. xxii-xxiii.
88. Ibid., p. xxvii.
89. Milner, *The Nation and the Empire*, pp. xvi, xl-xlii; 266-7, 300-1.
90. Ibid., pp. xvii, 155, 170; Milner, *Questions of the Hour*, p. 137; see B. Semmel, *Imperialism and Social Reform: English Social-Imperial Thought 1895-1914* (London: George Allen and Unwin, 1960), pp. 92-127, 177-87.
91. B. Kidd, *Individualism and After* (Oxford: Clarendon, 1908), p. 36.
92. Benjamin Kidd, *Social Evolution* (New York: Macmillan, 1900), p. 109.
93. Ibid.
94. Ibid., p. 50. For his evaluation of future British expansion, see pp. 49-62, 264-79, 326-42 and B. Kidd, *The Control of the Tropics* (New York: Macmillan, 1898).
95. Kidd, *Individualism and After*, p. 13.
96. Kidd, *Social Evolution*, pp. 149-50.
97. Ibid., pp. 236-7.
98. Kidd, *Individualism and After*, p. 29. See also B. Kidd, *Principles of Western Civilization* (New York: Macmillan, 1902), pp. 21-30, 68-91, 95-7, 148-9.
99. B. Kidd, *The Science of Power* (London: Methuen and Co., 3rd edn, 1918), p. 298.
100. L. Thompson, *Robert Blatchford: A Portrait of an Englishman* (London: Victor Gallancz, 1951), p. 217.

INDEX

alienation 6, 74, 140, 142, 183, 186, 216, 239
ancien régime 21, 24, 36, 64, 136
aristocracy 106, 143, 144, 150, 158, 166, 168, 178-9, 188, 190, 212, 251, 256
   aristocracy of talent 144, 167, 188, 212
   aristocratic principle 1, 43
Ashley, Earl of Shaftesbury 51, 79n, 152
axiology 8, 11, 14, 90, 145, 241

Blake, W. 4, 16, 25, 224
Blatchford, R. 13-14, 112, 199, 201-4, 206-29, 259
   and class struggle 220-1
   and industrialism 217-19
   and Marx 226-9
   and reform 224-6
   doctrine of the Hero 212-14
   ideological development of 201-3
   theory of history 208-11, 216
Bolingbroke, J. 159-60, 165
Burke, E. 1, 33, 45n, 50-1, 65, 68, 77-8, 122
Burns, R. 177, 199, 212
Byron, R. 7, 12, 78, 112, 125, 154-5, 171, 177

capitalism 151-2, 187, 205, 219, 241
capitalist system 10, 113, 114, 137-8, 144, 146, 215, 250
Carlyle, T. 2, 5, 7-8, 12, 14, 52, 64, 67, 79, 91, 94, 98-9, 106-7, 112-46, 152, 160-3, 165, 168, 170-6, 178-9, 181-3, 185-9, 191, 193n, 194n, 195n, 198-202, 204-7, 210, 212-13, 215-17, 219, 223, 227, 229, 230n, 235-6, 245-53, 255-7, 259, 260
   and capitalist society 138-43
   Carlylianism 160, 182, 199, 205, 211, 213-14
   doctrine of empire 14, 246-52
   doctrine of Heroes 42, 94, 114-15, 125-31, 176, 206, 212-14, 259
   French Revolution 114, 124, 126-32, 160-1
   Latter Day Pamphlets 113, 144-5, 248
   Past and Present 112, 115, 120, 140-1, 143, 145, 160, 163, 168, 171, 174, 179, 184-5, 187, 190, 198, 200, 206-7, 247-8
   Sartor Resartus 98, 114, 116, 120, 123-34, 160, 165, 173, 182, 187, 199, 202, 207, 223, 247
cash nexus 6, 99, 138, 151, 168, 179, 210
Chartism 12, 108, 151, 154, 159, 167, 168, 172, 205-6
Christian Socialism 52, 151, 205
Coleridge, S.T. 7, 11-12, 16, 18, 24-9, 33-4, 43n, 47-51, 53, 56, 59, 65, 68, 84, 91, 94, 115-16, 122, 137, 144, 146n, 152, 170, 194n
   and German Romanticism 33, 68, 122
Conservatism 8, 11, 13, 48, 52, 59, 68, 77-8, 91, 108, 112-13, 150, 156, 165, 173, 180, 229, 237, 257, 260
   Conservative democracy 151
   Conservative establishment 236
   Conservative Party 153, 160, 260

Dante 25, 40, 108, 129
Darwin, C. 112, 210
   Darwinism 211
Darwin, E. 4, 91
Davidson, J. 7, 240
Dickens, C. 201, 236
Dilk, C. 237-8, 240
Disraeli, B. 6, 12-13, 52, 79, 91, 107, 108, 112, 152, 153-70, 190, 192n, 193n, 222, 246
   and reform 167-9
   ideological development 153-60
   vindication of English Constitution 156, 159, 161, 164
   Young England trilogy 154, 160-1, 165

Eliot, T.S. 130, 252

Empire 14, 237, 246, 250, 252, 255, 257
  Roman Empire 67, 104, 251
Engels, F. 115-16, 211
epistemology 8, 10, 14, 19-20, 33-4, 53-4, 62, 91-5, 116-17, 241-2
  Carlyle's doctrine of 116-17
  Shelley's doctrine of 8, 91-5
  Southey's doctrine of 53-4, 62
  Wordsworth's doctrine of 19-20, 62, 116-17, 242

Fabian society 119, 202, 205, 222, 226
Feudalism 6-7, 69, 77, 162-3, 169, 171, 179, 185, 190, 240, 245
Feuerbach 31, 115-16
Fox, C.J. 41, 48, 83-4, 191n
Froude, J.A. 13, 237-40, 245

Garden City movement 7, 240
George, H. 200, 206, 222
Glasier, J.B. 14, 199, 209, 211, 214, 218-19, 221, 226-7, 229, 235-6
Godwin, W. 1, 17, 55-7, 73, 83-90, 96
Goethe, J.W. von 12, 115, 125, 130, 138
government 3, 36, 63-4, 70, 74, 83, 167, 180, 188, 237-8, 249, 258

Hardie, J. Keir 14, 112, 119-201, 203-4, 206-29, 235
  and class struggle 218-21
  and Marx 226-9
  and social reform 223-6
  doctrine of Heroes 212-14
  ideological development of 199-201
  theory of history 208-11, 215
Heroes 8, 24, 162, 165, 167, 169-70, 175-6, 182, 188-9, 212, 214, 223, 228, 236, 259
  see also Blatchford, Carlyle, Hardie

idealism 8, 27-9, 31, 114, 116, 211
imperialism 235, 244-6, 251-2, 255-6
imperialist ideology 14, 236-7, 240, 244
Independent Labour Party 14, 112, 199, 203-5, 210, 215, 223, 225, 227-8, 235-6
industrial brigades 74, 144-5, 189, 223, 248-9

industrialism 6, 50, 68, 72, 117, 151, 164, 216, 241, 244, 247
industrial city 40, 164, 201-2, 216-17, 239, 240, 243, 254
industrial civilisation 2, 137, 217
industrial order 10, 237

Keats, J. 7, 12, 49, 93, 101-3, 112, 120
  Hyperion 13, 93, 101-2
  The Fall of Hyperion 102-3
Kidd, B. 14, 236, 252, 257-9, 260
Kingsley, C. 13, 152, 170-80, 190, 205-6, 246
  and reform 178-80
  ideological development of 170-3
  theory of history 173-6
Kipling, R. 14, 246, 252-6, 258

Labour Leader 205, 218, 228
Labour movement 201, 205, 228, 259
Labour Party 151, 169, 260
laissez faire 4, 79, 157, 180, 234
Liberalism 37, 68, 157, 166-7
Liberal Party 150, 166, 199, 200, 229, 230n, 236
Locke, J. 3, 26-7, 29, 105
love 35, 37-9, 53-5, 58, 61, 96-9, 119, 129, 178, 203, 207, 218

MacDonald, R. 14, 199, 206, 210-11, 214-16, 220-1, 227
Malthus, J. 73-4, 83, 88, 90, 106, 166
manorial system 11, 61-2, 77, 143, 151, 162, 190, 239-40, 245
Marx, K. 31-2, 112-24, 136, 138-46, 186, 206, 211, 216, 218, 226-7
Marxism 173, 205, 218, 221
Marxists 210, 217, 229
materialism 6, 8, 20, 28-9, 31, 112, 116-17, 211, 246, 254
Maurice, F.D. 13, 171-2, 194n
medieval 10, 143, 162-4, 185, 190, 211, 215
Mill, J.S. 7, 13, 64, 106, 147n, 222, 235-6
Milner, A. 14, 252, 255-8
Morris, W. 7, 13, 198, 202, 212, 217, 226, 228, 240
myth 5-6, 14, 93, 138, 240-1, 244, 250, 252, 260

nature 17, 21, 24-5, 29, 32, 35-6, 39-40, 49, 53, 55, 85-6, 102, 115,

118-20, 125, 128, 139-40, 170, 173, 175, 181, 183-6, 191, 203, 209, 217, 238-44, 257, 261n
  estrangement from 39-40, 85, 139-40, 186, 203, 217
  forces of 40, 86
  laws of 36, 102, 120, 181, 183, 238, 261n
  power of 32, 191

Owen, R. 23n, 75-6, 141
Owenism 205-6

Paine, T. 1, 56-7, 83, 87
pantisocratic society 47, 60, 86, 88
Peel, R. 150-1, 153-4, 160, 165, 170
Plato 18, 37, 58, 72, 96, 209
Poet 8, 18, 27, 37-8, 41-2, 67, 101-3, 90, 93-9, 155
  Shelley's doctrine of 42, 90, 93-9, 115
  Wordsworth's doctrine of 18, 27, 37-8, 41-2
political economy 10, 74, 158, 176-7, 178-87
pre-industrial order 6, 10, 14, 61-2, 76, 89, 137, 152, 164, 237, 241, 250, 255

Quarterly Review 11, 48, 50, 52, 62, 67, 82n, 113, 137, 154
radicalism 8, 12, 48, 56, 68, 77, 108, 113, 156, 257
Radical Party 153, 156, 159, 204
revolution 1-2, 24, 57, 60-2, 64-5, 75, 78, 83, 87, 89, 107-8, 114, 125, 132-7, 142, 152, 156, 167, 172, 175, 221, 223, 228, 244, 247
  American Revolution 3-4, 105, 136
  French Revolution 1-2, 4-5, 11, 17, 20-5, 30, 35, 40, 59-60, 66-7, 87, 90, 105, 125, 134-6, 146n, 152, 165, 167, 171, 175, 191n
  Industrial Revolution 1, 4, 10, 17, 31, 68, 70, 139, 216, 243, 246, 256
Robespierre, 23, 59, 87, 135, 175
romanticism 16, 33, 114, 122, 124, 137, 210
  romantics 2, 7-9, 10-12, 14, 48, 84, 94, 115, 122, 124-5, 137-8, 145, 167, 170-1, 182, 190,
205, 224, 241, 245, 252-3
  romantic thought 12, 114, 211, 216
  romantic tradition 8, 13-14, 112, 152, 169-70, 181, 236, 259-60
Rousseau, J.J. 53, 58
Ruskin, J. 13-14, 152, 180-91, 198, 205-6, 213, 217, 223, 235-6, 245, and industrialism 185-8
  ideas of reform 188-91
  theory of history 182-5

Saint Simon, Count de 75-6, 118, 124-5, 210
Saint-Simonism 124-5, 147n, 206
Shelley, P.B. 2, 7, 11-12, 52, 64, 78-9, 112, 115, 120, 125, 145, 154-6, 160, 170-1, 177, 180-1, 205, 212, 214
  'Defence of Poetry' 42, 90, 94-7, 99, 103-7, 155
  ideological development 84-91
  Mont Blanc 91-4, 106
  philosophical view of Reform 86-7, 90, 100, 103-7
  Prometheus Unbound 90, 93, 98, 99-100, 155
  theory of history 96-101, 103-7
  see also epistemology, Poet
Smith, A. 4, 10, 128, 137, 227
social change 9, 68-70, 114, 123, 133, 237
social class 10, 35, 69-71, 73, 75, 84, 106-7, 127, 137, 139, 145, 152, 162, 188, 218-20, 252
  class struggle 76, 142, 145, 162, 210, 218-20, 241, 248
  social polarisation 10, 37, 73, 75, 139, 141-2, 186, 211, 215, 219-20
Social Democratic Federation 198, 202, 218, 226
socialism 13, 112, 181, 199, 201-4, 207, 213-14, 218, 220-1, 226, 229, 258, 260
  British socialists 14, 75-6, 108, 113, 182, 191, 198-9, 203-5, 211, 217-18, 225-9, 236-7
  continental socialists 124, 219, 225, 227
  socialist movement 201, 219-20
  Socialist Party 169, 203, 206, 220
social reform 41, 56-7, 60, 65, 74-7, 83, 86, 88, 143, 167, 178, 191,

205, 223-4, 229, 241, 248-9, 255-6
social reformism 11, 90, 190
social transition 51, 68-72, 74, 76, 89-90, 142, 147n, 158, 161, 167, 206, 252, 258
Southey, R. 7, 11-12, 42-90, 107, 115, 117, 121, 137, 139-45, 147n, 154, 157, 160, 170, 173, 189-91, 206, 212, 223, 244-6, 252
   Colloquies 50, 64, 75-6, 173
   early radicalism 47-62, 77
   idea of empire 14, 244-5
   Joan of Arc 47, 52-61, 64-6, 85-6, 113
   schemes of reform 72-8, 143-4
   theory of history 52, 66-72, 139, 143, 147n
   see also epistemology, pantisocratic society
State 11, 13, 51, 64-6, 72, 74, 76-7, 145, 152, 157, 177, 180, 182, 189, 200, 221-3, 226, 245
   and reform 11, 13, 51, 65, 74, 76-7, 145, 180, 182, 189, 200, 221-3, 226, 245
   and society 51, 66, 72, 74, 157, 189, 221-3
   supra sectional entity 13, 51, 64-5, 76, 145, 152, 157, 177, 180, 205, 221-3
St George Guild 189-90

Tamworth Manifesto 150, 165
Tennyson, A. 6, 8, 12-13, 15, 130, 254
Tory Party 51, 63, 151, 154, 156, 158-9, 163, 165, 169-70, 181, 191, 229
   Toryism 130, 150, 153, 156-7, 159, 165, 167, 170

Utilitarianism 105-6, 157

Whig party 63, 150, 153, 157-9, 163, 191n
   Whiggism 157, 165
Wordsworth, W. 11-12, 16-51, 53, 56, 62, 84-5, 91-3, 99, 101-2, 112-13, 115-17, 119-20, 131, 137, 171, 175, 180-1, 223, 241-6, 252
   experiences in France 20-3, 30, 35
   idea of empire 14, 241-5
   Lyrical Ballads 16, 27, 41, 47, 49
   The Excursion 11, 16, 18-19, 31, 38, 91, 101, 171, 181, 241-2, 244
   The Prelude 11, 16-31, 33, 35-6, 38, 41, 48-9, 62, 91-2, 131, 242
   'The Recluse' 18-19, 25, 40-1, 101
   see also epistemology, pantisocratic society, Poet

Young England 13, 52, 112, 161-2